TOLSTOY

TOLSTOY

Pietro Citati

Translated from the Italian
by Raymond Rosenthal

Schocken Books : NEW YORK

First published by Schocken Books 1986
10 9 8 7 6 5 4 3 2 1   86 87 88 89

Library of Congress Cataloging-in-Publication Data
Citati, Pietro / Tolstoy.
Translation of: Tolstoj.
1. Tolstoy, Leo, graf, 1828–1910. 2. Novelists,
Russian—19th century—Biography. I. Title.
PG3385.C5513 1986   891.73'3 [B]   86–10141

Design by Jane Byers Bierhorst
Manufactured in the United States of America
ISBN 0–8052–4021–7

CONTENTS

PART ONE

Youth

I

The first glimpse we get of the adolescent Tolstoy is in the act of looking at himself in the mirror. He is standing before the impenetrable glass, where "the impossible space of reflections" resides: he contemplates the cold blue eyes, the thick eyebrows, the mustache that slightly darkens the mouth, the graceless features which more resemble those of a worker or peasant than those of an aristocrat: or he sits before that other mirror which is his *Diary*; and with immense pleasure he continues to examine his face, his thoughts, his feelings, everything that the soul's enigmatic and frightening abyss sends to the surface. No man, perhaps, has ever known so vertiginous an intoxication with his own self. When he looks at himself, he believes—as he writes with feigned irony—that "*du haut de ces Pyramides quarante siècles me contemplent* and that the whole world would perish if I were to stop." If he looks even more deeply, he is convinced that he can see, behind the screen of his features, the entire surface of the world: war and peace, city and countryside, the French of the court and the Russian of the peasants, the living and the dead, past, present, and future. The most extraordinary thing is that in a few years he will not be at all mistaken. Inside the mirror, which for the time being sends back only the features of his face, is really hidden the created world, with landscapes, figures, clothes, objects, evoked by an infinitely precise and rapid hand: by means of the light, which emanates exclusively from him, he will illuminate the entire expanse of reality; and what could have been the mad dream of an egocentric or an illusionist became *War and Peace* and *Anna Karenina*.

There are many kinds of narcissism: gay and melancholy, delicate and emphatic, Olympian and Dionysiac; a narcissism that dissolves the world into a vague, euphoric mist or concentrates it robustly around the ego. Tolstoy knew its most terrifying form: the demonic, which secretly vies for rights and privileges with God the creator. He was proud of his aristocracy, his character, his feelings, the very letters that formed his name: he was convinced of being an exceptional person, ahead of his time, and that therefore neither a society nor a friend would be able to understand him. When he arrived at the Caucasus, he realized to what an extent this vanity obsessed his existence: "Vanity is an incomprehensible passion—one of those evils like epidemics, famine, locusts, and war, through which providence punishes men. . . . It is a kind of moral disease similar to leprosy—it destroys one part but mutilates the whole—it creeps in little by little without being noticed, then it extends to the entire organism; there is no attitude it does not corrupt—it is like a venereal disease; if it is expelled from one place it shows up with greater strength in another.—The vain man knows neither joy, nor sorrow, nor love, nor fear, nor envy that are true—everything in him is denatured, forced. . . . I have suffered much from this passion—it has ruined the best years of my life and deprived me forever of all freshness, all boldness, all the joy and initiative of youth." With the same intensity with which he became intoxicated with his ego, he found himself odious, repulsive, and detestable as only the great narcissists can hate themselves. He could not bear himself at the mirror. His face seemed to him coarse and vulgar: the eyes tiny and grayish: the features soft and flabby, the hands and feet big like those of a peasant. As for character, there was not a single vice of which he did not accuse himself. He was timid, cowardly, without energy and without pride, weak, he did not know how to live, he did not know any trade: and his will lacked that constancy which alone makes for greatness.

The quality the young Tolstoy lacked was perseverance: the firm continuity of the spirit which at first sight an observer would have attributed above all else to the author of *War and Peace.* There was no one more uneven then he: there was no one more versatile and changeable, more unstable and capricious; his moods followed a continuously broken line, an incessant neurasthenic zigzag, alternating high and low, gay and sad, anguished and profligate, like the graph of a rapidly fluctuating fever. In one day he had a hundred different faces. He fell in love with ever new things, changed passions like a dandy changes clothes: as soon as a thing was conquered and possessed by his mind, he threw it behind him, burning one experience after the other, going through life with the swift and furious rhythm of his Count Turbin. When he decided to go and fight against the Polish rebels one year after his marriage, his wife commented in her *Diary*: "To war. What is this aberration? Is he bizarre? No, that's not right, he is simply inconstant! . . . For men everything is a joke, a moment's whim. Today one gets married, and that's pleasant, one generates children. Tomorrow one feels like going to war and one leaves. . . . He's ready to abandon his children because he enjoys galloping on a horse, admiring the beauty of war, listening to bullets that whistle. . . . He's had enough with one year of happiness, and now he obeys this new fancy." At times the discontinuity was so radical as to pervade every moment of his life: every feeling became twofold and contradictory; and his face appears to us, at the same moment, with one eye tearful and the other merry.

Even though this discontinuity sometimes troubled Tolstoy, he understood that it constituted the armature of his existence. Without it, he could neither live nor perceive and absorb life: he experienced a "strange disquietude" when he felt "morally and materially tranquil." It is likely that Gorky, when he said that Tolstoy "was the most cunning of all gods," was thinking of this mobile and capricious spirit: Tolstoy was cunning because he incessantly changed shape, like Proteus, and one could not seize him in any of the temporary dens he occupied. But it was a fatal and dramatic cunning, like that which is needed by creators. Tolstoy's mirror—the mirror in which he contemplated himself and the totality of the world—shattered into thousands of scintillating and cutting fragments, because he wanted first of all to reflect the fragments of life. He was fluid, changeable, and discontinuous because he did not intend to let himself be imprisoned and rigidified by the banal round of existence. He tried to free himself from it; and seize the lights, vibrations, and colors of every minute, or of every molecule of a minute, that grazed his nerves' spasmodic inconstancy.

So young Tolstoy's nerves were always on edge and at the point of snapping. His soul's epidermis was ready to receive all the sensations and feelings that stirred the surface of the universe: they crashed against it like the sea's wave and even the smallest aroused a tempest. It was enough for him to listen to a piece of music—even the most vulgar and most poorly executed—for his dark or melancholy feelings, the mobile play of fantasizings, real or imaginary memories to be furiously awakened: he waited for this impact with voluptuousness and terror, with shudders and pallors of his entire being, because the slightest impact on the surface could generate frightful upheavals. Like a character in Sterne or a romantic hero, he was always ready to weep, whatever emotion might touch him: and with what pleasure did he shed tears as he bid goodbye, wrote letters, spoke, remembered. "I wrote a letter to Turgenev, then I sat on the sofa and sobbed tears without reason, but happy and poetic." When he did not cry, he fantasized. When he was a child, he hid under the blankets where, having abolished all connection with the world, he imagined that he was a foundling, or a hero, a savior of the country solemnly thanked by the emperor, or that he was dead and could hear his father and relatives talk about him, or of meeting in heaven his mother's soul; and imagination rendered these things vivid for him as though they were real. The *rêveries* of youth (as probably those of old age) were no less childish: dreams of evangelical ecstasies and redemption, of tireless study, of elegance, power, and strength pursued during the nightly hours when sleep did not come, or in the light of day. While he fantasized so freely he kept his imagination young and fluctuating, and prepared his qualities as a novelist. If he did not fantasize with a kind of obsessive obstinacy that he was other human beings, if he did not dream of being an animal or a color or a cloud, he would never have trained his prodigious novelistic capacity for identification.

Existence such as we live it—our gray existence composed of always the same repeated circumstances, dawns and sunsets, birth, adolescence, love, marriage, paternity, old age, and death—always seemed to him an unbearably tedious business. The ticking of clocks, which scanned the too-long minutes, seemed to him depleting. It was not worthwhile to live such an existence: one must invent a new one. Like Count Turbin, the protagonist of "Two Hussars," he dreamed of an existence imbued with violence, fury, speed, demonic tension, where the clocks ticked so rapidly that the rhythm of their ticking could no longer be noticed. He sought by all means—gambling, travel, love, war—to live more intensely and feverishly, attributing dramatic prominence to common feelings and imposing on superficial sensations the power of profound ones. Sometimes, like Dostoevsky's gambler, he tried to push all passions to the extreme, defying all human limits, so that they would turn into their opposites. Both in youth and old age the people who knew him were subjected to this contagion. "Lev has always had the gift," his cousin Alexandra wrote, "of experiencing everything with overwhelming intensity. The strength of his emotion was such that it imposed itself on others and led them to feel as he did."

Had he been asked why he sought this intensity, Tolstoy could have answered with a page of Baudelaire's: "There are moments in existence when time and space are more profound, and the feeling of existence is immensely increased. . . . There are days when man awakens with a young and vigorous spirit. As soon as his pupils are delivered from the sleep that sealed them, the external world offers itself to him with powerful impact, clarity of outline, an admirable richness of color. The moral world opens its vast perspectives, filled with new lights. . . . But what is most singular in this exceptional state of the spirit and senses, which I can without exaggeration call paradisial, if I compare it to the heavy darkness of common and daily existence, is the fact that it is not created by any visible or easily defined cause." During these hours, "veritable feasts of our brain," nature quivers with a supernatural tremor: the sky of a more transparent azure sinks as if in an abyss, sounds musically clang, colors speak, perfumes recount worlds of ideas, objects, dressed in more robust shapes, change, undulate, vibrate, trepidate. Within us, a spritual tension corresponds to this external tension: the senses are more attentive, feelings discover everywhere secret analogies, thoughts are accompanied by a nervous shock.

Baudelaire's "paradisial" moment was the same as Levin's and

Tolstoy's. While waiting to ask for Kitty's hand, Levin could not sleep. He opened the window of his room and saw a fretted cross on a church and the rising constellation of the Bear. He looked now at the silent cross, now at the light yellow stars, which were rising, and almost in a dream he pursued the images that flashed through his memory. Life seemed to him more intense, radiant, and acute: the blood coursed more swiftly through his veins, his heart beat louder, his brain was illuminated by sudden revelations. For two nights he hadn't slept and he hadn't eaten anything for a day: and yet it seemed to him that he was completely detached from his body, and he felt that he could do anything—even fly in the sky or shift the corner of a building. The next morning he left the house, strolled through the streets of Moscow, and "what he saw then, afterward he never saw again." Some children were on their way to school, bluish pigeons flew from the roof to the sidewalks, doughnuts dusted with flour were displayed by invisible hands in a shop window; and suddenly a child ran toward a pigeon and looked at Levin, smiling, the pigeon fluttered and flew away, shimmering in the sun among the grains of snow that trembled in the air. The morning spectacle which happiness had covered with its resplendent varnish made Levin cry and laugh with joy; and the children, the pigeons, the doughnuts did not seem to him "beings of this earth."

The boundless and intoxicated happiness that Tolstoy attributed to Levin—the happiness that from one moment to the next can break into the daily grayness of everyone's life—was an essentially physical sensation: to know and enjoy the body's vibration at a higher and more intense level, above all those of sight, so lucid and luminous, with pigeons "which shimmered in the sun." But in order to be happy one must at the same time dig out of the body sensations and intuitions that surpass it—an immaterial lightness due to which it seemed possible to fly in the sky, an unearthly joy that made everything one saw an unrepeatable spectacle. Tolstoy demanded that life should remain itself, nothing but an instant of body and time, without any transcendence: and yet it must leap beyond a barrier, becoming a mysterious *beyond*, an epiphany of the invisible and timeless. When he was happy, he knew neither past nor future: he lived neither in the memory nor in anticipation of joys: he inhabited the present, sucked up every drop of the present—with such intensity that past and future were embraced in the instant and he found on his lips the flavor of the eternal. For all of his life, even in old age, when he seemed to preach asceticism and sacrifice, he never desired anything but this. What mattered was to be happy in time and beyond time; and Christianity was but a road to this happiness.

Like Olenin, Tolstoy felt within him "the unrepeatable élan of youth": a force for which he could not find name and expression, because it was not yet divided according to the faculties of the ego, but had all its being in the moment when it poured into the light. For lack of other names, he called this force "love." He was there, on the surface of the earth, with his heart full of an immense joy, and he felt the need to clasp someone in his arms, someone he loved very much, to embrace him with all his strength, to hold him tight against his chest and make him share his happiness, while tears of *Sehnsucht** bathed his face. "Yes," he repeated, with a stupendous image he had stolen from Sterne, "the best way to attain true happiness in life is to spread outside oneself in all directions without any rules—like a spider—the prehensile threads of love and catch in them all that goes by; an old woman, a child, a woman, or a policeman." But to catch a woman or a policeman was not enough for him: the need for expansion broadened his soul infinitely. The spiders' webs must multiply, and in them catch all men and all women, without distinction, all animals, all things vibrating like creatures, and even the remote and enigmatic figure of God. "A marvelous night. What is it I wish? What is it that I wish for so ardently? I don't know, but not the things of this world. And how not to believe in the immortality of the soul!—when in the soul one feels such an immense greatness. Looked out the window. It is black, pierced and luminous. One wants to die.—My God! My God! What am I? And where am I going? And where am I?"

He needed to be immersed in the liquid atmosphere of love, like a child in its tub. During the years of late youth, the feminine world—that world which extended from the sparkle of dresses, the charm of smiles, to courtship and "the threshold of love"—gave him an irrepressible joy: he believed that only love could give him happiness, he

*Nostalgia, homesickness—TRANS.

wanted all human beings to share in his enthusiasm; and what did it matter if infatuations and tendernesses were first of all a game of his creative imagination? This force obeyed a strange law. Intoxicated and nebulous, it was turned to everyone and no one: it did not know precise faces to hug to the breast: one face was as good as the next, any object could set him on fire; his passions and his manias were pretexts that the "unrepeatable impetus" of youth donned in order to express itself. Some could say that it was only a matter of an intoxicated narcissistic projection. Thus, despite such an outpouring of universal love he remained cold, like the ironic dandy, or the most gelid, observing artist: as his wife accused him, "he never truly loved anyone." Tolstoy realized that there was even a greater risk. That obscure and undivided force of expansion, which pulsed and vibrated within him, had no definite direction: it could take him to the door of heaven; but also throw him, without his being able to prevent it, into the "bottomless pit" where all sensations, feelings, and things are confused.

Every time spring surged on the earth, the same lymph surged in his veins. "Spring has arrived!" he wrote to his cousin Alexandra. "In nature, in the air, in everything there is hope, future: a marvelous future. . . . I know very well, when I really think about it, that I'm an old potato scorched by frost, rotten, and what's more cooked in the gravy: and yet spring has such an effect on me that at times I catch myself in the full illusion of being a plant that only now is about to open up together with the other plants to grow simply, tranquilly, and joyously in God's world. . . . Make room for the extraordinary flower which swells its buds and will grow together with the spring!" "Before our eyes miracles are accomplished. Every day, a new miracle. There was a bare branch and look! now it is covered with leaves. God alone knows from what part of the underground comes all these green, yellow, and blue things. Some animals fly like cranes from one bush to the other and, who knows why, whistle with all their might: it is a marvel. Also at this moment, right below my window, two nightingales lacerate their throats. . . . Just think, I am able to call them to my window by playing the sixth on the piano. I discovered it by chance. A few days ago I was strumming as usual Haydn's sonatas which have sixths.

Suddenly, in the courtyard and in Auntie's bedroom (she has a canary) I heard whistles, peeps, trills, in tune with my sixths. I stopped and they stopped too. I began again and they too began again. (Two nightingales and the canary.) I spent about three hours at this occupation: the balcony door was open, the night was warm, the frogs were doing their job. . . . What a marvel. . . . There's no happiness more complete, more harmonious than this."

Nobody, perhaps, ever knew as well as Tolstoy the Pan-like and orgiastic impulse to merge—as Rousseau said—with the "system of beings, to identify with nature." After the spring rain, he plunged into the woods, ran among the bushes, tore off the wet twigs, rubbed against his face the inebriating perfume of the acacias, violets, rotten leaves, wild cherries, and mushrooms: or he slid into the apple orchard where he lost his identity, becoming the dark green nettle, which thrust up with its fragile blooming tip, disheveled burdock with the unnatural purple of its small, sharp-pointed flowers, the tender hop which luxuriated soft with dew in the shade, and even the burning rays of the sun which filtered among the leaves. . . . Nature offered him all the pleasures in which his happiness lay: it made him forget his unbearable person, abolished past and future, lured him toward the infinite, forced him to live where there was no longer "either place or movement, body, distance, and space."

When the spring moon shone on the earth, it seemed to reveal to him the divine inspiration and heart of nature. "Often, when there was a full moon I spent whole nights, sitting on my mattress, staring at the light and shadows, listening to the silence and sounds, fantasizing about different things, above all about the poetic happiness of the senses which at the time seemed to me the greatest happiness of life, and despairing at having only been able to imagine it, until then. . . . For me everything, then, acquired a different significance: the appearance of the old birch trees, which to one side gleamed with their leafy branches against the sky dominated by the moon and on the other with their black shadows gloomily covered bushes and road, and the quiet, majestic scintillation of the pond which regularly augmented in intensity like a sound, and the lunar refulgence of the dewdrops on the flowers in front of the porch which also cast their graceful shadows across the gray flower bed, and the call of the partridge beyond the pond, and the man's voice on the main road, and the subdued, barely perceptible creaking of two old birch trees against each other, and the hum of the mosquito near my ear, under the blanket, and the fall of an apple, caught among the branches, onto the dry leaves, and the leaps of the frogs, which sometimes came all the way to the steps of the terrace and with their small greenish backs shone under the moon in a certain mysterious way—all this acquired for me a strange significance—that of too great a beauty and I do not know what incomplete happiness." *She* appeared to him, the beloved woman, with her long black braid. "But always higher, always more luminous was the moon in the sky, the majestic shimmer of the pond, which regularly increased in intensity like a sound, became ever more clear, the shadows darker, the light more diaphanous, and staring at and listening to all this something told me that also *she*, with her naked arms and her ardent embraces, was not yet by any means all of happiness, that the love for her was absolutely not yet the greatest beatitude; and the more I looked at the high full moon the more true happiness and beatitude appeared to me ever higher, purer, closer to Him, to the Source of all that is beautiful and all that is good, and tears of a mysterious, unsatisfied, but joyous emotion filled my eyes."

Under the light of the moon, before looking at the pages of his *Diary*, or during the journeys that drove him across Europe—he prayed to God. Happiness flooded him. He did not supplicate nor did he express his gratitude: it was an aspiration to something superior and perfect, something he did not know how to express and yet understood very well: he asked, and at the same time felt that he had nothing to ask, that he could not and knew not how to ask for anything. Sometimes he repeated the syllables of the Lord's Prayer: "Thy will be done on earth as in heaven." Sometimes he slowly pronounced the words he had studiously written out in his notebooks: "Deliver me, O Lord, from illnesses and anxieties of the soul: help me, O Lord, to live without sin and without sorrows, and to die without despair and without fear—with faith, hope, and love I entrust myself to Your will." "Help me to do good and avoid evil: but as for my good and evil, let Thy most holy will be done! Give me the good, the true good! Lord have pity! Lord have pity! Lord have pity!" He needed God to be at his side like the most faithful presence, to extend His protecting hand over his head, to trace the providential path of his life. And yet he had no proof at all of God's existence, and not even that an idea of Him was necessary. As he would say many years later, at the time of *Anna Karenina*, the "living God, the God of love, is an inevitable deduction of reason and at the same time an absurdity contrary to reason."

An Orthodox Christian like his cousin Alexandra accused him of knowing God only in the feverish exultation of nature. "It seems to me at times that you gather in your single self all the idolatries of the pagan world, adoring God in one ray of sun, in one aspect of nature, in one of the innumerable manifestations of His greatness, but without understanding that it is necessary to go back to the sources of life to enlighten and purify oneself." He wanted to encounter God "in one of those exalted states of mind, in which he imagined he was somebody": sublime thoughts, enthusiasms, raptures, sudden élans, ecstasies; whereas men can know God much better in sorrow and misfortune, in the radical knowledge of finiteness and guilt. Alexandra was not mistaken. Like every Rousseauan pantheist, Tolstoy aimed "at the merging of his being with the supreme Being": at the soul's illimitable expansion and identification with God. But, in the youthful diaries, we also come across different accents. At times God assailed him with extreme harshness, with such violent blows to the heart that he felt like weeping; and he saw Him as the Alien, the Remote, the Inconceivable, the One who does not belong to the realm of names.

Beyond this intoxication, the young Tolstoy knew the other more frightening intoxication that is aroused in us by the vertigo of thought. He enjoyed thinking ever more abstract thoughts: to reach the point where he could sense the "unembraceable immensity" of the world of ideas: at such a moment he realized the impossibility of going any further—and yet he threw ever new ideas on the gambling table of the mind, until he was no longer able to express himself. Often he was attacked by the universal doubt: or he imagined that, outside himself, no one and nothing existed in the entire world, and that the objects were not objects but rather images which appeared only when he turned his attention to them, and that, as soon as he stopped thinking of them, they would immediately vanish. "There were moments in which, dominated by this fixed idea, I reach such a point of madness that I rapidly turn to look behind me, to the other side, or across the way, in the hope of catching unawares the void (the *néant*) in the place where I was not." He had the habit of thinking about what he was thinking about. Asking himself the question: "What am I thinking about?" he answered: "I'm thinking about what am I thinking," and so on and on, ad infinitum, victim of the vicious circle of intelligence, bent over himself like Narcissus over the water's mirror. Or he reflected on the multiplicity of causes: he discovered the cause of a thing or a feeling, and then the cause of this cause, and the cause of the cause of this cause. . . . While with his very fine scalpel he dismembered reality into its elementary parts, he risked becoming the victim of the mind's indefinite dialectic. This frightened him: even more than death; and perhaps also because of this he fell back, in an extreme attempt to save himself from intellectual vertigo, on the violent simplifications of his Christian preachings.

This continuous intellectual self-consciousness reinforced in him the metaphysical sense of the false. Like all prisoners of the vicious circle of intelligence, he could not help but consider false all the thoughts and feelings that one by one he detached and removed from his mind. He discovered in himself the feeling of falsity in the imaginary archetypal moment of his mother's death described in *Childhood*, with which he linked all the keys to his being. A deacon had entered the death room. That sound startled him: since he was not crying and was upright on the chair in a pose that did not look at all sorrowful, his first thought was that the deacon might consider him an insensitive boy who out of foolishness and curiosity had climbed onto that chair: so he crossed himself, bowed, and began to cry. At that moment an impulse of vanity merged with the true sorrow, the wish to show that he was more sorrowful than anyone else, the preoccupation with the effect he might have on the others, the pleasure of the consciousness of being a victim of misfortune. Precisely in childhood, the presumed heart of nature and innocence, the shadow of duplicity and falsity was formed.

Thus, little by little, everything was contaminated by this obsession with the "false." Life was a fake spectacle, simulated, recited, a play of masks, like the operatic spectacle that Natasha saw on the Moscow stage. Nothing escaped this: neither the deeds and proclamations of the heroes of universal history, nor the mannered words that we pronounce at every moment of the day; and not even our inescapably deceptive feelings, our contradictory sensations, the unconscious thoughts that overlap and swirl in our minds, or the "simulated" expression of sorrow that appears in *The Sevastopol Tales* on the faces of the dying. Sometimes the "false" seems to be the only terrain that Tolstoy knew: the only one on which he could build the labyrinthine construction of his novels. Precisely during those same years, Flaubert had described the modern world as the triumph of the inauthentic: commonplaces, literature, falsities, lies, dead words. Emma Bovary's desires, dreams, and loves are romantic clichés like the words of Rodolphe which are aimed at seducing her; and, in the womb of "reality," truth is equally remote, because Homais, Bournisien, and the Councillor employ opposed and symmetrical clichés. In *Notes from the Underground*, Dostoevsky had discovered a more dreadful form of the false. The protagonist does not share his feelings or feign feelings he does not have, repenting, taking offense, falling in love, flaunting his resentment, declaiming like an extraordinarily gifted bravura actor. As for the "truth" of the mind, it ceases to exist: it is a hoax, a smirk, a grotesque rictus, which attributes to "yes" and "no" the same degree of authenticity, as if the very principle of "noncontradiction" no longer had any cognitive value.

Since everything was false, Tolstoy denounced both the conventions of thought and those of society—the music of Bach or the beauty of mountains or love. At times his nihilism sounded youthfully gay: he pushed theories to extremes, demolished them, built new ones that he soon would demolish, with an enchanting mobility and a delightful sense of play; at times he was hostile, malicious, sarcastic, aggressive, ferociously Mephistophelean. He carried this nihilism in his mind throughout his life, down to the last writings on religion and art, without its losing anything of its puerile or childish quality. Only children do not know that deception and mystification lay the groundwork for man's most sublime pleasures, and only children destroy—because they are not the *things*—those toys they love so much. Without the sense of the false, we could not even imagine the greatness of Tolstoy the novelist. Always attentive to the duplicity of feelings, he sharpened his ability to divide the psychic material into separate parts: distinguishing their surface and what lies behind it, each of which was subdivided into smaller parts, and the whole was enveloped by a vibrant web of interactions. With this intuition in mind, Tolstoy intensified his tragic feeling of existence: all lies debunked, all illusions abolished, what was left if not the chasm of death?

Sometimes Tolstoy came to a halt, terrified by the complexity of the impulses that dominated him: the tragedy of vanity, the discontinuous sense of time, the neurotic excitation, the game of fantasizing, the dream of an atemporal happiness, the amorous dilation of the ego, the vertigo of thought, the intuition of the false. . . . What could he do with all these? How would he be able to order, regulate, arrange them in a structure? How could he manage to transform chaos into harmony? At the start, he chose the easiest road, although this easiness was jagged, moralistic, and far from smooth. He did not accept himself: he did not possess the tenacious indolence that led Pierre and Kutuzov to find freedom in the passive acceptance of life and history. He wanted to better himself indefinitely in view of a hypothetic good and an absolute perfection which sometimes he dreamed of attaining in a single leap. "To live honestly," he wrote, "one must become agitated, get entangled, thrash about, and start again and abandon again, and struggle ad infinitum, plunging in all directions. As for tranquility—it is a cowardice of the soul." And so in his *Diary*, which became his main weapon in the struggle for perfection, he began to write down his faults and weaknesses. He was vain, proud, lazy, apathetic, affected, untruthful, unstable, indecisive, imitative, cowardly, victim of the spirit of contradiction, too sure of himself, lustful, and he had a passion for gambling. . . .

Then he set up a severe and detailed life program which was to occupy a specific span of time. "In a week I'm leaving for the country. What shall I do during this week? Study Latin and English, Roman law and the rules. I specify: read *The Vicar of Wakefield*, learning all the words I don't know, study first part of the grammar;

read, both for knowledge of the language and of Roman law, the first part of *Corpus Juris*: fulfill the rules of my inner education, and win my return chess game with Liliya." "What will be the goal of my time in the country during the next two years? (1) Learn the entire course of juridical sciences necessary for the final exam at the University. (2) Learn practical medicine and part of theoretical medicine. (3) Learn languages: French, Russian, German, English, Italian, and Latin. (4) Learn agriculture, theoretical and practical. (5) Learn history, geography, and *statistics.* (6) Learn mathematics (the first-year course at the University). (7) Write a thesis. (8) Try to reach an average degree of perfection in music and art. (9) Put the rule in writing. (10) Acquire some knowledge of the natural sciences. (11) Write essays on all the subjects I will study." In the execution of these programs he could not permit himself exceptions: at all costs, no matter what labor and effort of the will was demanded, he must perform everything he had stipulated; and should particular circumstances arise, these too must be foreseen in advance.

When we reread these tables of the law, which Tolstoy was never able to apply, we cannot help but smile, faced by the mania for completeness of this dilettante encyclopedist who wanted to gulp down all of knowledge in a week or two years. The rules end on a comic note: "Win my return chess game with Liliya"; since all his life long Tolstoy employed the same ethical obstinacy in pursuing the highest ideals and the most frivolous aims, which someone else would have regarded as a game. The man who had set down this program was a man possessed, who wanted to kill in himself all unconscious spontaneity, all sentimental emotion, every amusement of the mind and imagination, every amiable abandonment to chance, in order to obey only that which was programmed, preestablished, foreseen. "Every morning," he insisted, "you will decide everything that you must do during the course of the day, and perform everything that you have decided upon, even if the execution of what you have decided should cause you some inconvenience" (or even: "meditate on my future actions, note them, and accomplish them, even if they are bad"). In the evening, on that tabulation of *the way to be* which was his *Diary*, he added up the accounts with meticulous precision, castigating himself like the most severe taskmaster. "I did not do my calisthenics seriously, that is, I did them without taking my strength into account: this is a weakness which in a general way I shall call *arrogance*, 'deviation from reality.' . . . I frequently looked at myself in the mirror; from this stupid physical love for myself can only come something bad and ridiculous. . . . I greeted Golicyn first instead of going straight to where I was supposed to. During my calisthenics I praised myself (boasting). I made an effort to give Kobylin a correct opinion of myself (petty pride). I ate too much at dinner (gluttony)." "I've broken rules (1) to avoid drunks, (2) to get up early, (3) not to think of the future, (4) not to play cards, (5) orderliness, (6) not to begin several things at the same time, (7) to act resolutely."

Without noticing their apparent contradiction, while he planned these moral reforms, he pursued a more futile ideal: to become a *dandy*, halfway between Dolokhov and Baudelaire. The first condition consisted in achieving perfect French pronunciation; the second was to have well-cared-for and -trimmed fingernails, the third, knowing how to bow, dance, and converse pleasantly; the fourth, the most important, a sovereign indifference for everybody and everything and a continuous attitude of refined and contemptuous boredom. When, in a drawing room, he was confronted by difficult situations, he tried to gain the upper hand; he dominated the conversation, spoke in a loud voice, slowly and distinctly, began and ended the conversation without ever exposing his feelings to the others. Wearing a fashionable coat and a top hat set at an angle on his dark red curls and carrying a silver-headed cane, he made a distinction between men *comme il faut* and *comme il ne faut pas* whom he despised and hated; and he spoke gladly only about futile subjects—cockfights, athletic contests. In reality, the moralist as well as the dandy set himself the same goal: to live a voluntary and mental life, composed of desperate tension and desperate artifice, pursuing the unnatural imperturbability of fashionable mannequins.

This ensemble of laws and rules was of very little use to him in the daily relations of existence. He feared the judgment of others: he flushed when others fixed their eyes on him: he suffered from a violent inferiority complex; and he wanted to be loved, fondled, the preferred of those others who seemed to him so remote and sublime.

As soon as he entered the magic circle of friendship and love, he was subjected to the influence of the beloved: he became as receptive as wax: if the other spoke emphatically, he did too: if the other spoke French poorly, he too stumbled over the pronunciation; the other's feelings having pierced his soul's nervous surface acted upon him like a contagion. But, at that point, precisely because every human contact represented the risk of making him lose his own ego, he reacted with violence. Flaunting his imaginary armor, he grew rigid, withdrew into the fortress of his self: he refused to undergo any influence that gave him the impression of being possessed; if it seemed to him that the amorous contagion brought inside him the hated and beloved other, he tried to wound, reject, and attack the other. He had a ferocious need for solitude, and refused to communicate his thoughts to anyone. After he had distanced everyone from his self, imagining himself to be at last able to enjoy the delights of solitude, he was desperate once again. "This solitude is killing me." He felt unloved, excluded, alien. "I am a kind of *badly loved.* That's it exactly, and I feel that I cannot be pleasing to anyone and that everybody is a burden for me. Despite myself, whatever I may be saying, with my eyes I say things that no one wants to hear, and I am displeased with myself because I say them."

Among the characters of his novels, he was without a doubt the most tragic: this mute character who will never appear on the stage and whom we nevertheless continuously sense like a restless, disquieting, and tormented shadow. Only his beloved Anna Karenina was marked in the same way by the seal of fate and tragedy. How many times did he not sense at his back the presence of *another* reality—unknown, immeasurable, hostile—that threatened to tear away the curtain, striking him in the back: how many times did he not sense death hovering over his days, expecting it from hour to hour, minute to minute; and love, to which everyone surrenders with so much trust, seemed to him a tragedy without remedy. The complaints about laziness, which he confided so often to his *Diary*, show us that this frenzied man sensed an abyss of apathy, a terrifying ocean of nothingness rising up to the gates of his soul and threatening to submerge him.

So I cannot imagine how anyone could have considered him a

"normal" person or writer—whatever this word may mean. Charles Du Bos said: "In his ultimate depths, Tolstoy was the most normal of beings. All the sensations that he brings to light have been experienced and lived by millions of men, women, and children in the same way that Tolstoy experienced and lived them"; and Stefan Zweig repeated: "He never goes beyond the restricted zone of the comprehensible, of what is evident to the senses, the palpable. He has no other poetic or magical qualities beyond the common ones. He never goes beyond the confines of normality." Tolstoy was a man possessed, a man pursued by the Furies, as few writers in a century when the Furies reawakened from their sleep. There was no person less "normal" than he: because it is not a normal person who carries all experiences to the breaking point: or who demands from everyday life absolute happiness, the miraculous leap beyond time. He could have recounted to us only his dreams, his deliriums, the startled moments of his perennially tumultuous ego. But, by an incomprehensible gift, the moment his hand picked up the pen, without his having done anything to obtain it, it was given to him to share the experiences of all creatures, by becoming the most mediocre of persons, or a dog pointing his prey, or a horse during a battle. He, who did not know and did not see others, *became all the others.* By a paradox, precisely he became the novelist of reality. He contemplated it with such furor and with such an excess of participation, with a gaze that reached *beyond*, from that mysterious world which he inhabited with terror and joy, so that the novelistic representation became electric, scintillating, intense, as perhaps it had never been—more fantastic than any dream.

II

On May 30, 1851, in order to "forget his complicated, unharmonious, monstrous past," Tolstoy arrived at the Starogladkovskaya *stanitsa** in the Caucasus. For almost three years, his surroundings did not change. No longer the plain and woods of Yasnaya Polyana, where he had pursued his dream of a Rousseauan landowner; nor the elegant streets and social gatherings of Moscow, where he had gambled away his life. He came to know the sad, arid expanse of the steppes, with its sand dotted with cattle tracks, a little wilted grass, and Tatar outposts here and there on the horizon. There was no shade: the sun rose and set always burning red: when the wind blew, the air carried along mountains of sand: when there was a calm, sounds had a feeble echo and were immediately doused and the quiet, veiled air inspired an impression of torpor and desolation. At first he did not like the mountains: then those steep rocks looming above the road, the furious crash of the Terek River, the foaming falls, the distant, snowy peaks seemed to him his soul's homeland; and "whatever he saw or thought, whatever feeling he experienced, took on for him the stern, majestic quality of the mountains." The Cossack village became his family. The moment he awoke, he saw the houses lifted above the ground, with large, luminous windows in front of which rose dark green poplars, acacia trees with their white, fragrant flowers, the sunflowers and grapevines. The horsemen with their tattered uniforms and precious weapons, caracoling down the

*Cossack village—TRANS.

roads: while the girls, with their varicolored *besmet*,* whips in hands, merrily chatting and laughing, herded the cattle back from pasture. Sado wished to be his *kunak*:† offering him his friendship in life and death, put at his disposal his house, his family, and his wife, and made him the gift of a splendid saber.

He went hunting. About six in the morning he slipped into a tattered cloak, boots rotted by water, attached his hunting knife to his belt, picked up his rifle and haversack: he called his dog; and returned around seven o'clock in the evening, tired and hungry. He roamed over the bald plains, the swamps and mountain slopes. He massacred pheasants and hares: chased elks, mountain goats, bears, and deer; or he would lie in wait along the bank of the Terek, shooting at the ducks that rose in swarms from the reeds. Close to the village there was a wood, a kind of pullulating and fiery terrestrial paradise filled with pheasants and mosquitoes: the myriads of insects suited the wild, almost monstrous richness of the vegetation, the abundance of birds and beasts, the somber greenery, the fragrant torrid air, the brooks of murky water filtering everywhere from the Terek and gurgling invisible beneath the projecting fronds. Suddenly into his soul there descended a strange sensation of motiveless happiness and love for everyone; and it was as though he had sloughed off the human shell, had become a fragment of nature, like those trees enveloped by the wild grapevines, like that teeming of pheasants, alive and ready to die, which raced by jostling each other and perhaps got a whiff of their murdered brothers, and the millions of mosquitoes which hummed among the leaves. At night, he lifted his eyes to the sky. The stars walked. He looked around: the wood soughed and seemed always expectant, waiting from one moment to the next for a boar to appear with a rustle. Down there he heard the young eagles and the roosters answer from the village, and the geese. He crouched there quietly and thought: fragments of ideas, memories, and fantasies were intertwined: he became a Cossack, a rebel in the mountains, a boar; and, as once upon a time before, he asked himself: "What is it I am thinking?"

*A Tatar garment with sleeves—Trans.

†A sworn friend for whom no sacrifice is too great—Trans.

At times he was gripped by a passion for uniforms, the desire for battle, a dream of military glory, the St. George Cross to pin on his chest. His squadron attacked the position of the Chechen mountaineers: a wheel of the cannon he was ordered to operate was damaged by an enemy shell; another shell killed a horse two paces away from him. When the Russian soldiers retreated, the rebel mountaineers shot at them with rifles. War, with its very concrete and real dangers, became in his *Diary* also a sort of childish fantasy. He wished that chance would have him meet with trials that demanded great spiritual strength: his imagination nourished by his pride suggested all these situations, and his presumptuous instinct told him that he would have enough courage to endure them. Whenever he behaved weakly or without courage he immediately found some justification, and convinced himself that the difficulties had not been so great as to demand the mustering of all his spiritual forces. His childish dream of omnipotence continued to measure itself against the unreal. Then he holed up in the village, which soon became unbearably boring for him. He studied the native language, compiled ethnological notes, jotted down Cossack songs: he read, played chess, lost desperately at cards, had conversations with his brother Nikolai, got drunk; and went back to hunting hares and pheasants, brutalizing himself.

A few years later he wrote that in the Caucasus he had begun to think—"as one has the strength to think only once in a lifetime." He lived in exaltation, concentrated in himself. "Never, neither before nor after, did I reach such peaks of thought, never again did I look *beyond* as during that period." If, before, he had lived by restraining himself and imposing on himself programs and rules of life, now he let the confused, contradictory, and tangled richness of his soul be reflected in the mobile mirror of consciousness. He dreamed of Yasnaya, the times of happiness he had spent there with Aunt Tatyana, the happiness that had slipped through his fingers without his knowing or taking advantage of it; or he envied the primitive existence of those steppes and those mountains, where men lived like nature: were born, mated, died, were born again, fought, drank, ate, made merry, and again died, with no other limitations than those that nature had imposed on the sun, the grass, the trees, and the wild beasts. Often, at night, he stayed awake. The sky was light, a fresh breath passed through his room and made the candle's flame sway. He breathed in the scent of the leaves of the oak and plane trees. The moon rose behind the hills, illuminating two small gossamer clouds, while in the distance, in the depths of the sky, a whitish band of very small stars which seemed to draw closer was barely visible. A cricket behind him sang its melancholy song. Far away a frog croaked. From near the village came the shouts of the Tatars and the barking of dogs. Then all fell silent again. "I said to myself: I will write what I have seen. But how? One must go, sit down before a table spotted with inkstains, take some gray paper, some ink; stain one's fingers and scribble some letters on the paper. The letters form words, the words sentences; but can one render what one feels? Is there not some other way to pour into someone else one's sensations when faced by nature? Description is not enough." Already then, when he was twenty-three, before he had even begun to write stories, Tolstoy sensed what one of his principal problems as a writer was.

So, almost by chance, he sought for this mysterious means, resigning himself to using letters and staining his fingers with ink. He began *Childhood.* He wrote without stopping, so as not to interrupt the tenuous stream of inspiration, which flowed ever more clearly within him. He copied and recopied. "I write with such ardor," he would say later, "that I become sick. My heart fails. I tremble when I pick up my notebook." In his Cossack village, or Fort Stary Yurt, or Tiflis, he narrated with his mind turned back, enveloped in a wave of regret and nostalgia for his childhood. Then the world was still a single cocoon, which concentrated around his life as a boy; and it seemed to him that everything existed for him alone. There was in his soul "a buoyancy, a sense of light and refreshment": an inexhaustible need for love impelled him to embrace all persons and all things, with tears and ecstasy; he lived in the luminous joy of the present, and at the same time in the hope that even more radiant times awaited him. But childhood was lost forever and he tried to recover it with the awareness that his attempt was certain to fail and could only leave him with a faint glimmer of the past.

The vibrant heart of *Childhood* is the image of the mother, who died when he was two years old. He did not remember her at all: he possessed no portrait of her, only a silhouette cut out of black paper, which portrayed her when she was ten or twelve years old—a convex forehead, round chin, and hair that fell like a curtain over the nape of her neck. Anxiously and with veneration he had questioned relatives and friends, so as to gather every bit of information about her. She was very cultivated for her time: she knew four languages, played the piano well, read Rousseau's *Émile*, commenting on it, invented beautiful fairy tales, similar to those that his brother Nikolai would later tell him: she loved and was loved; and she possessed two qualities for which her son would always envy her—those of never judging and knowing how to control herself.

With the passing of time, fantasizing around these bits of information, the mother had become for him the Oedipal image of the celestial woman who radiates a chaste and mild affection, without even the shadow of that erotic strength which in his late maturity he would abhor. Even as an old man he wept with great emotion, thinking of her embraces and caresses. Now, in writing *Childhood*, he imposed on himself a tremendous task. With letters, words, and sentences he wanted to recreate a past completely sunk in the abyss of his memory; and he brought his forgotten mother back to life, because this game with ghosts was the only way he could exorcize his sorrow. Finally at home in the falsity of literature, he lied to himself, imagining he could remember her face. "When I try to remember Mama, as she was at that time, before my eyes appear only her chestnut-brown eyes, which always expressed the same goodness, the same love, the beauty mark on her neck, just a little below where the short fine hairs curled, the small white embroidered collar, the tender, thin hand, which so often caressed me and I so often kissed."

The mother had died; and Tolstoy's tale, which from nothing created remembrances that had never existed, must contemplate and confront this death. He slipped into the almost dark room of the dying woman, immersed in the blended smells of mint, eau de cologne, camomile, and Hoffmann's drops: he imagined he saw the widely staring eyes that saw nothing, the agitated gestures, the head that slipped down from the pillows, the hand that rose and fell back, the attempts to say something. . . . He entered the drawing room, where the coffin had been placed. Amid the candles and the tall silver candelabra, the brocade, the velvet, the pink pillow adorned with lace, he saw "that diaphanous, wax-colored thing." Was that her face? Why had the eyes sunk in that way? Why that pallor, and on one cheek a blackish spot under the skin? Why was the expression of the entire face so severe and gelid? Why were the lips so pale? Confronted by this extreme experience of the imagination, Tolstoy touched for the first time on some capital scenes of his art: death as the judge of life, deception which corrodes existence at its gravest moments; at the same time he attempted one of the artistic processes that became most dear to him—to observe reality with the eyes of the protagonist. In the end, the feigned search for memory ended in horror. A five-year-old girl saw the dead woman's face, the sunken eyes, and the blackish stain on the cheek: she noticed the strong odor of the corpse, which filled the room and mixed with the incense: and she cried out with frantic revulsion. Then he finally understood where the strange odor came from. The thought that that face, which only a few days before had bent over him so sweetly, could arouse fear, made his soul overflow with despair; and he too let out a cry "which must seem even more terrible than the cry that had struck him."

As we read *Childhood* and the subsequent writings, we never cease being amazed. Everything would lead us to believe that the egocentric and tumultuous, contradictory and mannered character who expresses himself in the *Diary* should have written a book that resembles him: excessive and unnatural as he was. Instead, *Childhood* is an elegant and composed, fresh and wise book, where memories and literary echoes are woven together with great naturalness. So the act of writing had in him a healing function. What was strained was relaxed: what was turbid became purified by writing. By a sort of contagion, literature led him to also find in everyday life ease of behavior and the exactness of inner movements. It was enough to wait ten years. With a complete mental overturn, the abrasive moralist and the programmatic dandy became the strange wise man who, from the heart of *War and Peace*, proposed to men the quiet surrender of an almost Taoist wisdom.

Tolstoy possessed to an exorbitant, almost monstrous degree what we call the "capacity to objectify." Both in *Childhood* and *The Sevastopol Tales*, he drew his material from immediate biographical experience: while he wrote, this often burning material became the life of other characters. In narrating, he—who seemed so incapable of coming out of himself—freed himself from himself; and separated the entire world from himself. We might say that this process of transposition occurs in all great storytellers. But let us think of Flaubert, who achieved objectivity through labored expedients, very complicated metamorphoses; whereas the young Tolstoy arrived at them immediately with unheard-of speed and a magical naturalness that cannot be found in any other writer. He dipped his pen in himself; and immediately "these lights emanating from him alone" created perfectly objective figures and scenes. This is a spectacle before which I do not know whether admiration should prevail or a kind of stunned awe. Tolstoy's simple, immense secret lay in this. Thus his art, which might have led him to depict a completely solipsistic or illusionistic world (did not reality cease existing if he turned around?), which could have made him the most madly egocentric of romatic poets—allowed him to figure forth the entire created world, war and peace, youth and decline, love and despair and illusion, life and death and new life which is continually reborn from death, the infinite space around the resonant steps of his characters.

No one should be more grateful to literature than he—because literature had placated his anxieties, expanded his breathing and his experience, allowed him to become "the world." The *Diaries* of these years are filled with cries of gratitude. He sought no other happiness, no other glory, he desired no other pleasure than that of creation. "Reality has killed in my imagination all dreams of happiness, except the happiness of the artist": "My career is literature—to write and write! Beginning tomorrow I will work all my life, or send it all to hell: rules, religion, conventions—everything." A few years later he would add: "Thank goodness there is one salvation: the moral world, the world of art, poetry, and friendship. There is no one here: neither the commissioner nor the mayor disturb me: I live alone, the wind blows, outside there is mud, it is cold, and I play Beethoven with my obtuse fingers and shed tears of emotion, or I read the *Iliad* or invent characters of my own, women, I live with them, fill sheets with scribbles."

Dilettante that he was, he addressed to himself precepts of an almost cruel exactness. "Another condition of beauty—precision, the sharp definition of the characters." The vague and complicated must be excluded: one must pitilessly suppress "passages that are not very clear, prolix, out of place, in a word, all those that are not satisfactory even if good in themselves." Correcting is a dangerous exercise. "In rereading often, one judges oneself inexactly and unfavorably: the fascination and interest of the new and unexpected disappear and often one cancels what is good and seems bad only because of its frequent repetition." One thing among all others concerned him most: "I have the laziness of writing by giving details, I would like to write everything in lines of fire."

But the redemption that literature offered him was illusory. Literature purified him for a few months, or a few years: allowed him to find a provisional equilibrium with the world; and then? All the tangles, maelstroms, dissatisfaction, aggressiveness, the disharmonies of his contradictory nature showed up again, and after twenty, thirty, or forty years he found himself faced again by the same problems as in his adolescence. Nothing had changed: grown older, with many books on the shelves, infinite readings in his mind, he remained a young boy: a kind of Ulysses, who must always repeat his departure for Troy and his return through the dangers and monsters of the Mediterranean. So he accused literature with the same ardor with which he had exalted it. Literature was death, falsity. "And this horrible need to translate with words and line up in fly tracks on paper thoughts that are ardent, alive, mobile, like the rays of the sun that color the clouds in the air," he said, quoting George Sand. "Those who observe things in order to notice them, see them in a false light." He would not accept the idea of becoming, as Turgenev proposed to him, only a literary man: a servant of words. Even when he achieved the most extraordinary technical skill, even when he knew the novelist's art as no one, perhaps, had ever known it, he insisted on his essential status as a dilettante. He was on loan to literature. But in his inner spirit he felt was hidden "the germ of all possible qualities": he could become a soldier, the chief of armies, a schoolteacher, a pedagogue, a philosopher, an interpreter of God's word, a prophet, a vagabond, a monk, even a politician; and until death he tenaciously defended his multiform, protean freedom.

III

As in a systolic and diastolic process, after a long period of concentration in the Caucasus, Tolstoy's life broadened and expanded. He needed to see and know people of his own world, exchanging with them the futile conversations that were dear to him: he wanted primacy no longer in literature but in society. On March 12, 1854, he was at Bucharest where, during the Crimean War, the headquarters of Prince Gorchakov was located. He liked the fashionable life at headquarters. He was part of the general's circle: ate at his table every day, went off with the aristocratic, very *comme il faut* officers; he assiduously frequented the French theater, the Italian opera, and the fashionable restaurants, ate sorbets, and was so completely devoted to appearances that for three months he forgot to keep his *Diary*. Often the young, elegant aides-de-camp aroused his furious envy: one of them sang the gypsy ballads too well; with another he had a violent fight over a trifle. Unknowingly his mind stored up the scenes, the gestures, the words that he would use in *War and Peace*: Prince Sergei's cadet, *bon garçon, quoique n'ayant pas à lui seul inventé la poudre*, who would be reborn identical on the lips of Bilibin. When he took part in the siege of Silistria, war seemed to him a spectacle that some unknown God had organized as a feast for the eye. He climbed a hill through the superb gardens of Mustapha Pasha, the governor of the besieged city. From there, standing on a carriage, binoculars in hand, he saw the Danube, its islands and banks, Silistria, the fortress and the forts: he listened to the cannon and rifle shots which continued day and night: he could distinguish one by one the Turkish soldiers;

for hours on end he could not tear himself away from the spectacle, as though war seen from above lost all of its horror.

On November 7 he arrived at Sevastopol, assigned to the Third Light Battery of the Fourteenth Artillery Brigade. The city seemed to him "miraculously beautiful." When dawn began to tint the sky's vault over Mount Sapun, the sea's surface shed the somber colors of the night: cold and mist rose from the bay: the harsh morning frost bit into his face and crunched under his feet; and only the distant, ceaseless roar of the sea, rarely drowned out by the thunderous shots at Sevastopol, shattered the dawn's silence. The first figures bagan to move on the stage. Here they changed guard, with a clinking of rifles: there a doctor hastened to the hospital; and over there a soldier popped out of the barracks, wet his tanned face with cold water, and with rapid signs of the cross said his prayers. Then the sun rose in the sky, and under Tolstoy's eyes everything sparkled, as if the besieged city were varnished with light. The sea scintillated under the sun: the small black dots of the rowboats moved among the azure's foaming splendor: the white shore batteries appeared, the barracks, the aqueducts, the dry docks, the bastions, the city's elegant buildings tinged with pink by the morning rays: the foaming white light of the pier shone brightly with the sunken Russian ships, the black tips of whose masts emerged sadly here and there; until the sun, after shining with unchanging festiveness for all, reached the distant enemy fleet, which rocked along the rim of the sea. All along the line of fortifications, with a sudden lightning bolt which flashed even at high noon, swarmed globes of dense white smoke which grew upon themselves, taking on different shapes, and rose and stood out darker than the sky. Tolstoy had the impression that war made life's spectacle gayer. Everything was yellow, red, green, azure, with colors more intense than ever before: the shells, mortar bombs, machine guns, cannons, gun carriages, cases of ammunition, and rifles piled up as in a picturesque market. On the boulevards played the band of a regiment, the musicians stood stiffly: instead of music stands, other soldiers held up the scores; while all around, intent more on looking than listening, in a circle stood clerks, cadet offficers, nurses with their children, men of the navy, officers in white gloves, young women with kerchiefs on their heads.

When Tolstoy moved closer to the bastions and trenches, the frivolous music of the boulevards changed into the music of bullets: buzzing like bees, sibilant and swift, or twanging like a taut string. He heard the sentinel shout: "Cannon!" And he heard that sound, that thud, saw that fan of spray. When he heard the shout "Mortar!" his ear picked up the sibilant sound of a bomb, regular and rather pleasant: the sibilance accelerated until the shell struck the ground, followed by the explosion. Surrounded by these noises, he had a strange sensation of pleasure: a kind of mad desire that the next bombs should fall closer, ever closer around him; because war shattered the crust of habit, which made existence stifling to him, and offered him exciting and unusual sensations. At night he admired the extraordinary gracefulness of the artillery fireworks: the reddish trajectories of the shells interlaced in the air, the flashes of the blasts illuminated for an instant the deeper blue, thousands of small gleams revealed the rifle shots, while the crescendo of the cannonade reached the ear with increasing loudness. "*Quel charmant coup d'oeil*! Don't you agree?" said an officer's voice from a window, repeating the words a general had already uttered in "The Raid." "You know, it's impossible to distinguish the stars from shells at certain moments!" "Yes, just now I thought it was a star, and instead it came down . . . there, it's arrived. And vice versa that star there (what is it called?) really looks exactly like a shell." Nothing had changed since Silistria: even seen close up with the imperturbability, the sang-froid and dandyism of the young aristocrats, war had become a spectacle. So Tolstoy tried to be daring, as in the history books. He was thinking of an adjutant of Napoleon who, after having delivered an order, returned to him at a gallop, his head bloodied. "*Vous êtes blessé*!" Napoleon exclaimed. "*Je vous demande pardon, sire: je suis mort*!" and then he fell dead from his horse. But look! a shell came flying directly at him. Terror overwhelmed him: he took five unsteady paces and cowered on the ground while sweat burst pouring from all his limbs. Then he who boasted of never bending was seized by a great disappointment. When he heard a footfall he quickly straightened up, lifted his head, proudly rattled his saber. By now he felt like a different man. An officer of the engineers shouted to him: "Get down!" pointing to the small luminous dot of a shell which gradually became brighter as it approached with ever greater velocity. Grudgingly, he barely lowered his head and continued walking forward.

If in the Caucasus he had tried to allow only the voice of his original self to speak, now he was attentive to the voices and gestures of society. With his usual acumen, he noticed a paradoxical phenomenon: here, at Sevastopol, as shortly before at Silistria, war, with its daily risk of death, reinforced the officers' snobbishness instead of attenuating it. "For Captain Obzogov, Second Captain Mikhailov is an aristocrat and, because he wears a clean overcoat and gloves: for Second Captain Mikhailov, Adjutant Kalugin is an aristocrat, because he is an adjutant and addresses the other adjutant informally. . . . For Adjutant Kalugin, Count Nordov is an aristocrat and at heart he despises him and showers him with all sorts of abuse because he's the aide-de-camp of the commander in chief." Tolstoy knew this vice very well and he called it "the disease of the century." The first snob was he, who liked so much to be with people *comme il faut*; and he described his vice with an ironic and cruel elegance, which he would remember at the time of *War and Peace*. So he imagined that the honest, clumsy, tidy Captain Mikhailov did not wish to shake hands with Captains Obzogov and Suslikov, so badly dressed, in camel wool trousers, with no gloves and a tattered cape. He wanted to salute officers in white gloves: "pleasant people, and besides well informed on all the news." Doubly the prey to uncertainty, he walked past in sight of his aristocrats, until, gathering courage, he went up to them. Luckily, Adjutant Kalugin was in an excellent mood. The general had just spoken to him most cordially, his aristocrat—Prince Galtsin—had called at his house; and he did not deem it beneath him to shake Mikhailov's hand. Cavalry Captain Praskukhin, who very often met Mikhailov on the bastions, drank his vodka, and owed him twelve rubles and fifty kopeks, was much colder. Since he did not yet know Prince Galtsin very well, he would have preferred not to expose his friendship with a simple infantry captain; and only gave him a slight nod. Mikhailov's joy did not last long. Soon the aristocrats began to converse exclusively with each other, giving him to understand that he was free to leave. At the end, they just walked away from him. Nevertheless, Mikhailov was still satisfied. When in passing he grazed the Cadet Officer Baron Pesth, he felt in no way hurt by the contemptuous expression of condescension with which the baron came to attention before him and doffed his cap.

Tolstoy spent the period between the end of November and the beginning of April 1855 in the vicinity of Sevastopol: first at Esk-Orda, then on the banks of the Belbek River. War kept his vital spirits gay and lively: he played the piano and danced with the young ladies, hunted deer and fawn in the woods, listened, observed, and discussed. How easily his moods changed! In his *Diary* he wrote desolate notes about Russia: "I have become more than ever convinced that Russia must succumb or change completely. . . . Stupid exercises with useless weapons, brutalization, decrepitude, ignorance, bad maintenance, and bad nourishment kill attention, and the last spark of pride." Then he composed a poem, in which he expressed his condemnation and his election:

> When then, when will I finally cease
> To live my life without aim or passion
> And to feel in my heart a deep wound
> Without knowing how to heal it!
>
> Who has inflicted this wound in me, God knows,
> But I am tormented since birth
> By the bitter mortgage of the coming void,
> By a consuming sadness and by doubts.

He gambled for two days and nights in a row: he lost thousands of rubles: he was so disgusted with himself that he would have liked to stop writing and forget his existence: "Time, time, youth, dreams, thoughts, everything disappears without leaving a trace. I do not live, but I drag out my life." He prepared a project for reform of the army: he decided to enter the General Staff, then, suddenly, between one game of *stos* and another, between one fawn hunt and the next, he gave himself the task of reforming Christianity. "This thought is to found a new religion, corresponding to the evolution of humanity, a religion of Christ but stripped of faith and mysteries, a practical religion that does not promise future beatitude but grants beatitude on earth." Thus Tolstoyism was born in a moment of leisure of a young megalomaniac artilleryman who did not know how to spend his time.

At the end of March he was again at Sevastopol with his battery. On April 5 he spent a night in the Fourth Bastion, a hundred meters from the French lines. One hundred cannon shot at them, two thousand shells in twenty-four hours. The walls of the armored bunker split open, cracked, the floor shook, the acrid odor of gunpowder enveloped the bed, tables, clock, and icon. At first he did not like the hero's role: he was furious at being considered useless cannon fodder. Then he began to like the bastion: the continuous fascination of danger, the habit of observing the soldiers, the image of war were so attractive to him that he no longer wanted to leave. He implored God: "I thank You for Your constant protection. Set me on the road, and not to satisfy my futile aspirations but to attain the eternal and great goal of my life, which I do not know, but of which I am conscious." He spent his rest periods—four days out of every eight—at Sevastopol; and the feverish irresponsibility, under whose sign he had lived the entire year, made him like Adjutant Kalugin or any of the other elegant officers whom he depicted with so much irony. "I remained at Sevastopol until May 15 . . . and although four days out of every eight I had to stand guard at the Fourth Bastion, spring was so beautiful, there were so many people, my impressions were so rich, we lived in such comfort (I had a very elegant apartment with a piano), I went swimming in the sea, and we formed such a pleasant circle of distinguished people that those six weeks will remain one of my most agreeable memories." On the days of rest, he did not forget to write: a chapter of *Youth* and the first tale of Sevastopol, where he began to describe the reality of war from direct observation.

Perhaps it was precisely there at the Fourth Bastion, while the cannon shells burst against the armored bunker and the flashes, the smell of powder and blood tainted air, that Tolstoy got the idea of recounting the last minute of a fatally wounded soldier. His visionary qualities, which until then he had sensed only in himself, became grandiosely concentrated. With his eyes he saw and with his limbs he felt the sensations of a dying man. Like his mother's imaginary death years before, the war undermined his system for grasping and ordering reality: it compelled him to enter *inside* reality, breaking down any division between himself and the characters, and forcing him to make his first cognitive discoveries. Another writer would have described Cavalry Captain Praskukhin's last moments as a very swift flashing flare. Instead he prodigiously slowed down time, filling that moment with thoughts, memories, and sensations, like a small eternity.

As Praskukhin advanced at Mikhailov's side, a burst of light flashed behind him: the lookout shouted: "Mortar!": the shell's small incandescent dot seemed to halt at the zenith where it was impossible to tell its direction; then with increasing speed, whistling and giving off sparks, it fell toward him. He lay down on the ground, closing his eyes tightly: the shell thudded against the packed earth and a sparkling fuse whirled and crackled a meter away. While Praskukhin waited for the explosion a thousand thoughts flashed through his mind: not the noble and dreadful thoughts that we believe must be linked with death, but casual, petty, fragmentary sensations like everything that fills our superficial minds—the twelve rubles he owed Mikhailov, a debt in Petersburg, a gypsy tune, a woman's bonnet with purple ribbons, an insult received five years before. "Maybe it won't explode," he thought, and with desperate resolution he wanted to open his eyes. In that instant, still through his closed lids, his gaze was struck by the red burst of flame. Something struck him in the middle of the chest. The last instant of life was desperately long. Some soldiers flickered before his eyes: unconsciously he counted them; one, two, three, . . . five, six, seven soldiers, and one officer, his cape turned up. While they continued to graze past him, he was seized by the fear that they might crush him: he tried to shout at them that he was bruised: but his mouth was dry, his tongue stuck to his palate, a terrible thirst tortured him, he would have liked to drink the dampness that drenched his chest. Only by summoning up all his strength, he tried to shout: "Pick me up!" and from his mouth came such a horrible moan that he was afraid to hear himself. "Then certain red flames began to jump in front of his eyes;—and it seemed to him that the soldiers were covering him with stones: the fires jumped ever more sparsely, but the stones they laid on him crushed down more and more heavily. He made an effort to push the stones off his body, stretched out to his full length, and already he no longer saw, no longer heard, no longer thought, no longer felt anything." So, superbly, with a visionary capacity that perhaps in those years only Dickens possessed, Tolstoy visualized (the shrapnel in the chest that becomes a stone) the death of Captain Praskukhin. For many years, until the death of Prince Andrei, he did not attempt anything so bold.

Written in the heart of the battle, the first two Sevastopol tales remind us how in the besieged city blood coursed gaily in the veins of those men, happy to inhabit the world's colorful and mortal surface. They remind us of death in battle, death in the hospital, the horrendous spectacle of limbs amputated by a curved knife and flung in a corner: and yet anguish and horror confronted by human pain do not last long, as if their only function were to exalt the triumph of life and animal heedlessness. "Covered with still fresh blood, the bodies of hundreds of men, until two hours before filled with hope and different desires, sublime or petty, lay with now stiffened limbs in the flowering, dew-covered valley, which separated the bastion from the trench, or on the smooth floorboards of Sevastopol's funeral chapel; hundreds of men—with curses and prayers on their parched lips, crawled, rolled on the ground, and moaned—some amid the corpses in the flowering valley, some on stretchers, on cots, and on the bloodied floor of the ambulance station; and exactly as on the preceding days dawn flamed over Mount Sapun, the tremulous gleam of the stars paled, a white mist spread out from the dark rumbling sea, in the east a scarlet dawn lit up, the long, small purple-colored clouds dispersed at the luminous blue horizon, and exactly as on the preceding days, the splendid, powerful sun rose, promising joy, love, and happiness to the entire world returned to life."

The six weeks of light and ardor passed: on May 5, 1855, at the request of his Aunt Pelageya, Tolstoy was transferred to a mountain battery about twenty versts north of Sevastopol. He read *Faust*; *Henry Esmond*, *Vanity Fair*, and *Pendennis* by Thackeray, and "a stupid novel by Balzac" (perhaps *The Lily of the Valley*). He had been seized again by a furious passion for gambling, and he set for himself very detailed rules. Before playing, he must stipulate each time the amount he could lose: after losing it, he must immediately leave the table; and he went so far as to write in his *Diary* the amount to be gambled every month. With the help of numbers and calculations, he said he would learn to control and strengthen his character. In reality, his ambitions were greater. He wanted to subject gambling—the realm of chance, hazard, and the inexplicable, the area where he saw all the different human possibilities merge confusedly—to the abstract dominion of intelligence and kill the unpredictable that discomposes life. But *stos* and faro made a fool of him. He lost much more than he had set for himself; and then, chance—capriciously and royally as is its wont—allowed him to earn five hundred and eighty rubles, against all odds.

During the month of August, he went down to Sevastopol several times. The city was still very beautiful. The sun shone high above the bay, which varied its color in every part—with its stationary ships and the sailboats and rowboats moving about—all touched by a gay and tepid scintillation. A light breeze barely stirred the leaves, swelled the sails of the boats, rocked the waves. "Sevastopol, always the same, with its church whose construction is incomplete, the columns, the promenade along the sea, the green avenue on the hill, and the elegant library building: with its miniscule blue bays crowded with mainmasts, the picturesque arcades of the aqueducts, and the blue clouds of gunpowder, lit up in places by the purplish crimson of the cannon shots, always the same Sevastopol, beautiful, festive, proud, surrounded on one side by yellow mountains shrouded in mists, and on the other by the vivid azure of the sea playing under the light of the sun, revealing itself to sight beyond the bay." But something had changed. On the boulevards there no longer was music, no more cafés and cabarets, the women with kerchiefs on their heads no longer strolled on the streets, the bullet holes that riddled the houses had multiplied, the lamps in the windows were no longer there: war's illusions, braggings, and snobberies had disappeared; everything was marked by weariness, effort, and a burdensome expectancy. Sevastopol was about to fall, as had fallen the lives of the young officers cut down so prematurely.

On August 28, his birthday, Tolstoy witnessed the evacuation of the city, not a living soul was to be seen all along the line of the bastions. Everything was dead, deserted, but not quiet: everything still continued to go to wrack and ruin. Amid the loose soil, dug up by the recent explosions, everywhere lay abandoned twisted gun carriages under which Russian and enemy bodies had been crushed: heavy iron cannons, silenced forever, which a tremendous force had overturned at the bottom of the holes and half covered with earth: bombs, cannon shells, more corpses, holes, fragments of beams and armored bunkers; and again mute corpses in gray and light blue capes. All this, at brief intervals, shook and lit up under the flare of explosions which continued to rock the air. When he saw the French flags on the bastions, Tolstoy wept. He wanted to leave the army. On November 19, he arrived in Petersburg.

IV

A year passed. Time went by even more quickly. For a few months Tolstoy lived in Petersburg, sleeping on a sofa in Turgenev's house: he loved him and hated him; he met Russian men of letters whom he fascinated with the violence of his nature. He was present at the death of his brother Dmitri, his face consumed by tuberculosis and with an enormous hand which seemed welded to the bones of his forearm. He again saw Yasnaya Polyana, where the old wooden building in which he was born had been removed by its buyer; he tried in vain to free his peasants: he idly engineered a romance with a girl he didn't like—round, plump, insignificant, with porcelain eyes, ugly arms, and disgusting bonnets and smocks—and with a bad conscience he played the part of the suitor, educated, preached verbosely, and painted for her and himself the virtuous life of a young Rousseauan landowner, which at that moment he most likely detested. Meanwhile his hand, having attained an extreme point of refinement, drew with a very white brush the white light of the moon, the gelid luminescence of the snowstorm, the colorless whiteness of the sky, the now clear, now muffled tinkling sounds of the sleigh, the voices, the whistles, the crunch of clogs and ice skates, the torrid glare of memories, the night's blind race into the void over the immaculately white scenic flats of the snow.

On January 29, 1857, he left Moscow by mail coach. On February 4 he arrived in Warsaw, while the sun was rising, coloring the houses' walls: he took his first railroad train, which seemed to him inexpensive and comfortable; and on February 9 the train dropped him in

Paris. He was alone, without servants, confronted by that new city, that civilization which made him feel his ignorance, and he imagined that this trip would mark an "epoch" in his life. He stopped at the Hôtel Meurice, at 149 Rue de Rivoli: two days later he moved to a family pension recommended by Turgenev at 206 on the same street. The pension revealed to him Paris' first secret: a sociable and fatuous life where people had superficial relations with one another and gave each other superficial pleasures. The common meal was an entertainment: the conversation, interspersed with jokes and *calembours*, became general, and everybody trotted out whatever came to mind. He met a philosopher, a *bel esprit*, a ballerina in the opera, a Spanish countess known for her romantic adventures, an Italian abbot who declaimed *The Divine Comedy*, an American doctor who had access to the Tuileries, a young dramatist with long hair, a pianist who said he had composed the world's most beautiful polka, a hapless beauty who had been widowed and wore three rings on each finger; and a common laughing-stock. Immediately after the meal, they pushed the chairs aside and began to dance the polka. Tolstoy set himself a severe study program: at least "four hours a day of isolation and work"; and tutors came to teach him Italian and English. The first evening, despite his fatigue, he went to the costume ball at the Opéra. It was the last Saturday before Lent. A Frenchman had dressed up as a savage and hopped around all by himself in the center of the ballroom, his face and arms painted, his legs bare, waving his hands and yelling at the top of his lungs. "He wasn't drunk: he was an honest family man, he was simply having a good time." He played the tourist, relaxed, gay, *lebensfroh*,* as he said: full of eagerness, curiosity, and attention. He visited the Sainte-Chapelle, the Louvre, where he liked the *Gioconda* and Rembrandt, the Hôtel de Cluny, Notre Dame, Versailles, the palace and forest of Fontainebleau, the Bourse ("dreadful"), the Hôtel des Invalides ("deification of a scoundrel"), the Père-Lachaise cemetery; and it does not seem that the works of art made a profound impression on him. With his encyclopedic passion, he sat in on the lectures at the Sorbonne and the Collège de France: dramatic literature, political economy, philosophy of law, and comparative law.

*Joyous about life—TRANS.

Almost every night he was at the theatre. He saw *Les Précieuses ridicules*, *L'Avare*, *Le Malade imaginaire*, *Les Fausses confidences* by Marivaux, which seemed to him "a marvel of elegance," Alfieri's *Mirra* with Ristori, *Le Mariage de Figaro*, *Il Barbiere di Seviglia*, and *Il Rigoletto*; he detested Racine, who seemed to him "Europe's poetic sore"; and abandoned himself with a kind of intoxication to the futile, frothy, and feverish joys of light theater—the Bouffes-Parisiens, the Passe-Temps, Vaudeville, Variétés, the Folies-Dramatiques, the Folies-Nouvelles, and the *cafés chantants*. He liked to stroll along the streets, surrounded by the noise of the enormous crowd in which he too, like all the other novelists of the nineteenth century, loved to lose himself. He listened to the conversations of ordinary people, peddlers and coachmen, and on Sundays the verses of the *chansonniers* in the taverns on the outskirts of town. The "feeling of social freedom" was for him the chief attraction of French life; he liked to breathe it in everywhere; although it seemed to him that the only "poetry" felt by the Parisians was that of politics. "I've always disliked it, and now especially."

Immediately after arriving in Paris, he again began to see Turgenev, who lived at 11 Rue des Arcades. That soft, subtle, feminine, neurasthenic, disenchanted man who was as tender as he was uncertain, attracted him, just as Turgenev was fascinated by the complexity he sensed in him. The old seesaw of attraction and repulsion between the two men was immediately resumed. The very day of his arrival, Tolstoy observed with anger that Turgenev was morally in bad shape: he was sad, exaggeratedly troubled over his health; then he spent several evenings with him, drinking a bottle of wine in front of the fire, chatting about all sorts of things, and he let himself be enveloped by the amiable levity of Turgenev's conversation. On February 26, during a trip together to Dijon, he noted that Turgenev believed in nothing and loved no one: "he only loves to love." He was a cold man, bad, useless, heavy and boring, tired, and without faith. "I esteem him and rigorously speaking I even love him, but I have no empathy for him, and this is mutual." But what did he care for men of letters? In those days of gaiety and the dispersion of vitality, in theaters, operettas, and *cafés chantants*, he felt the need to be enveloped by women's looks, smiles, coquetry, and perfume. He was always falling in love with some woman, or his very mercurial imagination made him fancy that he was. At the pension there was the romantic Spanish countess, whom he found "delightful," and a ballerina of the opera, Louise Fitz-James, with lovely calves, who flirted with him and pronounced a sentence that opened an abyss before him: "*On n'est jamais aussi vicieux qu'on voudrait l'être.*" In the Russian salons, besides Marya Olsufyev, Princess Trubetskoy, and "an amiable young woman" without a name, he met Princess Alexandra Lvov. She was so pretty that for an entire day the fascination he experienced was so intense that it filled his life with joy. Excessive as usual, his feelings did not know half-measures, and he immediately thought about marriage and fantasized about a long, happy life. "I think I'm an imbecile if I don't try to marry her. If she should marry a man of parts and they were happy together, I could be sunk in despair." "Tell me frankly," he insisted a few days later with Turgenev, "whether the idea that I wish to marry her might seem disagreeable or ridiculous to her. I'm so convinced of the impossibility of such a bizarre thing that it seems to me ridiculous to write about it. And yet, if I could only believe in this possibility, I would prove to you that I too can love."

Driving his curiosity ever further, on April 6 he woke up early in the morning, took a carriage and went to the Place de la Roquette, where the guillotine was to execute a murderer. He was ill and nervous, and the spectacle perturbed him deeply. His eye was attracted by the smallest details, he saw up there on the scaffold a strong, white, and healthy neck and chest. He saw the sinister kiss of the Bible, while in the crowd a father explained to his daughter the practical elegance of the mechanism; he saw the blade fall on the neck; the head separate from the body and both roll with thuds into a basket. That night he could not sleep. A friend recounted that Tolstoy dreamed he was being guillotined and in the morning, awakening, discovered a scratch on his neck and was terrified by it, as if he too had been grazed by the monstrous machine. In the Caucasus and at Sevastopol, he had known the horrors of war, but what offended him in the sinister spectacle at the Place de la Roquette was a crime not committed as then under the wild impulse of passion but by a rational, calm, "civilized" spirit, certain and satisfied with itself. The judges had "the brazen ambition to carry out

God's justice." But human law was an absurdity: the State was a conspiracy, which had as its aim the exploitation and corruption of the citizens. The entire realm of politics was nothing but turpitude and lies. "As far as I am concerned, I shall never serve any government at any time or place." On April 8 he left for Geneva. He went to say goodbye to Turgenev: during recent days he had insulted him almost every evening in his *Diary*: suddenly this great sentimentalist, victim as no one else of the emotions that touched the epidermis of his soul, twice burst into tears after having said goodbye. "I love him very much, he has made and continues to make a different man of me." The train, which had seemed so pleasant to him on his journey from Warsaw to Paris, disgusted him and began to seem the mechanical symbol of evil and obsession that he was to describe in *Anna Karenina.* At Ambérieu he got off, and at eight o'clock in the evening he boarded a mail coach. He traveled through the night on the seat beside the coachman, while the coach traversed France and Switzerland. It seemed to him as though somebody had singled him out with a mark on his forehead. The spring night was illumined by a full moon: intoxicated, immersed in his natural atmosphere, thinking of Alexandra Lvov whom he had left in Paris, he took in the sounds and smells of the deserted road. His melancholy and malaise was changed into a moving and silent joy, and into love. "For the first time in a long time, I have again sincerely thanked God for being alive." At Geneva, he did not find his Tolstoy cousins. He returned to the hotel and spent the entire evening in his room, looking at the lake lit by the moon and reading the Bible. He was terribly happy, as he wrote to Turgenev: so happy he could cry. God had assailed him, as someone else could be assailed by an attack of hay fever. The next day he met Alexandra Tolstoy, who lived in the Villa Bocage together with her sister and the Grand Duchess Marya Alexandrovna. Alexandra was thirty-nine, had beautiful gray eyes, a contralto voice, exquisite social manners, and an elegantly ironic spirit. Though she moved amiably in society, among czars, princes, grand duchesses, and famous writers, she was animated by a scrupulous desire for purity. She would have liked to forget herself, hide her personal life as far away as possible, jump out of her body, rise above herself: at times her religious élan convinced her to lock herself up in a hermitage and leave behind the agitated "worldly anthill." She believed in Grace. "What matters is not what we give, but what is given to us, and by whom it is given to us." In those years of tumult and dispersion, Tolstoy was attracted by her virginal spiritual nobility: later, during the years of *War and Peace*, when he extolled the values of the family and the body, he perceived in her a certain lack of reality, and with a rare lack of tact wrote to her: "As soon as I come into contact with you, I put on my white gloves and tails (moral tails, it is true): after an evening with you, I always had, I remember, an aftertaste of something delicate, fresh, fragrant, while I wanted something more essential. There was nothing one could hold on to." But now, at Villa Bocage, Alexandra Tolstoy was not a pallid, unreal woman. What passionate vivacity animated her elegant gestures: what tranquil and ardent fire; what a desire to give herself to others! If Tolstoy had known how to listen less hastily, he would have sensed in her a hidden restlessness that religion, discretion, and pride could not hide: a vague sadness, and a regret for something that fate had not given her.

Tolstoy arrived at Villa Bocage, staging one of those *coups de théâtre* of which he was a master. "I come to you directly from Paris!" he said to her. "That city, that Sodom, has disgusted me so that I risked losing my reason. In the pension where I lived there were nineteen illegitimate couples and this revolted me terribly. Then I decided to test myself and went to the execution of a murderer. I was no longer able to sleep. Luckily I heard that you were in Geneva and I rushed to you like a madman, in the certainty that you would be able to save me." He chatted, laughed, joked wildly: he played students' pranks: a mercurial mood possessed him completely; in the heart of the nineteenth century he still seemed one of those inspired vagabonds, those crazed followers of Werther whom Goethe pulled along behind him ninety years before. When he was alone with Alexandra, with "scalpel in hand," he drew the portraits of acquaintances with marvelous precision, inspired by the color of an eye, a fold of the face, the shape of the shoulders, as if he had lived with them for a long time; or he made plans and programs that should have lasted him for the rest of his existence—beekeeping, the reforestation of all of Russia. Soon he confessed in his *Diary* that he was in love with Alexandra: perhaps a little more seriously than he had loved Louise Fitz-James or Princess Lvov. "It is frightful how easily I fall in love. If Alexandra were ten years younger . . ." "To my shame with Alexandra I have the clumsiness of a young man." "Alexandra is a marvel, a joy, a consolation. And I have never seen a woman who could reach to her knees." They spent the whole day together: they went boating, picnicking on the lake, played the guitar, explored Switzerland's mountains.

The enthusiasm of that spring settled into a tender, amorous friendship which bound them together for many years. Tolstoy needed her tact and breeding: her scrupulous and delicate hand, that purely spiritual dimension which he lacked and which with a part of himself he deeply despised. He felt protected. "Do you know what emotion your letters arouse in me? . . . It seems to me I am a child, who does not know how to speak: I am sick, my chest hurts; you understand me, you love me, try to help me, anoint me with balsam, and caress my head. I am grateful to you. I want to weep and kiss your hands for your love, your caresses, and your sympathy." He liked being corrected and converted—even if he knew perfectly well that nobody would ever be able to correct or convert him. As for Alexandra Tolstoy, perhaps her young cousin aroused in her heart a more intense emotion. She felt a great tenderness for him. "I mentally throw my arms around your neck in one of those impulses of sympathy that I adore, as if I were a schoolgirl." She needed his face, his hands, his words: it seemed to her that from him flowed a "young and vital element" which gave her new life; if he was not there, she yearned for his presence. "I have for you a real and proper *mal du pays.*" "I would very much like to take a small trip not around but inside your head. And if this were possible, I warn you that like a mineralogist I would dig and grub in every corner: then, on tiptoe, I would descend to the region of the heart because that is where the precious stones nestle." With great naiveté, without understanding to what a morose and enigmatic man she was speaking, Alexandra believed she was tied to him by a magnetic fluid or a kind of "harmonic correspondence," and she insisted that they were "in the same key, even if they seemed to sing in different tones." With even greater innocence, she hoped to convert him to her form of worship.

"After having roamed, after having sought this and that without finding satisfaction in anything, perhaps you will attain the truth." "On your account I am at peace. The work begun by God will certainly be accomplished in your soul. For the time being only one veil is lifted: you believe in and wish for the good with all your soul. And then one after the other the various veils will lift and so on till the end of your life."

Rather than a woman, that spring Tolstoy loved the lake of Geneva. From the windows of the Pension Keterer in Clarens, in the places dear to Rousseau, morning or evening he didn't stop gazing at its water and banks. The lake, pale blue and ultramarine, sparkled before his eyes with the white and black dots of sails and boats. Near Geneva, at the borders of the resplendent lake, the warm air formed dark and trembling blotches: on the opposite bank the green mountains of Savoy rose abruptly with small white houses on their spurs and cleft rocks which had the appearance "of an immense woman dressed in white, wearing an ancient costume." "To the left, above the rust-colored vineyards, in a clear and close fashion and in the heart of the dark green orchards one could make out Montreux with its graceful church hanging from the side of the mountain: Villeneuve on the edge of the water with the metal of the houses that glittered vividly under the noon rays: the mysterious gorge of Valais with the mountains piled one on top of the other; Chillon, white and cold, sheer above the water, and the small islands that rose in an artificial but no less beautiful fashion, right in front of Villeneuve. Fine creases wrinkled the water, the sun fell vertically upon its azure surface, and the sails strewn over the lake seemed immobile." The beauty penetrated his soul through his eyes and blinded him. In an instant, a tangle of emotions filled him: love for himself; but above all love of others, the need to embrace someone in his arms, press him against him, tickle him, pinch him, communicate his great joy to him. He thought with regret of the past, hoped for the future, felt a desire to have a long life: "the idea of death was surrounded by an aureole of infinite childish poetic dread." In the end, there was no longer past or future for him. There was only the present, which like a ball of thread very slowly unwound and disappeared. He continually made excursions on foot along the borders of the lake and among the mountains. On April 30 he left for Amphion together with Mikhail Pushchin, an old Decembrist, and walked until late evening along the fragrant Savoyard roads. Two boys carried their knapsacks and told—chirping, almost singing—tales of ghosts and apparitions in the Swiss castles; while Tolstoy and his friend listened in silence, breathing the perfume of the road. When it was completely dark they reached Amphion, right on the shore of the lake they discovered in the dusk a very beautiful garden and villa: three huge white Newfoundland dogs and a servant did the honors of the house. "Mikhail Ivanovich and I have decided that we are simply happy people: we have eaten, we've drunk, we've made music."

On May 15, Tolstoy began a longer journey with an eleven-year-old boy, Sasha, the son of friends for whom all of life's impressions were new. At four in the afternoon, leaving Montreux behind, they began to climb a small stair in the vineyards, headed for the mountain. Sasha was a great help to him; with his presence he freed him from the thought of himself, and this gave him strength and moral gaiety. While the lake before their eyes became ever narrower and more brilliant, he began to reflect. Man, especially civilized man, is blocked inside himself by self-consciousness and reflection which are for him what life imprisonment is for a convict. Closed inside the narrow walls of his self, man is impotent. How can one free oneself from this incarceration? Tolstoy needed to expand and open up his forces, lose himself in the infinite: if he loved others, drank, slept, worked, expunging thoughts of himself, if he dug deeply into his unconscious, he felt his strength become unfettered and liberated. Then he felt able to achieve omnipotence, the hidden dream of his life, like Faust or a romantic magus.

Meanwhile they had climbed so high that the vineyards' dark yellow plots and the fruit trees were no longer visible, but the dark green trees of a wood cast their shade. The air was cool, the road, dug through the rock, was clay-lined and winding; they smelled the odor of dampness and newly cut fir, the birds sang loudly in the woods. Suddenly they were struck by an unusual odor, happy, white, springlike. Sasha wanted to get hold of that perfume: he ran into the wood to gather cherry blossoms, but they did not give off a scent yet. The scent became ever sweeter and heady. After a hundred paces there opened before them a large, declivitous clearing of a white-green color, filled with white narcissi. Sasha gathered them with both hands: he brought Tolstoy an enormous, intolerably odorous bunch; and then, with the destructive greed of children, he ran to trample and rip up the lymph-rich flowers.

They came to the village of Les Avants on a vast clearing covered with narcissi: behind, the wooded mountains spread out below, and lower down appeared a small fragment of brilliant lake with barely visible boats and sails, while in the sky stood motionless a young, opaque moon. The two travelers entered a pension: Tolstoy sat down to write in his *Diary*; everything was already black, the moon lit up the vast clearing, the river, undisturbed by the day's noises, roared uniformly in the valley's bottom. The white and heady perfume of the narcissi inundated the air. In the morning they left at dawn, directed to the Dent de Jaman. Walking seemed easier: water from the melting snow streamed around them. As they crossed a bridge, the Dent de Jaman appeared with its crevasses and snow and bushes around its peak: the sun had not yet risen from behind the ridge; everything was empty, damp, and deserted, they did not feel or hear anything, on all sides bare tree trunks and sparse vegetation. Tolstoy did not stop to look around: he did not like the mountains' gelid aloofness. Nature was for him a mother that enveloped him in her womb: he felt immersed in it on all sides; at the same time his eyes followed the things unfolding in the distance and losing themselves in the infinite, so that in a single sensation he experienced the constricted and expanded: "I like nature," he wrote a few days later, "when the warm air surrounds me on all sides and that very air is engulfed in the infinite distance; when the succulent blades of grass I have crushed by sitting on them call to mind the green of illimitable fields; when these very leaves which, stirred by the wind, shift a shadow on my face, compose the line of a distant wood; when the very air we breathe calls to mind the depths of the infinite azure sky; when you are not alone in your exaltation by and enjoyment of nature; when close to you myriads of insects hum and swarm, ladybugs graze you, and birds fill the air with their song."

Returning to Clarens on June 11, he left again for Berne on the 22d, and on the 24th for Lucerne, where he stopped at the Hotel

Schweizerhof. When he opened the windows of his room, the lake's beauty overwhelmed him, like Lake Leman's. All the colors, lights, shadows, nuances, contours, and lines were fused in a single whole which immediately affected his soul. The lake, bluish like burning sulphur, with the boats' small dots and the evanescent wakes, spread out immobile and levigated, almost convex among its varied green shores: it narrowed between two enormous promontories; darkening, it gradually meandered and disappeared amid a massing and superimposing of mountains, clouds, and glaciers. In the foreground, a humid, light green, swift succession of reed-covered shores, meadows, gardens, and villas: farther away, the dark green of the overgrown crags and the ruins of castles: at the end, the jumbled purplish-white mountain backdrop with its peaks rocky or opaquely white with snow; and everything was submerged by the indispensable tender azure. "Neither on the lake nor on the mountains, nor in the sky, a single unbroken line or a single unbroken solid color nor a single uniform detail: everywhere movement, asymmetry, an infinite mixture of shadows and lines. In everything a placidity, a softness, a unique and infallible beauty," like that *fondu*, that *vernis des maîtres* which he tried to reproduce in "The Snowstorm," "Two Hussars" and "The Cossacks," and before long in the vast, mobile, and asymmetric canvas of *War and Peace*.

Precisely there, in the midst of that beauty which was so irregular, colorful, soft, and blended, modern man had erected his sinister monument to the straight line. An old wooden bridge had been torn down; and in its place someone had built a lakeshore avenue straight as a rod or a white stick: sumptuous, rectangular five-story buildings; and in front of the buildings a double row of linden trees surrounded by robust props and banal green benches. At seven thirty, when Tolstoy was called to dinner, he discovered that the dreaded straight line was dominant in the dining room too. The silent assembling of the guests, almost all English, lasted three minutes: the rustle of women's dresses, light steps, exchanges of words with the extremely courteous and irreprehensible waiters; the places were occupied by those men and women dressed so charmingly, even richly, and above all looking exceptionally neat. From all sides flashed extremely white laces, extremely white collars, extremely white teeth (real or artificial), extremely white faces and hands: that white was the color loved by the straight line. All the guests were polite, formal, composed, calm, indifferent, satisfied with themselves and their polite, calm, rectilinear, and mediocre life: they had no need whatsoever to look others in the face, know them, attune themselves to them, speak to them; and even less to make them happy, as would have been liked by Tolstoy, who was still overwhelmed by the lake's harmonious beauty. The very white hands covered with rings and half-gloves moved only to straighten collars, cut boiled meat, pour wine into the glasses. No inner agitation was reflected in those movements. No one ever uttered a lively, colorful, and ardent word: boring speeches about hotels, the weather, Mount Rigi, the place one came from and the place one was going to, silly echoes of the news read in the papers. Tolstoy was seized by a feeling of oppression, contrariness, and sadness. He had the impression of being guilty of something, as when he had been punished as a child and from the next room heard his brothers' happy shouts. Around him, knives and forks moved on the dishes with a barely perceptible sound: the food was consumed little by little: the fruit was eaten with a fork, the waiters asked in a whisper what wine do you wish to order; he had the impression of being dead and of eating among the dead.

Overcome by sadness he left the hotel and began wandering aimlessly through the town, down the narrow, dirty, unlighted streets, past closed shops; and the more he walked the more darkness descended into his soul. He was alone, he felt cold, everything oppressed him. When he was returning to the hotel, he heard from afar the strains of a strange and pleasant music. These strains instantly had the effect of uplifting him: it was as though a gay light penetrated his soul: his attention, which had become torpid, turned again to all things; and the beauty of the night and the lake gave him a feeling of exultation. In the middle of the street, in the half-darkness, he saw a semicircle of people crowded around a small, squat man, a Tyrolean wandering minstrel dressed in black. He clearly heard—so far away and sweetly trembling on the evening air—the full chords of a guitar and several voices which, rising in turn over each other, did not sing the theme, but here and there intoned its salient moments and let this suggest the rest. The voices seemed now close, now far: now a tenor voice stood out, now a bass, now a throaty falsetto together with a cooing of Tyrolean trills.

"Those voluptuous, languid guitar chords, that dear, easy melody, and the small, isolated figure of the man in black against the fantastic backdrop of the somber sky, the moon which was beginning to shine . . . and the black poplars of the garden formed a bizarre but inexpressibly beautiful ensemble, or such at least was the impression that I received. . . . It was as though the perfumed freshness of a flower had blossomed in my soul. Instead of weariness, distraction, indifference for all things, which until only a minute ago were within me, I suddenly felt a great need for love, an overflow of hope, and—just like that, without reason—a joy at being alive. What is there to want, what is there to wish for? I spontaneously said to myself: here it is, surrounding you on all sides, beauty, poetry. Draw it into yourself in deep, full gulps: take delight in it with all your might: what more do you need? Everything is yours, everything is good." Tolstoy's elation was shared. Elegant ladies in their full skirts, gentlemen with very white collars, doormen, waiters in gold-embroidered liveries stood listening at the entrance to the Schweizerhof: among the linden trees along the boulevard stood impeccably dressed waiters, cooks in snow-white smocks and hats, girls with their arms interlaced, and people out for a stroll. They all stood with their mouths shut, surrounded the singer, and listened intently. The silence was deep: only in the pauses of the song, from afar, who knows from where, spread the cadenced beat of a steam hammer and the rippling trill of frogs.

When the small minstrel held out his hand, no one among those hundreds of people threw him a cent. Someone even cackled. The singer put his cap back on and left, moving with rapid steps toward the city. Tolstoy was invaded by a sense of sorrow, bitterness, and shame for that little man, that crowd, and himself, as though he had been the one "to ask for money, and he had been given nothing, and had been laughed at." In the throes of an inexpressible anger at those people, he rushed through the darkness in the direction of the town, caught up with the minstrel, who was mumbling something to himself, and suggested that they go back to the Schweizerhof together.

He led him into a room where the people of the town went to drink: while Tolstoy was ordering champagne for his new friend, three waiters, the doorman, and a hunchbacked maid sat down to stare at him, and laughed scornfully at the minstrel's words. At that, he gave free rein to the fury of indignation which for some time had been boiling inside of him—the fury that he enjoyed igniting and stirring up in himself, which imparted an elasticity and alacrity to his physical and moral strength. He called the headwaiter and made him lead the way to the dining room, near the table where an Englishman and his wife were eating mutton chops. The English couple looked at them at first with amazement, then annoyance: the husband pronounced the word *shocking*; the wife pushed back her plate, rustled the silk of her skirts, and vanished through the door.

The next morning Tolstoy began to write a very long letter to Botkin, which he changed into a short story. He felt that the occurrence of the evening before was much more significant than those published in newspapers and history books: the fact that the English had killed another thousand Chinese, the Russians a thousand Chechens, the French a thousand Kabyles, and that the Emperor Napoleon III strolled on foot in Plombières and was preparing the farce of an election. Rousseau was not mistaken. Such an inhuman event would not have taken place in a Russian or Italian village, where "barbarity" reigned. It had been possible here, in Lucerne, in the realm of the straight line, where civilization, freedom, and equality had attained the highest level and where the most civilized people of the world's most civilized nations gathered. What had become of man's original, natural feeling? It was no longer there. It gradually disappeared with the spread of civilization, that is, the interested, rational, and selfish association of men, which was opposed to the instinctive association founded on love. Not one of those rich, educated, and civilized men had found within his soul the impulse to do a good deed. Not one of them had recognized the maligned voice of poetry. Must all values then be overturned? Was barbarity a good and civilization an evil? Was slavery a good and freedom an evil? Tolstoy rejected other subdivisions in the eternally fluctuating, infinite, infinitely stirred-up chaos of good and evil. The man who recklessly tried to fathom the laws and purposes of God's world saw contradictions everywhere, like that between the wandering minstrel and the English lord. God does not know contradictions. With a gentle eye He looks down from His incommensurable heights and rejoices in the harmony in which all of us—the minstrel, the lord, even Tolstoy with his tantrums and furies—thrash about in apparent contradiction.

At this point Tolstoy could leave Europe. He had learned all he needed: the levity and horror of the great cities, the education of the heart, the amorous élan aroused in us by beauty, the abolition of time, the omnipotent dilation of the self, the engulfing and infinite in nature, the straight line and the blended color, the fate of poetry in the modern world, the end of all contradictions in God's eyes. He stayed another fifteen days in Switzerland. On June 26 he left the big hotel and found refuge in a pension, where his eye lingered with pleasure on the owner's daughter, a seventeen-year-old in a white blouse who bounded about like a cat and the thought of her held something "light and sweet." On July 1 he climbed Mount Rigi, where the inflamed globe of the sun stood still over an illimitable sea of mist. On July 4 he began to read *Wilhelm Meister* and a biography of Charlotte Brontë: the 8th found him in Zurich, from where he planned to reach the Rhine, Paris, and England. The Rhine falls at Schaffhausen left him cold: in Stuttgart he thought of opening a school at Yasnaya Polyana for the peasants' children. When on July 13 he reached Baden-Baden, he played roulette from morning to night: lost, won, the next day lost everything down to the last cent: on the 15th he lost another two hundred rubles he had borrowed: he lost again during the following days; and turned for help to the poet Polonsky, Botkin, Alexandra Tolstoy, and Turgenev. On July 24, in Dresden, he was moved by Raphael's *Sistine Madonna*—the same painting that enchanted Dostoevsky.

On July 30 he was at Petersburg.

V

Two years after his return to Russia, Tolstoy tried to put into effect the plan that had flashed through his mind in Stuttgart. For some time now literature was not enough for him: he believed he had forever renounced writing short stories or novels: the artist's illusions in which he passionately believed after the Crimean War seemed to him "cowardice and falsehood"; he felt the need for a clearer, simpler, and more solid activity that could give him the impression of having his feet planted on the ground. So, in the autumn of 1859, he opened a school for the children at Yasnaya Polyana. At first the peasants had no confidence in it, there was someone who even said that if they were to send the boys to "the Count" he would send them to the czar to soldier against the Turks. On the set morning, twenty-two boys assembled on the village street: clean white shirts, heads greased with butter and oil; while the poorer wore *lapti** which were too wide, the too-long caftans of their older sisters, and wetted their hair down with *kvas.*† "The Count" appeared before them with a black beard like a gypsy, long hair like a peasant, and a flattened nose; he began by having them repeat the letters of the alphabet. In a few months the boys rose to seventy and became attached to him—"like pitch to the cobbler's thread." They became inseparable: only night parted them; when they left him for an hour, it was as though they hadn't seen him for a whole day.

*Plaited bast shoes—TRANS.
†Russian beer—TRANS.

In July 1860 Tolstoy departed for Europe. In Berlin, Leipzig, Dresden, Marseilles, Weimar, and London, he visited public and private, lay and religious schools, kindergartens and orphanages, scandalizing the old professors with his aristocratic hauteur and the capricious and rapid staccato of his questions. What he saw made him indignant. Four-year-old French children obeyed at the shrill blast of a whistle like soldiers, executed drills among the desks, at a command stood up with hands at their sides, and then in strange and tremulous voices began to sing the praises of God and their benefactors: the German schoolchildren had souls closed in their shells like snails, an expression of boredom and terror on their faces, and repeated alien words in an alien language. In Marseilles he roamed through the streets, taverns, *cafés chantants*, museums, shops, the docks of the port, and among the bookstalls and realized that the true European education was acquired spontaneously. For a few cents tens of thousands of people purchased the illustrated editions of *The Three Musketeers* and *The Count of Monte Cristo*: they went to the theater, or the large and small cafés where playlets and sketches were performed or verses declaimed; so that at least one-fifth of the city daily received an aural instruction, "like the Greeks and the Romans in their amphitheaters." In April 1861, he returned to Russia, bringing with him trunks full of pedagogical books. His mind was a tumult of ideas and projects which for a year would fill his existence. Perhaps his road—he thought—was not to write tales of war and love but to become a teacher of the millions of young Russian peasants just released from serfdom.

For the schools of his time, Tolstoy felt only aversion, fed by a plebeian nihilism which grew more ferocious with the years. What good was school? There the teachers taught Latin grammar, the study of Greek and Latin poetry in the original language, the history of Alexander of Macedonia, and the geography of Guadeloupe—that the earth is round and the air composed of nitrogen and oxygen—things, without exception, that were useless and harmful. As for the children, if you ran into them at home or on the street you met happy, curious creatures who joyfully wanted to learn. At school they were locked up in a jail, where conversation, questions, and free movement were forbidden. Forced to remain tied to their books for six hours, obliged to learn in one day what they could learn in half an hour, they were trained in the most complete laziness: all the nobler faculties—imagination, the ability to understand, creativity—were erased from their minds while the semi-animallike qualities were favored—to pronounce pure sounds, count numbers in a row, perceive words without permitting the fantasy to enrich them with images. With his anarchic conservatism, Tolstoy prized only one form of education: the traditional education in which the boy learned the father's trade. The son of a landowner learned to manage his fields: the son of a sacristan to train in the choir, the son of a Kirghiz cattle breeder to raise cattle; and so from the very early years direct relations with life, nature, and one's fellow men were established.

In the articles he published in the review *Yasnaya Polyana*, Tolstoy denied the possibility of constructing a pedagogical science, just as later he would deny an art of war; and with merry scorn he derided all of reason's attempts to impose a rule on the variousness of life. Education is only a way of adjusting to the multiplicity of events. With an always renewed psychological insight, the teacher adapts his intelligence and his culture to the needs of the children sitting in front of him, desirous of venturing with their hands clasped in his into the forest of existence; in exactly the same way that the good captain assesses the temperament of his troops and the nature of the terrain before attacking the enemy. The teacher cannot be a god, who molds the children in his own "image and resemblance": who imposes on them his own character, his own culture, his own unrealized dreams, his own concept of the world. Like every excellent mediator, he must agree to be only the conduit between the children and the wealth of the universe. Teaching is the most complex and dramatic of all arts. The true teacher is a great aural narrator, an actor capable of playing every part, a man endowed with a very lively imagination and incomparable psychological flexibility. As he teaches, he renders all things clear and visible, leaving intact around them the irradiating force of mystery; and he arouses in his pupils a spirit of tense, vital animation.

Without any claims to healing, unsupported by any conception of the world or morality, without the imposition of any truth, he must perform an almost sacred function. When in a classroom he sees tattered, dirty, weak children with shining eyes and often with angelic expressions—he is seized by an anguish, a terror, similar to that experienced at seeing someone drown. "Oh, my God, how can we pull them to safety," we say, "and whom should we pull first and whom next?" The children who crowd the desks in front of him are already leaving behind the unselfconscious and perfect harmony of childhood when nature deposits in them truth, beauty, and goodness. Every minute of their days, every step on the path of existence, only destroys part of this harmony. Therefore the good teacher looks back into the past, to early childhood, where perfection hides. He is the only person who can prevent the fall into the mire of time. He understands the uncertain and confused things that mingle in a boy's frail soul: he identifies his living form; and with extreme delicacy he sees to it that the hidden germs develop in him, preserving the indefinable aura of childhood harmony.

When Tolstoy departed for Europe, the boys "were left like orphans." They went to school, but everything seemed sad and empty to them: there were neither games nor jokes nor fantasies; and their minds were even closed to their studies. They wrote to him to come back as soon as possible, but Tolstoy did not return. One day the rumor spread: "Lev Nikolaievich is back." That morning the boys refused to go to school and ran around the garden of the main house, waiting for him. When he came down, already from a distance they began to shout at the top of their lungs: "Welcome, Lev Nikolaievich! Welcome Lev Nikolaievich!" He had just awakened: he brushed his hair with two brushes while they examined him from head to toe, patted his jacket and trousers, questioned him about his journeys. From that day on, teaching was resumed with the old gaiety.

The school at Yasnaya Polyanya was located in a two-story stone pavilion. The classrooms were painted blue and pink: minerals, butterflies, plants, flowers, and instruments for the teaching of physics were displayed on shelves lining the walls. Every morning at eight, the bell called the children from the village: the frost-covered windows of the *isbas* had for some time gleamed with candlelight; half an hour later, in fog, rain, and snow, under the first slanted rays of the autumnal sun, or the full rays of the spring sun, little figures appeared, talking animatedly. Farther back a straggler arrived, running and out of breath. When the teacher had not yet come, some of the boys gathered around the front porch, pushing each other off the steps or skating with their feet on the ice; and still others entered the blue and pink rooms. None of those children, bundled up in their fur jackets or winter coats, with heavy peasant shoes and *lapti* on their feet, brought books and notebooks from home, just as they would not take home lessons, homework, and pensums. Each of them brought only "himself, his receptive and passionate nature, and the conviction that again today he would have fun in school as he had fun yesterday."

The boys sat on the benches, desks, windowsills, or floor, or in the armchairs. Friends coming from the same village sat next to each other. No sooner did one of them decide to go to a particular corner than all his companions, shoving each other and rolling under the benches, went to the same place and, looking about, showed on their faces such an expression of happiness and satisfaction "as though they were destined to be happy for the rest of their lives, since they had managed to conquer that particular place." The lessons lasted from eight to twelve and from three to eight or nine. Tolstoy and the other teachers taught grammar and carpentry, voice and the Old Testament, gymnastics, drawing, and composition. Perhaps the best-loved lesson was reading. The boy read almost through clenched teeth, his eyes shiny, seeing only his book. Then Tolstoy began to tell stories: the war of 1812, the war in the Crimea, life in the Caucasus, the Cossacks' customs, and Hadji Murad's heroic death. He tried to address himself to the peasant experience of his pupils. He told how a bear was on the point of killing him; how hares at the break of day cross the snow-covered fields in leaps and bounds, how hunting dogs always chase wild animals from the side, so as not to be blinded by the scent; how his dog Bulka chased the carriage that took him to the Caucasus for twenty kilometers, and there was wounded by a boar. In the end, he no longer observed the limits of time and space. He told the story of the geese that saved Rome, the story of Polycrates of Samos, his excessive good luck and his death which he had read in Herodotus: a *bylina** about the metamorphosis into bird, carp, and wolf of the hero Vulgar: the customs of the Eskimos and about St. Bernard dogs: the balloon flight of an English aeronaut, when high up there he felt he had become king of the entire city and all the people in it; and the legend of an Indian princess transformed into a silkworm. One day he came to school with a collection of folk proverbs and told the pupils to write a story around one of them. "How can you write that?" the boys aked, convinced it was too difficult. "You write it!" one of them told him; and Tolstoy wrote a story. When he read it aloud, nobody liked it, and he suggested that the boys should compose it: he would set down on a sheet, like a scrupulous mediator with the world of books, the words and images they dictated to him. They were all very interested; almost all of them participated in the composition; but especially Semka and the small and delicate Vaska Morosov. Gathered around him, lying on the floor or on the desks, the children saw what they imagined: the *lapti* of an old beggar stiff with the cold, the wretched, tattered coat and torn shirt beneath which appears a thin body drenched in melted snow; or the neighbor wearing a skimpy woman's fur. The images traversed their minds with great vividness, bursting into excited and emotional words, so that Tolstoy's pen could barely keep up with them. Vaska ran ahead of the action: he told how the peasants fed the old beggar, how the beggar fell during the night; so that Tolstoy had to ask him not to go so fast. As he spoke, Vaska's large black eyes glittered with an unnatural light, fixing a point in the distance: his small hands, black and skinny, gesticulated feverishly: he got angry, continually prodded Tolstoy, asking: "Did you write that? Did you write that?"

Soon the other boys returned home and the story was left to Semka and Vaska Morosov's imagination. Each had a different talent. Semka had a taste for minute description and truthful details: Vaska a rich and ardent imagination and that sense of measure which some novelists manage to acquire only after tenacious efforts. Without ever having been educated, he practiced the same principles

*Heroic or epic tale—TRANS.

of narrative art that Tolstoy had for some years tried to apply. Whereas Balzac at the beginning of a novel devoted long descriptions to the main characters, places, and settings, Vaska made the different characters known with an artistic hint thrown with offhand negligence into the midst of an ongoing action. Above all, he possessed what a critic would have called the "objective touch." He only had to put down a concrete detail, such as that strange little woman's fur worn who knows why by her neighbor, and a multitude of thoughts and images were awakened in the reader's mind.

Tolstoy's pen continued to write for hours at the dictation of the two excited and happy boys who never seemed to become hungry or thirsty. He felt he was discovering a creative talent, which he was accustomed to see in Homer and Pushkin, personified for the first time in the two small peasant boys: poetry was there, before his eyes; and it was a great emotion to see exteriorized this awesome force, which he had felt boiling within him so many times. In the end, his heart was torn by fear and remorse. On that day he had opened to the little peasants a new world of joys and suffering, the world of art, and it seemed to him that he had contaminated their inviolate souls with a subtle poison. He would have liked to disappear on tiptoe, leaving the mysterious flower of poetry to bloom far from his eyes. Instead he had caught sight of it, as one watches the work of bees, which must remain hidden from the eyes of men. But at the same time he was happy, "as a man must be happy who is able to see what no one else has seen before."

Toward sunset, no light was seen from the school's windows and the silence was almost perfect. Only a faint and muffled sound behind the doors, and an urchin climbing the stairs two steps at a time, showed that the pupils were still in class. Tolstoy read the Old and New Testaments: he thought that no other book could, like the Bible, lift for the boys a fold of that veil which had hidden from them the world of knowledge and of poetry. If anyone else entered that shadowy half-darkness, he saw the older boys clustered around him: their heads upturned, they stared at his mouth as if to swallow every word. The foreheads of the smaller boys frowned with attention: if the visitor caressed their heads or tickled their necks, they did not smile but shook their heads as though to chase away a fly, and then once again immersed themselves in the mysterious and poetic story. "It was terrible and beautiful for them to hear how the curtain of the Temple was torn and how darkness had fallen upon the entire earth." When Tolstoy closed the book, they all crowded around him, and shouting one louder than the next tried to tell him what had remained impressed in their minds.

At eight or nine in the evening, school ended. The boys began to separate, going off in different directions through the countryside. One of them, to go down to the village, used a large sleigh: he fastened the shaft, climbed up in the middle of the sleigh, and with a great shout disappeared in a whirl of snow, leaving behind all along the road the dark clumps of those who had fallen off. While Tolstoy was accompanying them home, three of the boys told him stories about the wizards and devils in the forest, who play pranks in the woods and make peasants lose their way, appearing before them dressed as gamekeepers. They approached a wood where often there were wolves. It grew darker. The path could barely be seen, and the lights of the village were no longer visible. Semka stood still, listening: "Stop, boys! What's that?" They heard nothing, but the fear increased. As in an amoebaean song, in the shadows that aroused and excited terror, Tolstoy told them about the death of Hadji Murad and the murder of Countess Tolstoy. Semka walked ahead, taking long strides with his big boots. Vaska walked at Tolstoy's side and, at the story's most frightening moment, slightly grazed him with his sleeve: then with his whole hand he grabbed two of his fingers and did not let go of them. When Tolstoy had come to the end of his tales of death, in an agitated and imploring voice Vaska asked him to go on telling stories, so as to experience the fearful atmosphere with even greater pleasure. They passed through the wood and began to approach the village. "Let's go on," said the boys, when the lights came into view; "Let's go through the woods again." They walked in silence, again and again sinking down on the path soft with snow. The white darkness seemed to tremble before their eyes: the clouds were low: there was no end to the whiteness in which they walked, making the snow crunch; and the wind rattled through the bare crowns of the poplar trees.

Never, perhaps, did Tolstoy exert such charm—his tremendous

gift, which he was to abuse so much—as during that period of his life. To the boys of Yasnaya Polyana he appeared now like an ancient boyar: now like a fanciful teacher: now like an affectionate father: now like an athlete; now like a big, playful dog. He possessed their souls and made them love him: he guessed their thoughts: infused their day-to-day existence with gaiety, vitality, joy; he knew he had the keys to their hearts. When he married, the school continued for some time. But everything was different: the instruction was entrusted to mediocre and eager teachers, he appeared rarely, the lessons dragged on sluggishly; and the pupils began to leave one by one. After a few months, only about ten were left, and in 1863 the school closed down. Talking to Tolstoy had become difficult. It no longer was as it used to be, when one could run to him and open the door without being announced. Now one must ask Alexei Stepanovich for permission, and Alexei Stepanovich answered that the countess was still asleep, or she wasn't dressed yet, or that the count was writing, that he was busy, so he couldn't announce them. When finally the boys managed to get to him, Tolstoy saw them for only a brief time: joking, reading from a little booklet, presenting an easy little problem in arithmetic; then he said: "Well, goodbye, come again. Now I'm going to write," while Sonya appeared at the door and looked at them—cold and distant—through her lorgnette.

Fifty years went by. The most intelligent of those boys—Vaska Morosov, the one who wore his sister's *lapti* and caftan, who dictated the story with eyes shining with tears, the one who told and listened with so much pleasure to images of terror—lived in Tula where he was a coachman, "like a convict doing his time, manacled and shackled to a heavy chain." Old, mourning over his failed life, he returned in memory to the happy years when he studied in the pink and blue school at Yasnaya Polyana. "Here then," he wrote, "are all my memories of the time in school. By now fifty years have passed. I am already old. But the memory of Lev Nikolaievich's school and of him has remained with me, bright and clear, and lifts my spirit, especially when I am afflicted by adversities and life seems difficult. In those painful moments, I concentrate within myself and begin to remember the time that was. How did my life go by? Who have I been? I penetrate further and further into my memory and stop at the Yasnaya Polyana school and Lev Nikolaievich, and memory paints everything clearly for me down to the smallest detail. Here I am: I am a ten-year-old pupil, here is Lev Nikolaievich, young and merry, here are the sled races down the hill; here are the pranks with Lev Nikolaievich, here we bury him in snow, here is the game with the ball, the strolls through woods and fields, the conversations on the terrace, our tales of wizards. . . . Then, as though awakening, I no longer feel an old, decrepit man with a life that didn't turn out well, but a pupil in school, a ten-year-old boy. I never lost and never will lose the memory of those bright and happy days. My love for Lev Nikolaievich which began to burn in me then shines radiantly in my soul and illuminates my life."

VI

On September 23, 1862, Tolstoy married Sofya Andreyevna Behrs*, and six coach horses drew the enormous *dormeuse* with the bride and groom to Yasnaya Polyana. The obsession with marriage which had tormented him during recent years, conjuring up fantastic betrothals, flinging him at every female face because it might contain the image of all earthly happiness, had subsided. Tolstoy wanted to get married; he had coldly decided to plunge into marriage, as many times in the Caucasus and the Crimea and at Baden-Baden, sitting at the roulette table, he had coldly challenged chance. But perhaps no voluntary decision or challenge to chance had ever generated such a tumultuous violence of emotions, which he excited, increased, exasperated, so that they took him over completely and swept him away, like a fatal wave of passion. "I did not sleep until three. I dreamed and tortured myself, like a sixteen-year-old boy. . . . Another night of torments and without sleep, I suffer, I who have always laughed at lovers' sufferings. . . . Nobody can help me, only God. I pray to Him. I am in love as I never thought it is possible to be. I am crazy, if this continues I will kill myself." He wanted his marriage to be an event unique in the earth's history. In all the marriages he knew, he had seen the sad victory of the "quotidian": boredom, petty quarrels, money, banal talk, the children's upbringing, and slow decline. He expected to descend into the hor-

*The name "Sonya" was often used by Tolstoy as a term of endearment for his wife, Sofya.

ror of the quotidian, seizing from it an "immense happiness," always unchanged on the always unchanging and yet different horizon of his days, superior to any happiness he had ever glimpsed in his dreams.

A few months after the wedding a page of his *Diary* tells us that his dream had failed: had he been overwhelmed by the limitations, conditions, proximity, restrictions, and jealousies of life *à deux*? "Where is my self, the one I loved and knew, which sometimes pours out of me all at once to my joy and fright? I am small and nil. And I am like this since I married the woman I love. All that is written in this notebook is almost a falsehood. The thought of her being there reading over my shoulder diminishes and denatures my truth. . . . It is enough to read this . . . to make me relapse into all the banalities of life I have detested since my youth. And I have lived in them for nine months now. . . . It is terrible, senseless to tie one's happiness to material circumstances—a woman, children, health, affluence. The simple spirit is right. One can have women, children, health, but happiness does not lie in that." He could not tolerate the petty scenes that took place between them as in other families; and it seemed to him that the "powerful interests and passions" that once animated him had been completely lulled. And for whom had he sacrificed his old self? For whom had he become domesticated? He would never possess that pure, inexorably virginal woman at his side: she would always elude him, depriving his joy of all fullness. Sometimes it seemed to him that the well-brought-up young girl of good family he had married was only a porcelain doll: her shoulders and neck cold and bare, her black dyed hair arranged in wide waves on which in the more prominent spots the color was gone, her empty eyes half closed, her smooth hand cold and pleasant, her tiny porcelain feet poised on a small green porcelain strip which represented the grass-covered ground. In writing to his sister-in-law Tatyana, Tolstoy bantered delightfully, telling her how Sonya had become a statuette to be carried in one's vest pocket: he composed an elegant caprice *à la* Hoffmann; but how can one not sense a shadow of bitterness behind that playfulness? Then the shadows receded. Every instant knew the marvel of conjugal love: so physical and intense as to leap beyond itself, becoming fantasy, inspiration, madness, as happened to Levin when he walked through Moscow's streets and saw the bluish pigeons fly on the sidewalks and the children racing toward the pigeons. "When at night and in the morning I wake up and see her looking at me and loving me, I love her. And nobody—especially not I—stops her from loving as she knows how, in her own way. I love it when she sits next to me, and we know we love each other as much as it is possible, and she says: 'Lyovochka'—and she stops—'why do the pipes of the fireplace rise so straight?' or 'Why do horses take so long to die?' . . . I love for us to be alone a long time, and I say, 'What are we going to do? What are we going to do, Sonya?' She laughs. I love it when she gets angry and suddenly, in a flash, she has a thought or a word that sometimes is brutal. 'Stop, it's boring'; a minute later she is already smiling timidly. I love it when she does not see me and does not know it, and I love her in my own way. I love it when she is a little girl in her yellow dress and she juts out her lower jaw and sticks out her tongue. I love it when I see her head thrown back, and her face serious, and frightened, and childish, and passionate, I love it when . . . "

Sometimes he felt that his happiness was "frightening," just as Hawthorne was terrified by his happiness as a husband, and prayed. Hawthorne was terrified because his amorous happiness was composed of the "fabric and substance of eternity," so that spirits still tied to the body must rightly tremble before it. Tolstoy, instead, was frightened by it because the happiness of lovers is at the mercy of time: because it was so extreme that its violence and tension could only generate catastrophes, and because it touched such profound and chthonic regions of his being that he feared he had ventured too far. And besides, who could assure him that this joy was really his? Perhaps he did not deserve it; perhaps he had stolen it; it was something illegitimate, which God and his destiny had not assigned him. While children filled the house and his hand filled sheets of paper, this terror of happiness lessened and perhaps disappeared. The temperature of his life declined without falling into quotidian grayness, as though that instantaneous amorous intoxication had been multiplied by millions of instants. He was tranquil and serene, without secrets, or desires. The fabric of his existence was like everyone else's: the children who got themselves dirty and yelled, Sonya who suckled one and carried another and at every moment reproached him for not realizing that they were both on the brink of disaster. The tasks in the fields, the strolls, the hunt; and yet happiness painted all those small events with its brilliant colors.

If he had wanted to sum up his life, he would have had to copy into his *Diary*, which during those years he abandoned almost completely, the reflections of Pierre Bezukhov after his imprisonment. He too, like Pierre, had for years sought a goal in life. He had done nothing but seek in the distance, who knows where, over the heads of the people who were around him, trying to find the sublime, inaccessible, and infinite in all things. He had not found them. In all that was close he found only the limited and mediocre; and so he picked up a pair of binoculars and searched in the distance where mediocre things shrouded in mist seemed to him sublime and infinite only because they were indistinct.

Now, however, he no longer sought a purpose. He had the feeling that none existed, and this gave him the joyous awareness of being free. He renounced his dreams of love for men and their redemption which had possessed him especially during the time of the school. As an old adage says, it seemed to him that the *mieux* was the *ennemi du bien*, and he withdrew into his family selfishness. He understood at last what his old nurse had told him long ago: God is everywhere. He had learned to see the infinite and sublime in all nearby things and, throwing away the binoculars, he joyfully contemplated around him "eternally mutable, eternally sublime, inaccessible, infinite life," and the longer he looked at it from near at hand, the happier and more tranquil he felt. Immersed in quotidian existence, wholly devoted to the here and now, he accepted the limits and conditions of conjugal life. "I feel," he wrote to Alexandra Tolstoy, "like an apple tree that before grew with all its branches stretching upward and on all sides and that life has now pruned, lopped off at the crown, tied, and propped up, so that it does not inconvenience others, so that it sinks its roots deep and grows straight." His existence, which at times had spread wide to the point of perdition, contracted and concentrated, to allow the unlimited expansion of novel writing. Like every writer who aspires to the infinite, he had to kill it in himself.

Completely enclosed in the circle of his family, he had never before felt his spiritual and intellectual forces to be so free, lively, and vibrant, so ready to undertake an immense labor. At the beginning he felt only a general desire to narrate, as one has the desire to go for a walk: he felt that his hand was "tranquilly sure"; and it seemed to him that he could have written on any subject whatsoever, like a prodigal god of the novel. Then, in the autumn of 1863, he fell into the maelstrom of *War and Peace*. He lived locked up in his study, occupied by the characters who filled his mind. "When Papa works in his study." one of his sons was to write, "one mustn't make noise, and it is forbidden to go to see him. What he does when he *works*, we children don't know at all." At the table he was also serious and silent, his mind lost in his creations; he didn't even notice that his infant daughter had begun to laugh, had learned to hold an object in her tiny hands, and recognized her mother and her nurse. The whole house lived suspended from the activity of its indifferent, distant master; and only on rare occasions would Sonya timidly enter the study. The task was tremendous, frightful: as if he had to create the world all over again. When his pen raced over the paper, his spirit was alert and gay, a high spirit* as his sister-in-law Tanya would say: thoughts and images attacked him with extreme acuteness, with violence and joy; when he left his desk, he spoke about his characters as if they were flesh and blood, then came the difficult days. He had dark and somber thoughts—thoughts of death, or creative impotence—which gave him no rest. He was submerged by the vortex of possible combinations: he did not know in what style to write; all the details wanted to be set in the foreground—and he had to push them back in their place, reestablishing the novel's hierarchies. He had no hope for himself or anyone: he worked with effort and without élan, and everything became forced, sterile, too diffuse.

When summer came, he often stopped narrating: since for him writing was a surrogate for the vital force that raged in the world during the summer months. Then he devoted himself to the estate. "Only the hunter and landowner," he said, "feel the beauty of na-

*English in original—TRANS.

ture." He set up a beehive close to the wood, had apple trees planted in the orchard, grew cabbages, built a distillery, chose camellia and azalea seeds: imported Japanese pigs ("a few days ago I saw a pair of them and I know that for me there will not be happiness in this life until I have these pigs"); he bought three hundred merino sheep and during the summer when the entire flock of white females with their bells passed following the shepherd and his dog, and then the lambs were born on his land, his heart swelled at the sight of all that was alive, grew, and propagated. In the summer he discovered the children. In 1865 Serezha walked by himself; the game of life, which until then his "coarse man's eyes" had not seen, was beginning to become comprehensible and interesting for him; at the same time he had no feelings whatsoever for little Tanya. When the children grew older, he played with them. He took them swimming in the Voronka, rode with them through the forests and brush, skated and did gymnastics, observed with them the life of butterflies and ladybugs, guided them into the distant Samara steppes. Sometimes he pretended he was afraid, clutched two children by the hand, and, walking on tiptoe, trying to make as little noise as possible, went to hide in a corner of the room. "There it is, there it comes," he whispered in a dismayed, alarmed voice. Huddled in the corner, their hearts beating wildly, the children waited for *it* to go away. Tolstoy squatted on the floor, pretending to watch intently an imaginary figure. He followed it with his eyes, while the children, clinging to each other, said nothing for fear that *it* might see and hear them. Finally, after a few minutes of tense silence, Tolstoy became calm and gay: "It's gone away," he exclaimed.

Despite his fits of amorous intoxication, it is not certain that Tolstoy understood the girl with the dark hair and the large, black, slightly myopic eyes the *dormeuse* had brought, almost in tears, to Yasnaya Polyana. She was not a "porcelain doll," although before her marriage she did all the things that girls from good families did; read, wrote short stories, painted watercolors, played the piano, dreamed of romantic loves and children to raise. As soon as she arrived at Yasnaya Polyana, Sofya Behrs revealed a temperament as tragic as her husband's. There was in her a desire for the absolute, a somber force of concentration, a tendency to exasperate all her feelings, using them as weapons with which to wound herself above all; and continuous swings in mood which transported her from joy to anxiety, from love to hate. But, unlike Tolstoy, who was happy as few human beings ever were, she never knew the art of being happy. A kind of unceasing, self-destructive fury possessed her. Now she was inhabited by a feeling of guilt which made her choke with tears: now she experienced anguish, the void, cold, boredom, the feeling of being alone, absolutely alone, abandoned in a corner like a miserable reptile, pregnant, with bad breath and two spoiled teeth; the grimmest imaginings and obsessions filled her mind. She suffered from anxiety. She was afraid her husband would die, and the picture of his death unfolded before her eyes with frightfully precise details. She was afraid that everything would decline, fade away, everything would end: in fact already had ended at the very moment she wrote in her *Diary*: "It continually seems to me that autumn is already here, that soon everything will end. . . . But what does *everything* mean? I don't know myself. . . . As for imagining that winter will follow autumn, I am absolutely incapable of it. What boredom not to feel up to anything, not to find pleasure in anything, as if I were an old woman."

Sonya's love for her husband was jealous and fierce. She would have liked to possess his present, his past, his most distant youth, his childhood—that immense dark dimension of time, that chasm of hours and minutes which she had not shared. With a stupendous sentence she wrote: "If I could kill him, and then recreate him exactly the same, I would do so with pleasure." She dreamed of taking over her husband's soul and, with a scrupulous mental broom, cleaning it of all thoughts, feelings, and fantasies that were not she, as though she could be the only source of his imagination. She could not stand his love for "the people," in whom she saw her rival. "He disgusts me with his people. I think that he must choose between me who, for the time being, personifies the family, and the people, whom he loves with an ardent love. Is this selfishness? Too bad. I live for him, I live through him, and I want it to be the same for him, otherwise I feel beleaguered, I suffocate." She accepted only her husband's tenderness for Alexandra, with whom— "I'm too young and foolish, not poetic enough"—she could not compete.

Although she protested that she did not feel drawn to "carnal relations," her furious jealousy was above all erotic. When she read "The Cossacks," she fantasized around Tolstoy's loves in the Caucasus and felt "such disgust that I could have burned the whole book." When she imagined her husband's amorous relations with Aksenya, thinking about "that vulgar, fat, whitish" peasant, she voluptuously thought of daggers and shotguns, gripped by homicidal frenzy. One time, she had a dream in which she took Aksenya's and Tolstoy's son and dismembered him. "As soon as Lev came, I told him I would be deported to Siberia, but he picked up everything, the legs and the arms, and told me it was only a doll. I looked and, instead of a body, there was hemp and cotton wool. I was very disappointed."

With the passing of the months, confined as she was within the walls of Yasnaya Polyana, Sonya's mental world concentrated around her husband. She thought only about him. If he was close by, she spied out the expressions on his face, trying to understand what was in his heart. If he was away, she went into his study, tidied it up, arranged the linen and the things in his chests, glanced through his papers, and with all her will tried to enter inside him to understand him: or she drew almost mechanically, turning her ideas over and over in her head, imagining him from every aspect and with every possible and imaginable expression: when he returned, it seemed to her that everything was light and easy. She loved him so much that she felt ill from it. Much as she scrutinized his face, she did not understand her husband. With his ambiguous and enigmatic world, obscure even to himself, he remained a stranger for her. He lived his own life, unable to give himself to her or any other human being, unable to entrust himself completely even to literature, in an incomprehensible no-man's-land, and he did not let Sonya venture into it. At times, he seemed to her cold, indifferent, animated by a perverse, hostile will. What would become of their love, which she dreamed would last as long as time? She was afraid of losing it, as an old man is afraid of losing his only son on whom his existence rests. With all the strength of hysterical passion, she clung to her happiness: it seemed to her that it was only a gift of chance: she was certain that one day fate would take back what it had bestowed on her, and she would be left without anything, in the desolate void of her life.

At first, she was overcome by the solitude of Yasnaya Polyana. She had left her house in Moscow, full of sisters, noise, animation, visits: she still heard in her ears the joyful burst of young voices; and now, in the snow-covered village, all she could do was sit all day, sew, do needlework, play the piano, without anyone paying attention to her. She had a curious sensation. She felt she was in a deep sleep, like the princess confined in the fairy-tale wood, or the porcelain doll her husband had written about: she was full of a mortal torpor and weariness: she knew that she must wake up very soon if she too did not want to sleep for a hundred years; but who would help her to wake up, bestir herself? Everything around her was old: Aunt Tatyana, the servants, the furniture, and even her husband seemed an old man, who existed only to impose on her prohibitions, restrictions, to say to her: "Stop that!" She would have liked to flirt with someone, go to a ball, do somersaults, chat about frivolous and amiable things with a friend; she would have liked to have her hair waved, buy ribbons or a new leather belt.

With the birth of the children and the great book that sprouted and extended its branches beside her, Sonya was placated and grew serene. She became the all-seeing, omnipresent spirit of the house. With the large bunch of keys hanging from her waist, she ran from cellar to attic, visited the courtyard and the stable, kept the accounts: nursed the babies, sewed expertly at her sewing machine, prepared medicines for a sick peasant woman, taught the smaller children, illustrated some books with watercolors, painting terrifying wolves, a swim in the river, a fire, cabbage and cart thieves. She watched over the house, over her husband and children with feverish, bustling anxiety. According to her sons, "she knew everything better than anyone else." "She knows that one must wash every day, that at meals one must eat the soup, that one must speak French, be well behaved, not drag one's feet on the ground, not put one's elbows on the table. If she says that one mustn't go out to play because it's going to rain, one can be sure that it will really rain, so one must obey her."

In the evening she knitted in silence, at her husband's side: or played four-hand pieces at the piano with him; or lay at his feet on a bear skin, falling off into a quiet sleep and waiting for the time to go to bed. When her husband was writing *War and Peace*, her head, with its well-combed black hair, bent to decipher the manuscript full of deletions, sometimes written in every direction, crammed with corrections in every corner. The next morning Tolstoy found his pages copied in a clear handwriting on his desk; and he always added new sheets, covered in a black, incomprehensible scrawl.

PART TWO

War and Peace

I

When we enter *War and Peace* through the doors of Anna Pavlovna Scherer's *salon*, Tolstoy takes us at once into the immense realm of the "false." During those years, there was nothing for which he felt a more profound attraction: it was so complicated, labyrinthine, and full of secrets, all of which engaged his abilities as a novelist. It was like a challenge. As soon as Tolstoy's sixth sense warned him that there, before his eyes, life and imagination had distilled something "false," his precise and subtle hand quickly scraped away the surfaces, discerning the truth that hid behind them; and he scraped away surface upon surface, ever lighter veils behind which at times he despaired of seeing anything. What does the "feigned laughter" of old Prince Bolkonsky or young Prince Andrei conceal, or Prince Vasily's languid manners? Often, as in Bilibin's or Speransky's case, the "false" does not allow its surface to be lifted: it is not pretending or hiding, it does not mask anything: it is something smooth, levigated, and impenetrable, a kind of blinding mirror behind which there extends no truth and no secret. In such cases, it is the triumph and mystery of pure surfaces.

With what perfidious and destructive elegance Tolstoy described the rituals, ceremonies, words, and displays of the "false"; and at the same time with what enchanting amiability—as if he were thankful to the society of Moscow and Petersburg for giving him the opportunity to represent it. He had no illusions: the greater part of Anna Pavlovna's, or Helene's, or the Rostovs' *habitués* are empty-headed. But he loved the elegance of the receptions: the carriages that arrived and departed with their red lackeys, and the servants with their plumed hats: the glitter of wax candles, the splendor of silver and crystal, the gold and silver of epaulets, the soft clash of knives, glasses, and dishes. He loved the levity, the aerial weightlessness of the women's dresses; at times he seems to become a woman, because like a woman he falls in love with a Bordeaux-colored velvet gown, a gown of white tulle with a pink silk petticoat and small roses on the *corsage*—because he knows, like one of them, where to pin a ribbon to a *toque* and what a misfortune too long a dress could be; and in the end all the faces, the laughter, the *tulles*, velvets, *toques*, rosebuds, diamonds, pearls, whites, light blues, and pinks are reflected in the mirrors lining the staircase, becoming confused and merging together. In the deceptive and flattering light of the ball, all fools are redeemed for an instant: Helene Bezukhov really is the queen of Petersburg instead of a stupid and corrupt woman, and Anatol Kuragin a beautiful young knight instead of an obtuse womanizer. Tolstoy knew that splendor, wealth, luxury, pomp, and ostentation are vain things: but he caressed them at the same time that he branded them as vanity.

Even more than the lights, the gold and silver, Tolstoy adored the ephemeral glitter of the words that resounded in Moscow's and Petersburg's salons: futile, frivolous, absurd words to which he listened with infinite patience, collected in the sound box of his memory, and fitted them together as in a precious melodic game. Now a character speaks Russian, now French: Russian words are mingled with French sentences, French words creep into Russian sentences, French words are transcribed in Russian, and the play of the two languages, carried out with marvelous felicity, is accompanied by the sound of knives and forks, the tinkle of glasses, the discreet steps of waiters, the names of the dishes and wines. Never perhaps has anyone described the insubstantial with more grace. Before these prodigies we ask ourselves how it was possible for him at the same time to describe the lofty sky over Austerlitz behind which there is God or nothing, or the eye of death which looks upon our life.

The game of fashionable chatter culminates in a name—that of Countess Apraksin. This is a character who never appears on the scene, of whom we do not know the face, character, history, and habits: a pure *flatus vocis*. At Petersburg Prince Andrei's wife, little Lisa, with her small, upturned, fuzz-covered lip, describes how she attended a reception given by the Apraksins: a few days later in Moscow during the name-day gathering at the Rostovs, female voices resound, feverishly excited, overlapping each other: "*Chère comtesse, il y a si longtemps . . . au bal des Razoumowsky . . . et la comtesse Apraksine . . . j'ai été si heureuse . . .*": a few hours later, during dinner at the Rostovs, Tolstoy mockingly repeats the same words: "*Les Razoumowsky . . . Ça a été charmant . . . Vous êtes bien bonne . . . La comtesse Apraksine.*" We don't have to wait long for the grotesque return of this name: Julie Karagin interrupts the second page of the romantic, gossipy, and mystical letter she's writing to Marya Bolkonsky, because Mama must take her along to dinner *chèz les Apraksin*. We assume that the countess' life must go on eternally in this way, like a phantom invisible to us between a reception and a dinner, the object of unending comment by Petersburg's high society, when, lo and behold, disaster. As soon as Prince Andrei's wife arrives at her father-in-law's estate, she informs him of the latest city gossip: "*La comtesse Apraksine, la pauvre, a perdu son mari, et elle a pleuré les larmes de ses yeux*" So we see that the *flatus vocis* has taken on flesh: Countess Apraksin has lost her husband and sheds all her tears: but this apparent life is only the gleam of an instant, for her sorrow has once more become a pretext for the inexhaustible conversation that weaves around her name, making her forever a prisoner in the labile world of words.

The reception that takes place on a July evening in 1805 at Anna Pavlovna Scherer's house—the symbol of and substitute for all the salons that are not described—unfolds in a spot very far from the heart of *War and Peace*, as though Tolstoy wished to describe his characters with reversed binoculars and hint from afar at the events that will shortly erupt on the stage. This reception has no dramatic or novelistic function, although in it some plots are prepared: it is just a fragment of the web of existence, and so Tolstoy immediately announces to us that he will include in his novel many other casual days or hours and indeed that he would make the casual the very fabric of the book. And so we see the guests arrive one by one: Prince Vasily Kuragin, his children Helene and Hippolyte, Lisa and

Andrei Bolkonsky, Vicomte Mortemart, Abbé Morio, Pierre Bezukhov, Princess Drubetskoy, and other figures that Tolstoy leaves in the shadow. During the book's long rewritings they multiplied: the *petite conversation* turned into a *grande conversation*, the sonata for a few instruments into an expansive symphonic overture; and meanwhile, in accordance with the process of reality's fragmentation so dear to Tolstoy, many small inlaid motifs have replaced more fluid and ample motifs, many brief portraits have expunged richer portraits, while present scenes have taken the place of later, subsequent scenes. As is natural, our characters discuss the topics of the day, among which Napoleon predominates. But not one of them is a jarring or isolated instrument: not one of them can play a solo, as continually happens in the novels of Balzac, Dickens, and Proust, where the verbal effluvium eternally overflows the banks. Anna Pavlovna, behind whom hides Tolstoy the conversational virtuoso, is an excellent orchestra conductor. If one of her violin–guests stands silent in a corner, she sweeps him into the whirlpool of the music: but if another violin or another bass is too violent, passionate, or impetuous, she induces him to lower his tone; if a group shuts itself up, elaborating only its own motif, she blends and intertwines it with the group next to it, thus conducting with an infallible baton her salon's great musical interplay and mosaic.

As the symphony of voices unfolds, Tolstoy intimates quite clearly that we are at the theater. Each character wears over his face (granted that he has a face) a mask that he himself has chosen, or that life, society, and habit have induced him to choose. Prince Vasily always speaks languidly, with detachment, indolence, and indifference, "like an actor playing a part in an old play." Anna Pavlovna's mask is the opposite: all vivacity, élan, and enthusiasm; except when she speaks of the emperor's mother and an expression of devotion and veneration suffused with sadness spreads over her face. Prince Andrei recites the part of boredom and snobbish indolence. Helene exhibits her radiant and monumental beauty; Princess Drubetskoy wears a gelid, tear-stained mask; and even the servants stand there like rods, listening to the French conversation (for them unintelligible) with certain faces that appear to understand everything but do not wish to show it. There are those who have two masks: Princess Drubetskoy, who suddenly removes her tear-stained mask and by mistake dons the one she wore when young ("the smile of a young coquette, which at one time no doubt suited her, but now clashed so violently with her devastated face"): a passage that reminds us of how many things Proust learned from Tolstoy, the man-about-town. Only one character arrives at Anna Pavlovna's with a naked face: Pierre Bezukhov, who has no mask, does not know how to playact, does not know the hidden rules of the universal theater, and by his spontaneity and improprieties offends the realm of good form and convention.

Some of the actors on that evening in July do not know that they are playacting, like innocent Lisa Bolkonsky: some, instead, know very well that they are on stage, like Prince Vasily or Anna Pavlovna, who underlines the consummate art of her playacting with a smile of self-irony, and so introduces us to the joys of theater within the theater. Among these innocent or knowing masks, Tolstoy moves joyfully, fascinated by the pure pantomime. When we read: "With the graceful, free, and familiar manners that distinguished him, Prince Vasily took the lady-in-waiting's hand, kissed it, and then rocked it for a moment leaning back in his armchair, his eyes looking elsewhere"—how can we think that *behind* this meticulous precision of gesture is hidden the traces of a soul? But then immediately afterward, with one of his rapid and cruel strokes, Tolstoy lifts the mask and reveals the naked face. In the scene we are considering, this happens twice. Precisely when Prince Vasily addresses one of his most unnatural and vivacious smiles at Anna Pavlovna, the lines around his mouth pucker and something "disagreeable and strangely coarse" appears on his face: shortly after, on Princess Drubetskoy's mannered and tearful face there gleams for an instant "an acrimonious irritation." As we shall soon know, Prince Vasily and Princess Drubetskoy are the two great enemy–protagonists of the world of the "false"; Tolstoy relentlessly concentrates his attacks precisely on them, even though they are the most skillful and consummate actors, and reveals their turpitude or shadowy nature. Nothing authorizes us to say that that something "disagreeable and coarse" and that "acrimonious irritation" are our two protagonists' deepest faces: perhaps they are only two more involuntary masks; and we still do not know whether Tolstoy will ever be able to tear them off.

Amid the play of the dialogue, Tolstoy insinuates two ample comparisons which are on one hand a jocose parody of Homeric comparisons and on the other offer a first form of the formulation of those metaphors to which Proust entrusted the significance of his high-society descriptions. "Like the owner of a spinning mill, who after having ordered his workers to sit at their places, paces about the plant and notices the breakdown, the unusual creaking, or too-noisy sound of a spindle and hastily rushes to it, to slow it down or give it the correct movement—so Anna Pavlovna also circulating in her salon approached a group where silence had fallen, or which spoke too much, and with a single word or gesture reactivated the conversation's correct, decorous mechanism." "Just as a *maître d'hôtel* knows how to offer, as if it were something wonderful and supernatural, the piece of boiled meat that, seen in a dirty kitchen, you would have no wish whatsoever to swallow, so during her evening Anna Pavlovna served up to her guests first the vicomte, then the abbé as if they were supernatural delicacies. The vicomte was served up to the company in the choicest and most flattering style, like a slice of roast beef on a hot plate surrounded by vegetables." The high-society performance that begins at this moment is therefore a play of automatons, a concert of talking robots, like those dear to the Chinese during the eighteenth century: a society dinner where Prince Vasily or Viscount Mortemart or Lisa or Helene have the same function as a slice of roast beef; he, Tolstoy, is its great director, its impeccable scene shifter, the extremely elegant *maître d'hôtel* who at every step presents us with a new surprise.

A few hundred pages later, in a completely similar situation, during the reception given in Bagration's honor at the English Club, we are surprised by three natural comparisons. The guests shuttle back and forth between rooms and converse animatedly, "like bees at the time of the spring swarms": then, scattered here and there through the rooms, when the bell sounds they crowd together in a single knot, "like grains of oats bounced on a shovel," and stand motionless in the large drawing room; finally they take their places in the dining room, the closer to Bagration the more important they are, "like water which spreads more abundantly in the spots where the terrain is lowest." How different the comparisons of the first scene seem to us! There mechanisms and artifice, here bees, grains of oats, rivulets of water—the phenomena of nature. Has society really changed? With his metaphorical irony, Tolstoy tells us that not even his descriptions of automatons must seem stiff, and that perhaps a distant echo of the movements, rhythms, and sounds of nature is heard precisely here, in the very heart of artifice.

A few days later, no longer in Petersburg but in Moscow, Prince Vasily and Princess Drubetskoy clash in a battle on whose outcome depends not only Bezukhov's immense estate, but the preeminent position in the society of the "false." Everything that happens is seen through the naive, bewildered, and sleepy eyes of Pierre, who does not understand a thing, or by a narrator, who in the same way pretends he does not understand, and willfully mixes up the narrative information. The result of these optics is the description of death in the world of the "false": fatuity, irreverence, lack of respect, senseless rituals, fake tears, automatic gestures, greed unleashed by the passion for money; as if in a contest, Tolstoy opposes to the concealed perfidy of society his own declared, scintillating perfidy. Nothing that is repugnant about modern death is spared us. We hear the lackey's voice, bold and sonorous, "as if by now everything were permissible": the banal and offensive conversations that are held at night in houses visited by death; we watch the atrocious violation of the dying man, when everybody comes into his room, stares at him, offends him, shifts him about, handles him like a thing.

While Count Bezukhov is dying, Princess Drubetskoy reveals to us the subtlety of her cunning machinations. With her puny dyed silk dress and small shoes worn at the heel, she goes through the corridors and rooms of the mansion, ignoring and sweeping aside all obstacles: the doorkeeper's and servants' contempt, Prince Vasily's cold, insulting glance, the young prince's hostility. She continues to wear on her face the tearful mask. Now, according to what is opportune in a given situation, her voice becomes softer and tender, tears bathe her face, and she seems to carry on her frail shoulders the sorrows of all men and the knowledge of all the rituals to be performed. But, behind this tearful veil, she does vile things. Bold, shameless, brazen, pitiless, implacable, she violates the room of the dying man, uncovers maneuvers, like the most intriguing of Machiavellian politicians. Her secret lies in her step. While the large, tenebrous house is immersed in the silence and slowness that precedes death, she seems to augment her agility. She darts lightly up the stairs in her small, shapeless shoes with the brio of a dancer: she bends, sways, glides, runs with a small, pattering gait, slips in everywhere, with an elf's speed and slyness.

Her great rival, Prince Vasily, reveals with his very first remark his inferiority in the face of this bedeviled enemy. He does not have the familiarity with death that women so often have. He is indecisive, incapable of the inspired solutions that will assist him on other occasions: he looks gaunt, as if greed were devouring him: his cheeks contract and quiver spasmodically; now his eyes have a provocative glitter, now they look about frightened. While Princess Drubetskoy glides about everywhere with the brio of a dancer, he is slow and clumsy and trips along heavily when approaching the dying man's room, where his rival has slipped in, tiny and quick as a mouse. In the comedy that will decide his fate, Pierre for the first time reveals his nature: he is passive, plunged in a sort of torpor of the consciousness, and he falls asleep everywhere, in a carriage or an armchair, as though his only desire were to regress into sleep. Like a big puppy, dragged along on a chain, he lets himself be led by Princess Drubetskoy, who arranges things for him to become the heir of an immense fortune, without his grasping the reason for even a single one of her moves. He does not understand anything of what is happening: all the gestures and scenes are incomprehensible to him; and he accepts without discussion what he sees or what is imposed on him—the presence of the employees of the funeral establishment, the bold, impertinent voice of the lackeys, Princess Drubetskoy's strange sentence about "your interests," the bathtub in the middle of the room, the sudden deference shown him by others, the necessity to sit in an armchair or kiss his father's hand.

The scenes of this final ballet, which forms perhaps Tolstoy's high-society masterpiece, are overwhelmingly comic. Nothing is funnier than the kiss that Pierre, following Princess Drubetskoy's advice, applies to his father's broad hand: than when he believes that the new apoplectic "stroke" his father has suffered is the blow of a cudgel; or than the struggle over the wallet containing the will—

between the short-legged princess and Princess Drubetskoy, with her small, scuffed shoes. Seen with the eyes of Pierre who does not understand, or the narrator who pretends he does not know and withholds certain information from us, everything seems to us absurd, phantomatic, unreal, as is the life we lead in the world of pretense. Count Bezukhov's death is also the death of a paralyzed automaton: the swaying leonine head, the gaze that does not know where to rest, the confused, raucous sound that issues from the convulsively twisted mouth, the desperate impatience, the feeble arm that falls back upturned, the last, weak, suffering smile, which expresses a kind of irony about his impotence. As in a seventeenth-century religious play, earthly power, derided and offended as it dies, reveals its weakness. And yet, despite the vulgarity of the living and Tolstoy's perfidy, there still is a shadow of greatness in this death: the allusion to another space, we do not know whether to God or to nothingness. "When Pierre approached him, the count looked into his eyes, but with that look whose sense and value it is not given to man to understand. Either that look said nothing at all, save that as long as the eyes are there one must after all look somewhere, or it said too many things."

When the battle between the two rivals ends, it is with the victory of Princess Drubetskoy, who secures for Pierre—the *bâtard*, as the young princess says—the father's controversial inheritance and a little something for herself and her beloved son Boris. She, the queen of the "false" and playacting, does not stop playacting until the end, without making the slightest mistake, weaving the prodigious colored tapestry of her lies. When Count Bezukhov is dead, she calls Pierre (who is indifferent to the death of a father he didn't know). She kisses him on the forehead, bathing him with her tears. Then she falls silent, pauses. " '*Il n'est plus. . . .*' " Pierre looks at her over his glasses. " '*Allons, je vous reconduirai. Tâchez de pleurer. Rien ne soulage comme les larmes.*' " The next morning, chatting in all of Moscow's drawing rooms, she begins to laboriously weave her *legenda aurea*, transforming the sinister and farcical ballet into "not only [a] moving but edifying" death. "She did not know who had behaved better in those terrible moments: the father, who during those last minutes had remembered everybody and everything and said words so moving for his son, or Pierre, if yor just looked at him it broke your heart he was so distraught, and yet tried to hide his sorrow so as not to embitter his father." As soon as the count dies, the other protagonist, Prince Vasily, leaves the room, walking unsteadily: pale, his lower jaw quivering and jumping with a feverish shudder. " 'Ah, my friend!' " he exclaims, taking Pierre by the elbow, " 'how much we sin, how much we deceive, and for what? I, my friend, am close to sixty . . . And for me . . . Everything ends with death, everything. Death is terrible.' And he begins to weep." Precisely Prince Vasily—the hero of the "false," the undeterred intrigant and manipulator, who tomorrow will begin to study some new cunning move—casts his mask aside for a moment, condemning the deceptions of his life. Has he attained truth because he was defeated, because he is old, because the sleepless night has prostrated him? Who can tell? With another of his strokes of genius, Tolstoy shows us that every soul is double, perhaps multiple; and that truth can live anywhere, even in a heart most worn out by the habit of pretense and playacting.

This defeat does not tame Prince Vasily's multiform spirit: his mind is always full of schemes, prospects, projects; and, as soon as the situation is favorable, he seizes the instant and takes advantage of those involved. Tolstoy denies that war can be compared to a game of chess: but the social life of Moscow and Petersburg, where the situations, causes and concomitant causes are by far less numerous, is precisely a chessboard, and Prince Vasily is the Napoleon of high-society strategy. Immediately after the defeat suffered at the hands of Princess Drubetskoy, he tries to settle the score with a startling victory over his adversary: if Count Bezukhov's millions have eluded him the first time around, he will capture them the second, by making the young, inexperienced Pierre marry his daughter Helene. So he begins to take an interest in him, with the manner of a man overburdened with business deals, tired and exhausted, who is too compassionate to leave a defenseless young man to the mercy of chance and scoundrels. He guides him, educates him, commands him, speaking to him in his throaty voice, like the uninterrupted cooing of a dove, the voice to which he has recourse in cases that call for unusual persuasion.

Pierre is attracted by Helene's body: by her marmoreal bust, the enchantment of her shoulders and neck, her perfumes, the creaking of her corset, the warmth she emanates like a lacy and radiant animal. Eros dominates him: the barriers fall, the powerful pleasure of proximity triumphs. At this point, tying his destiny to hers seems to him inescapable, like certain actions ponderously performed in a dream. And yet he despises her, and a voice tells him: "This happiness is not for you. This happiness is for those who do not have in them what you have." Perhaps the situation would have been prolonged indefinitely if Prince Vasily did not have a stroke of genius. On the evening of Helene's name day, he invites a small number of intimates to dinner: they all wait for Pierre to declare himself and the sexual desires of the couple to be fulfilled. After dinner, Pierre and Helene chat, sitting by themselves in a small drawing room. Suddenly Prince Vasily gets to his feet, throws back his head, and with a resolute stride, in rapid steps, with a jovial and solemn expression, comes into the small drawing room. "God be thanked!" he exclaimed. "My wife has told me everything! My dear Lelia! I'm very, very happy . . ." and, his voice trembling with feigned emotion, with one arm he clasped Pierre and with the other his daughter. He has invented everything: there has been no decisive word between the two young people, and his wife has not confided anything to him; but this inspired lie breaks through Pierre's passivity. His lips join the lips of Helene, who appears disagreeably perturbed; he exclaims: "*Je vous aime!*" remembering what one must say on such occasions; and his words sound so squalid that he is ashamed of himself. So the new marriage is born under the double sign of Eros and the false. Meanwhile an old lady says: "*Les mariages se font dans les cieux*," with ecstatic submission to the celestial will. But never did a marriage take place more on earth than this one.

As the years go by, the old Petersburg and Moscow salons lose their glitter. The princes of high-society conversation recede into the shadows, Anna Pavlovna Scherer, Prince Vasily, Princess Drubetskoy are on the point of being forgotten and the salon of the young Countess Helene Bezukhov assembles the cream of Russian society. It is not by chance that Prince Vasily's daughter has the same name as the Helen of Sparta and Troy. Hers is the calm, tranquil, marmoreal beauty that emanates an incessant erotic irradiation, arousing a kind of ecstatic fear in those who comtemplate her. She stands at the heart of *War and Peace* like a monumental allegory of sex: but if one compares her to Natasha, to that frenzy of sensual vitality, one understands that her sensuality is dull, opaque, sterile, lifeless, like that of a statuesque and resplendent automaton. Helene's smile does not gleam in her eyes, her mouth, her face, always flattering and attractive in different ways: it pours out always the same and unchangeable, addressed to all and to no one, and does not say anything to those who know her. And yet Helene fascinates almost all the male characters in *War and Peace*, except for Prince Andrei: like an empty receptacle into which is discharged the imagination and sensuality of others. Her resplendent emanation is not the vital light of the young Tolstoyan protagonists: but rather a maleficent source which seduces, corrupts, contaminates everything that it touches.

The first time we meet her, in Anna Pavlovna's salon, she seems stupid. While around her the conversation swirls, Helene gazes at her well-rounded arm resting on the table, or her beautiful bosom, on which she straightens a diamond necklace: she adjusts the folds of her gown; and studies Anna Pavlovna's face so as to imitate her expression. Some years later, Helene has acquired the reputation of a *femme charmante*, *aussi spirituelle que belle*, of *la femme la plus distinguée de Pétersbourg*. Ambassadors entrust diplomatic secrets to her: young people read books on the eve of her receptions so as to shine before her: the witty Bilibin saves up his *bons mots*, to say them for the first time in her presence, the Prince of Ligne writes her letters eight pages long. When he attends her receptions, Pierre experiences a kind of fear or suspense, as though faced by the trials of a dice player. Every time he is astonished. In her soul his wife is vulgar and coarse, and yet she gives proof of an infallible social tact: she is stupid and yet she courageously ventures into politics and philosophy, delivering her *bons mots*, or pronouncing banal words in which the others discover profound significance. The transformation of a stupid woman into a high-society genius is one of the great mysteries of *War and Peace*, no less great than those revealed to Prince Andrei by the lofty skies and death: a mystery that enchanted Madame Verdurin's creator. Where did Helene learn tact and discretion? Is she only a clever snob able to imitate the appearances of intelligence? These questions remain without an answer. But, with Helene's triumph in elegant Petersburg society, Tolstoy has meant to condemn once and for all the world of the "false," in whose glitter and mysteries he has indulged for so long. All its wealth, splendor, intellectual complications, and *mise en scène* create a monument to a stupid and lifeless woman. Form, so loved and idolized, ends by cancelling itself.

II

When students of Tolstoy complain about the scant historical reading he did before writing *War and Peace*, one is reminded of an anecdote told by Henry James. An English woman writer had received much praise for the reconstruction of the French Calvinist world she had presented in one of her stories. When she was asked from what books she had obtained so much information on so little-known a subject, in what library she had so scrupulously documented herself, the writer gave a strange answer. When she had lived in Paris, she had passed the open door of a pastor's house: having finished eating, some young Protestants sat around the laid-out table, with its glasses in which sparkled the last of the wine. That one glance was enough for her: like a spider which works with ever thinner silken threads, the mind had seized that flashlike glance, the small suggestion of an instant, changing it into the fabric of a story. I believe that Tolstoy would have loved this anecdote. In writing *War and Peace* he made use (although not exclusively) of an impalpable documentation, composed of family memories, old readings, the vibrations of the air.

Tolstoy did not wish to evoke the historical age of his grandparents in a minute and precious manner, describing clothes, rooms, figures, as a novelist with an antiquarian vocation would have done. He could not tolerate the fatal distance that history would have placed between him and his characters: he needed to have them before his eyes, in that ideal present which constitutes the time of his mind. He would never have understood the Dutch taste of Manzoni's *Betrothed.* If he had to evoke past times, he did so like Stevenson, who with a single tricornered hat, a single white wig, a snuff box, and some tarred pigtails resuscitated out of nothing the eighteenth century of gentlemen and pirates. He too was satisfied with a light 1805 odor, a delicate 1812 perfume; and, as in *Treasure Island,* we are immediately swept away, we immediately feel ourselves the contemporaries of Napoleon and of those romantic times. This historical color is not distributed uniformly. Pierre, or Natasha, or Nikolai Rostov almost lack it completely: whereas the color becomes dense around the pre-Romantic Julia Karagin, the neoclassic Helene, the Pushkinian Dolokhov, around Prince Andrei the *enfant du siècle,* and above all old Prince Nikolai Andreyevich Bolkonsky.

The moment that Nikolai Bolkonsky comes to greet his guests at his Lisye Gori estate, we breathe a very sharp eighteenth-century perfume. His daily activities are those that the "enlightened," in their industrious idleness, most willingly cultivated. He is busy from morning to night: now in the writing of his memoirs, now in high mathematical calculations, now in the manufacture of snuffboxes on the lathe, now with his daughter's algebra and geometry lessons. His favorite maxims could not be more typical of the Enlightenment. He likes to say that the sources of human vices are only two: idleness and superstition; and that there are only two virtues: activity and mental lucidity. His bright, sparkling eyes under thick, frowning eyebrows and his youthful gay step convey to us something of the quick, bright rhythm of Voltaire's stories. The old prince adores the abstract and precise law of numbers and wants to impose it on life—so fluctuating, changing, and diverse. In his house, all clocks must strike the same hour: all occupations must be repeated at the same instant; every day he devotes the same amount of time to the lathe, to algebra, to an antemeridian nap and sits down at table always at the exact same minute. He understands nothing about the inner time of other men, which changes according to the individual, the days, the imagination, and cannot obey the crystalline rhythm of clocks. He understands nothing of the passions of hearts, not even his own; so at times, despite his dislike for them, he seems to us strangely akin to the German generals who want to impose an abstract strategy on the multifarious circumstances of war. Reason, whose victim and prisoner he is, grants him a single privilege. His gaze is precise, no illusion clutters his mind: and his cold and negative laughter derides the ridiculous, unmasks appearances, like the gaze and laughter of Tolstoy and Prince Andrei.

This small laugh—dry, cold, disagreeable, which the distrustful eyes never share—is the emblem of his persona. He never laughs fully, with eyes, mouth, and heart, as Pierre and Natasha laugh, because he does not know how to dissolve in laughter all the feelings that choke his soul: love, disillusionment, frustration, hatred, melancholy, contempt; the greater part of his life remains unexpressed, incapable of liberation and naturalness, shut up in the frail jail of reason, to which it has sacrificed all of itself. Therefore—as Tolstoy emphasizes at every turn—his laugh is "false." So, at least in part, Prince Bolkonsky belongs to the same world as Prince Vasily and Anna Pavlovna, even though his persona is so much greater and more desperate.

He nourishes only one profound passion, that for his daughter, Princess Marya. He cannot say it in words: he tortures Marya with his selfishness, the ferocious feeling of possessiveness, the perfidy of an amorous and sadistic torturer. Incapable of speaking and laughing, he lives his old age in a lie and worship of his own past, madly trying to immobilize the hands of the clocks, like—Tolstoy seems to say—all worshipers of reason. Until death comes, and with death the only truth of his life. Struck down by paralysis, frail, small, wretched, the prince lies with his back propped up: he rests on the cover his small, bony hands, marked by a livid tangle of veins: his left eye stares straight ahead, while his right eye slides askew; eyebrows and lips are immobile. He tries to speak for the first and last time, he rattles and moans, seizes his daughter's hand, presses it against his chest here and there, as though searching for the place that suits it. " 'Always thoughts! For you . . . thoughts . . .' he manages to say. . . . 'I called you throughout the night,' he enunciates slowly. . . ." " 'My little one'—or—'my dear'—Princess Marya cannot understand which but, from the expression of his eyes, the word pronounced surely was a tender, affectionate one, such as he had never said."

When Tolstoy first imagined Prince Andrei, his mind fondled the idea of a high-society fashion plate, halfway between an effete hero of Pope's and a bored epigone of Pushkin's Eugene Onegin. At that time, Prince Andrei's hands were of an extraordinary delicacy and whiteness: they seemed unable or unwilling to do anything, except twist the wedding ring on his finger, smooth down hair by hair his well-groomed mane, and rub against each other. "He spoke a bit through clenched teeth and as though lazily, and his face remained tranquil. His beautiful eyes gazed with weariness and indifference. In all his ways he exhibited feminine softness which was unnatural but evidently affected with premeditation. He walked and moved, as a rule, slowly, dragging his feet, he always sat down, lounging back at his ease and even rolling his eyes, as though they were tired from looking." In the final draft of *War and Peace*, Prince Andrei does not forget the refined effeteness from which he was born. At army headquarters, in the drawing rooms, the military parades, we find him with a snobbish boredom on his face, in which the fire of existence seems to be extinguished: while he gesticulates with his small white hands, lounges indolently, or speaks Russian with a French accent, like the lowest of dandies. Almost until the end of his life, he loves artificial elegance, high society's conventions and *bons mots;* and the "naturalness" in which Pierre and Tolstoy are prepared to see a positive value often seems to him a coarse, banal quality. He cannot endure familiarity and bad manners. When we see him speak and act—small, elegant, proud, refined, sure of himself—it seems to us that the world of the false has found in him its perfection and its consecration. He is the flower of form, although he is so very superior to form, despises it, and seeks an unspecified ideal behind it.

Like his father, Prince Andrei encloses the fire of his feelings and the fervor of his thoughts in an impenetrable expression. While Pierre's sweetness leads him to confide in everyone, Prince Andrei reveals to no one what he carries in his heart. His face and his soul seem to belong to two distinct spheres: when new joyful desires and vital dreams erupt in him, almost by contradiction he is dry, full of severe resolve, and above all "disagreeably logical"; if sorrow strikes and almost destroys him, he displays a small smile, "cold, mean, disagreeable," like his father's. He cannot endure everyday reality: reality is composed of dirt, chaos, confusion ("*notre chère* Orthodox army"), senseless orgies, fantasies, the gossip and boasts of hussars, and little religious picture cards; that reality which does not obey either form or rational order, and which Pierre will learn to venerate during his imprisonment. Whenever it touches him, he flaunts his intellectual pride as a weapon of defense or offense; and the shadow of this style remains in him during his enthusiasms and moments of tenderness. A note of Tolstoy's reminds us that originally he was "Mephistophelean." Something of the intelligence of "the lord of flies and mice" marks him until his death: irony, mockery, contempt, the ruthless and corrosive rationalism with which he derides platitudes and brings to light the minute atrocious and odious truths in which Mephistopheles delights.

During the time he frequents Natasha's house, he gives the Rostovs the impression of "being someone belonging to an alien world": in reality he is an alien as regards any milieu, any town, any worldly limitation. He lives, speaks, acts, commands, mocks like one of the princes of the earth: he bears none of the stigmata of the outcast; and yet life resides at an insurmountable distance from him. During the 1812 campaign, not very far from Lisye Gori under the hot noon sun the soldiers of his regiment swim in a small muddy pond: "The pond had risen approximately by one-half its height again, submerging its banks because it was full of human bodies, white, naked soldiers' bodies which splashed about with arms, faces, and necks brick-red in color. All that naked white mass of human flesh splashed about amid shouts and laughter in that dirty pool like carp crammed together in a bucket." When Prince Andrei sees those splashing human bodies he has a shudder of aversion: at that moment the very substance of life is revealed to him in a flash—the flesh destined to die, to be killed, to be reborn inexhaustibly—and he rejects it in fright and horror. Whereas Pierre discovers in Karataev the symbol of the "roundness" and complexity of existence and sees God in all things, Prince Andrei fears and hates the world of bodies in which God has wished to enact the mysteries of the incarnation.

This estrangement from the flesh gives birth to the impetus of Andrei's nostalgic yearning. He experiences it for the first time on the Rostov estate, when Natasha appears before him, a slim "young girl with dark eyes, in a simple cotton dress, her head covered by a white kerchief"; Natasha shouts, laughs, exults, is happy; and he looks at her, listens to her, watches her. "What makes her so exultant? What may she be thinking about? . . . And what is she so happy about?" he asks himself. He would like to possess through her the heart of life that is alien to him and eludes him. In order to possess life, he would like to have her love—but, to reach Natasha, one must traverse that perishable flesh which splashes about in muddy ponds, Karataev's round complexity which God has scattered in all things. For an instant Prince Andrei contemplates Natasha; and then she escapes him, destined for his rival–friend.

So the fire of yearning burns inextinguishably in him: it is not only the yearning for love, but also for that infinite which we cannot attain on earth; every experience disappoints us because it cannot encompass it and we continue searching for it always—farther on and elsewhere. In the universe of *War and Peace*, Prince Andrei is the only one who knows metaphysical passion, pure and without blemish: he ventures twice into the world that is beyond ours; with his lucid powers he explores what exists beyond the barrier, and tells us the only things we know about it. In so doing, he reveals to us the complexity and ambiguity of his personality. He stands guard like a Vestal over form, aloofness, restraint, irony: the faculties that Tolstoy is never willing to give up; and, at the same time, he offers us the greatest depiction of the infinite yearning that disquiets, torments, and gives happiness to men.

When he converses with Pierre in the novel's first scenes, Prince Andrei is tortured by the desire to emulate Napoleon. He already possesses everything that fortune can bestow on him: he does not need to "arrive," like Julien Sorel or Lucien de Rubempré; and his Napoleonic mirage becomes a pure, childish, ruthless dream of glory, which nervously animates every muscle in his body and makes his eyes glisten and shine. Literature and abstract thought do not attract him: at the moment he cannot have a political career; all that he has left is military glory, his Toulon and his Pont d'Arcole. Like his father, he believes that mathematical reason rules the world: he thinks that war is a chess game between two generals; in his mind he elaborates battle plans and counterplans. At Schöngraben war shows him how chaotic and unpredictable reality is: neither plans nor military directives exist, and great generals, such as Bagration, only confirm history's casualness. But he is stubborn, childish, incapable of grasping life's suggestions on the fly; and a short time later, at Austerlitz, he is again in the grip of his absurd strategic plans.

We all know what remains of these dreams. At Austerlitz, hordes of retreating Russian and Austrian soldiers tumultuously return to the same place where five minutes earlier they had passed in orderly review before the emperors: Kutuzov receives a leg wound; and, at the moment of extreme disaster, in the midst of approaching ruin, Prince Andrei seizes a flag and, with bullets whistling around him, runs toward the enemy. A few minutes later, he is lying on the ground, seriously wounded. Above his head, there is only the sky: a high sky, not limpid, but nevertheless immensely high and immensely quiet, with a silent gliding of gray clouds, beyond which could be sensed, suffused with azure, an infinite depth. " 'How silent, how peaceful, how solemn! Not at all like the way I fled,' thought Prince Andrei, 'not the way we all fled, yelling and fighting: not at all like that Frenchman and that gunner, who, with nasty, frightened faces, struggled over the gun mop. . . . Yes, these clouds glide through this lofty, infinite sky in a completely different way. How is it that I was not aware of this before? And how happy I am at having recognized it, at last! Yes, everything is empty, everything is a delusion, except this infinite sky. Nothing, nothing exists, but this.' "

What is the meaning of this sky, so lofty and calm, that suddenly fills Prince Andrei's mind? What is the meaning of this very profound quiet, which suddenly halts history's tumult and the novel's pace? What is confided to us by this ecstatic vision of a mysterious beyond? What we have before us is the supreme religious revelation, which illuminates Prince Andrei's mind: the only one he can attain through his acute mathematical rationalism. At this moment, in the calm and through the tatters of the clouds, he does not discover his sister's Christian and personal God: but rather an "indefinite, inscrutable, inconceivable, and supreme" God, an obscure God similar to that of negative theology, a God none of us can describe in words or images and of whom only the sky's quiet emptiness offers a visible image. We do not know whether to call it God, or the Great All, or the Great Void. We could not be any further away from Pierre's omnipresent God, nature–God, fullness–God, creator–God: even though this void has absorbed into itself all things, nullified them, and transformed them into illusion.

So, when Prince Andrei, at the point of death, contemplates earth with the gaze of the lofty sky, everything appears vain and illusory to him: vain and insignificant Napoleon with his petty exultance over his victory and his schoolbook sentences; vain and insignificant history's events and personages, so futilely quarrelsome. "The nullity of life, whose sense no one has ever been able to understand, and even the greater nullity of death, whose meaning no one among the living has ever been able to understand and explain," become clear to him. But, at this moment, there is nothing sad, mournful, or disconsolate about such thoughts, and they do not even constitute a prelude to death. Prince Andrei does not want to die: never has existence appeared more beautiful to him than now that he understands it so differently. He wants to live, with the thought of that lofty, quiet sky fixed forever in his mind. He would like to act with the knowledge of the profound delusiveness and vanity of all things and even of his own actions, like—Tolstoy might have remarked later on—a wise Buddhist.

The Austerliz battlefield is the highest observatory that Tolstoy constructed in *War and Peace:* the gaze that Prince Andrei casts from it on the world is broader and vaster than the one he will acquire by his exploration of the realm of death. He will never again be able to live at this height, as he had hoped, lying on the battlefield, under Napoleon's vain eyes. His destiny is the same as that of all of Tolstoy's main characters: Natasha, Pierre, Levin, and Anna Karenina, who all come to know the apogee of life during an ecstatic revelation, an unearthly illumination, which interrupts the course of their existence and of the narration. In that quick, fleeting instant, they taste a drop of eternity, which forever fills their minds and hearts. But these moments have no relation whatsoever to time. It is impossible to place them in a historical context, set them in the continuous and gradual courses of an existence, like stages of a career that must always lead them farther and higher. They are fulgurating and instantaneous like the light with which God reveals Himself to His initiates. Then life returns, with its progressive time and its conventions; and the great moment volatilizes, leaves no traces, it is not brought to fruition, or leaves behind only a fugitive, intermittent memory, like the sky of Austerlitz in Prince Andrei's mind.

Some time later we again hear Prince Andrei discussing with Pierre: his wife has died in childbirth, his eyes are dull, and a thin line furrows his brow, "indicating a long concentration on something fixed." Pierre joyfully describes his new hopes as a Freemason and reformer: but Andrei cannot participate in what he is saying, as if he no longer had anything in common with him. Enclosed in the solitude of the countryside, he has given up all general principles and all illusions: he does not believe in God or evil, justice or injustice; he has cast behind him his dream of glory, his desire to be loved, his love for his fellow man, his hope of reforming Russia. While Pierre expounds his naive philanthropic philosophy, he describes his own sad, desperate egotism, his melancholy epicurianism, which has survived disaster. He now lives only for himself and his family, "without harming anyone." "I am alive, through no fault of mine: therefore I must go on living, in some way or other, the best possible without bothering anybody, until I die." He has a new God now: no longer the inscrutable and empty God that hid beyond the sky of Austerlitz; nor even Pierre's God, the Supreme Architect, the master of *harmonia mundi*, who holds the invisible chain of the universe. How can he believe in a *harmonia mundi* when all around him he sees nothing but failure and distress? If he arrives at God, as at a hypothesis that alone can comfort his melancholy, it is because he sees the scandal of pain and sorrow, the abyss that opens, beyond all places, when a loved one disappears; and he thinks there must be some mysterious *beyond* which requites us for this scandal. Whereas Pierre is alchemical and a follower of the Enlightenment, Prince Andrei, for once, is simply Christian.

A new period of his existence begins with these conversations. The force of love again erupts in him: he sees Natasha for the first time, running and chatting in the garden in the moonlit night; an unexpected tangle of youthful thoughts and hopes softens him. In the old oak tree, which puts out fresh, new leaves and wraps itself in a green canopy, he recognizes a symbol of himself. An unmotivated emotion of springlike exuberance transforms him, of all people, who seems the person most remote from biological rhythms: and once again he has the desire to live for others and with others. The sky of Austerlitz, with the memory of the vanity of all human affairs, is by now very far from his path. The first activity to which he devotes himself is another mistake: for a few months his collaboration with Speransky revives the Enlightenment ideas of his youth which Bagration's example should have dispelled forever. But the mistake does not last for long. The meeting with Natasha saved him: when he abandons his activity as a reformer, it seems to him that he is throwing off the suffocation of laws and principles and entering God's free world. Now all barriers between him and happiness seem to have fallen. He looks at the splendor of Natasha's eyes and smile: when they dance he clasps her body in his arms, and the "wine of her charm goes to his head." This love makes him live for the first time: wipes out the melancholy, disillusionment, and contempt, buries the last shadows of the past; imparts to his cheeks a strange, childlike animation. His eyes shine with light—and he joyously enters the realm of light that Natasha radiates like no other human being.

This luminous flare lasts for an instant which Tolstoy avoids describing: Andrei must leave, forced by the novel's God; and Natasha falls in love with Anatol Kuragin. When Andrei is back in Moscow a "deep vertical crease" is etched between his eyebrows, as after his wife's death: his laugh is the same as his father's; only these physical signs let us sense the pain and disappointment that ravage his soul. Now he is cold, arid, full of rancor and hatred: he cannot free himself from the bite of memory; vital strength abandons him. Reality reveals to him the innumerable fragments into which it is divided and disintegrated. It was always like this, bescause reality, according to Tolstoy, is not a continuous fabric but a great puzzle* of millions of details joined and fitted together; but at one time life's music, intoned by Natasha's lips, threw a veil, a delicate melodic paste over the cracks. Now Natasha's music has vanished; and existence appears to him as it is—absurd, lacerated phenomena without meaning and without connection.

One thing he has learned once and for all: it would be senseless to think that this connective impasto between things can be human reason, which lays out plans, designs, excogitations, machinations, and, by using millions of the puzzle's* pieces, arranges disasters and then tries to tell us what has happened. Reason has no power in human life; and with his acrid, Mephistophelean spirit of contradiction Prince Andrei enumerates the instances that render senseless all the predictions of intelligence. When he listens to the scientific German strategists, or before the battle of Borodino to Pierre talking to him about the war as a game of chess, Prince Andrei laughs bitterly. War a science? "What sort of science can there be in a situation where, as in every practical matter, nothing can be foreseen and everything depends on innumerable circumstances whose meaning will manifest itself at a moment, which nobody knows when it will take place?" War a chess game? "With this little difference: in chess you have the right to think about a move as long as you want to, you are outside the conditions set by time, and with this further difference, that the knight is always stronger than the pawn, and two pawns stronger than one: whereas in war sometimes a battalion is stronger than a division, sometimes weaker than a company." By now Prince Andrei, precisely because of the analytical acumen of his rationalism, has abandoned the rational illusions of youth which still confuse Pierre. He has understood very well the importance of his conversion; and he compares himself to Adam and Eve when they tasted the fruit of the tree of knowledge of good and evil.

A strange comparison. Does this mean that negating human reason, revealing history's horrors and casualness is therefore something forbidden to men, who are because of this driven out of the earthly paradise? Is understanding the truth a sin, like the sin of Adam and Eve? Prince Andrei is desperately alone: life has abandoned him, love has disappointed him atrociously, reality has gone to pieces, reason has served him to destroy reason, and the distant God of Austerlitz does not comfort him with His image. At that moment it seems that his entire past existence—the relation with his father, the wars, the love for Natasha, the French invasion, the imminent battle of Borodino—was a magic lantern show, at which

*English in original—Trans.

he had looked through a lens and under an artificial light. Under this light, how those images had exalted him, troubled him, made him suffer! Now the illumination has changed. Someone has removed the magically colored glasses from the lantern. The light of early morning has appeared: the light of death—white, gelid, without shadows, without perspective, without variety; and all images, once so flattering, seem to him simple, pallid, coarse, badly painted. He looks around: he looks at the yellow, green, and white of the birch trees' barks, which sparkle under the sun in the late August light, the clouds curled in the sky, and the smoke of bivouacs on earth. He imagines that he is dead, and is seized by a sense of horror. At the center of this vision, where his eyes were before, there is no longer anything: or, rather, there is this monstrous thing—a total absence, something aggressively negative: and at the touch of that empty and inimical gaze all things are contaminated and the birches with their contrasts of light and shadow, the curly clouds, the bivouacs' smoke take on a menacing and frightful aspect.

Tolstoy was always attracted by the unknown country of death. He always questioned and knocked at that door, behind which he thought resided the supreme secret of the universe. What is behind it? What do we understand about death, before dying? With what eyes do the dead look at us? And with what eyes do they look at themselves and their country? This was the one science he really would have liked to possess; he envied the dead and the dying for it; sometimes he would have liked to pass *beyond*, together with some of his family, his brothers Dmitri or Nikolai, and return among us to tell us about it. This was the one dream that destiny did not permit him to realize; and so he wrote around this point again and again, as if words could reveal to him what his eyes could not contemplate. He did not tell about death just for the horror and terror of it: or because he was tied to earthly bodies. Death was for him the unique *other*, whom we perhaps have the possibility of knowing: his interest was not physical but grandiosely metaphysical. He felt that it was not a dimension, a lessening and then an end to life. When a body ceases to live, like old Prince Bolkonsky's wretched body, with its livid veins and its halting speech, something in that body takes over—Princess Marya thinks—"something extraneous, hostile . . .

a dreadful, horrifying, repugnant mystery"; or, as Prince Andrei will sense, *that thing*. Death is not a void, a negative, the obverse of life, an absence: but a radically different reality, something obscurely full, which occupies the place occupied by existence.

Prince Andrei's death experience goes through two stages. When he is wounded on the Borodino battlefield and sees Anatol Kuragin in the same dressing-station tent, he is overwhelmed by an exultation of compassion and love, by ecstatic tears of tenderness for men, for himself, for their and his own mistakes. He thinks about his sister's religion and rereads the Gospel. "Yes, love," he thinks with a once more perfect lucidity—"but not the love that loves in view of something or for some motive, but the love that I felt for the first time when, at the point of death, I saw my enemy and yet loved him. I experienced then the feeling of love that is the very essence of the soul and does not need an object . . . to love one's fellow man, to love one's enemies. To love everything: love God in all of His manifestations. A beloved person can be loved with human love: but only an enemy can be loved with divine love . . . nothing, not even death, can destroy it. It is the very essence of the soul." This total love has nothing in common with the total passion for reality, which Pierre knows during his imprisonment: it is an incorporeal, disincarnate love, which prepares him for death, since to love everything and everyone means not to love anyone, not to live this earthly life, to deny it.

If he wants to penetrate into the heart of the country of death, Prince Andrei must go beyond this stage: as happens at decisive moments in Tolstoy's novels, a dream makes this transition possible for him. He lies in his room, and wants to go to the door to shoot the bolt and lock it. He starts to move, hurries, already knows that he won't lock it in time: nevertheless, spasmodically, painfully, he summons all his strength. Beyond the door, there is *that thing*. But at the very instant when with so much effort and so clumsily he manages to drag himself to the door, the terrifying something on the other side already pushes at it, batters it. Something superhuman batters at the door, and it must be stopped. He clings to the door, makes an extreme effort (since it is by now impossible to close it) at least to hold it: but his attempts are weak and maladroit, and the door opens, and then shuts again. Once again, from the other side *that thing* pushes; and both leaves of the door silently fly open. The *thing* enters, and the thing is death. After this dream, Prince Andrei enters the country of death: if not into its heart at least on its periphery; and from there he looks at our existence. By now he is alien, distant, like someone who has arrived among the icy expanses of Tibet or the North Pole: he lives amid a cold that seems to us unbearable: he has difficulty understanding anything that is alive; and he is severe, jealous, hostile to anyone who thinks of life. All the persons dear to him—Natasha, Marya, his son—surround his bed: he has loved and perhaps still loves them most tenderly; and yet he turns to them with an indifferent, alien, or ironic voice, as though he no longer cares for anyone. In a certain sense, he has again found himself: the impenetrable crystal that has kept him at a distance from all things. His coldness and estrangement from life, his repugnance and hostility for the "flesh," culminate here, in the frozen territory he inhabits: with one part of himself he has always been a dead man, and by dying he simply realizes his destiny. Over his shoulder with an even more gelid eye (as gelid as the other eye is enthusiastic), Tolstoy watches the tragicomedy he has staged.

The icy territory is only the periphery of the country of death. Tolstoy tells us that, after his dream, Prince Andrei understands "something else, something that was not and could not be understood by the living"; and he insists that a great light pervades his inner being and, before his eyes, the curtain that had hidden the unknown from him rises. What is illuminated by that great light? What is revealed by that lifted curtain? What does Tolstoy learn, in the course of the most profound discription of death he has ever attempted? Despite all the words that seem to promise us that they will depict the "inscrutable Eternal," "something formidable, eternal, occult, and remote!" Tolstoy remains silent. The heart of the country of death is still unknown to us. We do not discover what lies beyond the ice. We only know that in Prince Andrei death causes a "strange levity." Nothing else. We can only advance some hypotheses. Perhaps that great splendor behind the curtain is the radiant light of God—the God of Austerlitz, so long forgotten. Or, more probably, it is only the light of death: an atheistic, negative light, incomprehensible to the living.

III

As with all great books, we can read *War and Peace* for what it seems to tell us. The surface enchants: we follow the destinies of innumerable characters, entering a drawing room, suffering the passion of love, visiting military headquarters, experiencing the disasters and senselessness of war, relishing the joys of the ironic happy ending, through a horizontal, infinitely meticulous reading. We can, on the other hand, consider the novelistic surface a veil, behind which a secret truth is hidden: in that case, we concentrate our attention on a number of points that seem to us to hide a more intense thickness, and *War and Peace* will appear to us as one of the supreme philosophic–symbolic novels of the past century. But if we ask ourselves what the hidden symbolic textures wish to tell us and what the definitive truth of *War and Peace* is, we are at first perplexed. Tolstoy seems to proclaim the yes and the no of all things, presenting an idea, image, or symbol, and immediately afterward its opposite. There is no reason for our anxiousness. Tolstoy has meant to describe precisely this duplicity, this yin and yang of the universe. Prince Andrei Bolkonsky's and Pierre Bezukhov's faces, characters, lives, experiences, and thoughts correspond at every point, like front and back, the image and its mirrored reflection. Unlike most of his readers, we must not take sides: nor fight on behalf of one or the other, or seek a compromise or a way out. Like Tolstoy during those very laborious years of gestation, we must keep clear and ultimate in our minds only the fatal antithesis of reality, following in turn Andrei and Pierre to the end of their separate experiences; and then resolve this antithesis on a higher plane, as is taught by the epilogue of *War and Peace*.

At Anna Pavlovna's, Pierre is the only character to appear without a mask, incapable of behaving in accordance with the universal theater's rules. He cannot playact because he does not belong to the realm of form, where Prince Andrei moves about as a sovereign: in the variations he carries the sign of formlessness even in his face's features ("turgid, coarse, ill-defined," while Prince Andrei's are "fine, hard, and clearly delineated"). He does not know contempt, irony, the cutting retort, in which the ways of the salons educate all men. What is enchanting in him is naturalness: a simplicity and joviality filled with candid grace; goodness that does not know intentions, programs, and purposes, but is born spontaneously from the depths of the heart. No one can resist him, neither children nor adults: everyone approaches him, while Prince Andrei keeps people at a distance; even the old, arid, and ironic Nikolai Bolkonsky is warmed by his conversation.

A good upbringing teaches not to reveal one's feelings: Prince Andrei is supremely well brought up; but what obliges Pierre to restrain himself, when impulse stirs within him? As soon as he meets Captain Ramballe in Moscow, the latter, with the vulgar, superficial, and naive familiarity of the French, tells Pierre about his ancestors, childhood, adolescence, and youth: about all his dealings with relatives, property, and family: about *ma pauvre mère* and especially love, with the childishly deep conviction of being the only one ever to experience all of its seductions. Any other person would not talk about himself in the company of this perfect traveling salesman: Pierre, swept along by the wine, Ramballe's joviality, his own amiability and lack of inhibition and irony, confides in him, of all people, the secret of his life: his love for Natasha. Like Tolstoy, we laugh, conquered. In this smiling and effusive naturalness, we like the hidden childlike quality, the "boyish smile" that accompanies his acts. While all the other characters, even Natasha and Nikolai, become adults, he is the only one to live firmly and at the same time unknowingly in a children's world. He dreams, fantasizes, imagines like a young boy: for him these colorful fantasies are more real than reality itself and drive him to action: as when he cultivates the absurd dream of killing Napoleon, the "Beast of the Apocalypse."

Pierre does not know the stress of the will, the effort and rigidity of programs and intentions: if Tolstoy has attributed to him so great a part of his own thoughts, he has taken away from him all that which in himself was stubborn, programmatic, and willful. While Prince Andrei is a hard, cutting flint, he is soft and fluid, meek and enveloping like water which adapts its shape to the place where it is poured. He could repeat the words of *Tao:* "He dulls what is sharp, disentangles what is tangled." Throughout his existence all he does is accept passively what is imposed on him or proposed to him: his father's inheritance, the marriage to Helene, his conversion to Freemasonry, his participation in the patriotic war—there is not a stage of his experience in which he is not swept up and dominated by others. He is obedient to Anna Pavlovna, Princess Drubetskoy, Dolokhov, Prince Vasily, his wife, Osip Bazdeyev, Prince Andrei, and then endlessly, beyond the end of the book, he obeys Natasha, finding in obedience the same beatitude others may find in the affirmation of the self. We always surprise him as he is agreeing, accepting, welcoming, letting rise up in himself the voice of others, of life and fate, almost as though in the universal harmony his role were that of echoing the music of others. As Tolstoy understood and forgot, this is the supreme wisdom: "not to act," and in *War and Peace*, together with Pierre only Kutuzov knows it. The old general bows to history's mechanical and dreadful necessity: Pierre bows to Natasha's wonderfully sweet but equally dreadful necessity, and the two characters are in perfect correspondence in the novel's economy. The voice of common sense could charge both of them that by not acting battles are lost, the army falls apart, and one's life is consumed in futile experiences. But the voice of destiny answers that by becoming passive, acting in a sinuous and shapeless manner, like water, changing ourselves into everything that is proposed to us, we receive the gift of what matters most: the feminine secret of life and history—victory, Natasha.

Thus, shapeless, soft, and aquatic, Pierre lends himself to his task as the novel's hero, who, as Goethe said, "must be passive, or at least not active to a high degree." If he had narrated too many episodes through the eyes of Prince Andrei, Tolstoy would have imposed on reality the aggressive, now ironic, now metaphysical light of his world. Through Pierre's eyes he presented a larger part of it, the struggles between the protagonists of the "false," Freemasonry, the battle of Borodino, Moscow under the French, and imprisonment. This was for him a privileged viewpoint: Pierre's passive eye allowed him to mirror reality as it was: his naive and farcical eye allowed him to describe its strangeness and comic aspects; his astonished eye made it possible for him to present events as an empty, absurd, and horrible nightmare. The prodigious comic culmination of this narrative process is the battle of Borodino. Pierre does not realize that he is on the battlefield: he does not hear the sound of the bullets and cannon shells that whistle by on all sides, he does not distinguish the enemy, he sees neither dead nor wounded, although they fall quite close to him. Then he reaches the center of the battle, Raevski's Redoubt: with his tall white hat he perches peacefully on an escarpment and with a shy, abstracted smile, politely moving out of the way of soldiers, he strolls through the battery, under the cannonades, with the same tranquility as though he were strolling on the boulevard. We are in the very heart of history: but history as seen by one who does not understand a thing and imagines that in it he occupies an insignificant place; and thus history is faithfully presented, derided, and nullified.

Nobody in *War and Peace* possesses an imagination as limitless as Pierre's: reality as he sees it is always enveloped by a laughing or euphoric ideal mist, which blurs its outlines, shades off its contours. Except for some metaphysical élans, Prince Andrei's thought tends toward action: Pierre's thought, on the contrary, is thought sunk in itself which does not want to compare itself with things. Locked in his room, or at a chance stagecoach halt, sitting down or standing, without noticing external events he spends hour upon hour meditating: in reading we have the physical impression of his mind which attempts, strives, connects, and disconnects, becomes entangled and lost in itself, has sudden illuminations and sudden discouragements; only very rarely does Tolstoy let us know exactly what these thoughts are, because he attributes to Pierre a pure and uncontaminated faculty of thought, the play of the mind with itself, which does not reach any logical conclusion whatsoever. Like all abstract men, he always lives on the brink of a revelation. The following morning, or even within ten minutes, he will happen to do something extraordinary, capable of consuming his life: he is the man of Utopia, of imminent catastrophe, of the comet that, fixed in the sky with its long splendiferous tail, scintillating and changing colors among the innumerable twinkling stars, announces to him the total renewal of soul and universe. In recompense, minute and complicated quotidian reality interests him very little. He does not have a head for business, he is unable to carry through the reforms he has planned for his estates, whereas Prince Andrei always accomplishes what he sets out to do. Thus the true "alien" in the cluttered thicket of existence seems to be none other than he.

And yet this abstracted man, with his head always lost in who knows what realm of dreams, is the most down-to-earth character is *War and Peace*. When Tolstoy brings him to life on stage, he tells in the first place the adventures of a *body:* a massive, almost enormous body, which eats, drinks, gets drunk, lazes in bed, joyfully performs all vital functions. We never see Prince Andrei eat: instead, from the very beginning of the book, Pierre is seated at table, devours the *soupe à la tortue*, a fish mousse, a partridge and accompanies them with dry Madeira, Rhine, and Hungarian wines. During his father's illness and death, he seems to live almost outside consciousness, in a mysterious torpor. This torpor never leaves him: his unconscious activity is very intensive and no intellectual suspension arrests or interrupts it. Prince Andrei is only visited once by a dream that announces his imminent death. Passive, aquatic, contemplative, Pierre dreams all the time: vast dreams which are prolonged into wakefulness, creating an ambiguous, semioneiric, semireal reality, where he loiters gladly with such pleasure; erotic and philosophic dreams which contain revelations of the beyond, where thought has an intellectual precision absent during the day. If Pierre had seemed to us a stranger to everyday reality, his full existence in the body, the richness of his unconscious activity, the passive bent of his mind allow him to live in the very heart of life. He is at ease in it, with perfect enthusiasm and naturalness: from there he speaks with others, converses with us; and conquers Natasha, the flower of life.

With exquisite intelligence Tolstoy has incarnated in Pierre's body the two comic archetypes, Don Quixote and Sancho Panza. Pierre has Don Quixote's abstract and intellectual as well as Sancho's earthy comicality: he struggles with windmills and the fish mousse: he does not understand because he is too immersed in thought, and because he is too dominated by the body; because he is too idealistic and too realistic, filiform and massive, vertiginous and crude. This alliance between the two Cervantean archetypes could not be more delightful. Everything that Pierre does—inherit, marry, duel, join the Masons, participate in battles, try to kill Napoleon, save little girls, fall in love, marry again—is supremely comic: Tolstoy loves him, makes fun of him, laughs behind his back, and is enchanted by everything he does, like a child with his most amusing puppet. As for Pierre, he is well aware that he amuses Tolstoy and is amused by what he does. Even though he is constantly occupied with the greatest of man's problems, he is never able to take himself seriously: he plays at philosophy, or at war, or at marriage, as one might play chess: he does not forget that he is an amateur, a man without a profession, a bungler; he never participates completely in the thoughts and actions of which he is in fact so convinced, and precisely because of this he floats without danger over all of history's horrors. Finally, he knows how to laugh at himself, with his massive, jovial laugh, while Prince Andrei only knows the subtler pleasure of irony.

His laughter does not exclude anguish, melancholy, and despair: the interminable days that Pierre spends stretched out on the sofa, without eating, without getting dressed, without leaving the house, without seeing anyone. Then it seems to him that in his brain a screw has lost its thread, a screw on which all his existence depends: the screw does not go in, does not come out, but continues to turn on itself without catching. He thinks: "What is evil? What is good? What must one love and what hate? What must one live for, and what am I? What is life, what is death?" All things seem to him vain, arbitrary, unreasonable, invented at whim: devoid of all importance in comparison to eternity, and so on and on, always again the same question confronts him: "For what purpose?" When he listens to banal chatter or hears talk about human baseness and foolishness he is horrified: he asks himself why men bustle about and spend so much time intriguing when everything is so brief and obscure. At times the world collapses before his eyes in a heap of senseless rubble: he feels that there is neither salvation nor a way out for himself and the rest of mankind. Once Tolstoy explicitly says that "Pierre is not far from madness." Like his author, he constantly lives at the limits of the human mind, battered by an excess of thoughts, sensations, dreams, attacked by the real and unreal, the impossible and unthinkable; and a little push would be enough to throw him into the abysses of dementia. So this Sancho Panza is a tragic character: we do not know how far the dark zone of his mind extends; only his sudden dreadfully violent outbursts of fury allow us to glimpse something of his dark side.

The crowd of memories does not besiege Pierre, while a part of Prince Andrei always faces the past. He has done nothing but make mistakes: the wrong marriage, attempts left dangling halfway, absurd undertakings; but he only has to shake his head, reach out with one hand, for the past's burden to lift from his spirit and for him to stand again at the beginning of life, ready to start all over again. Like Tolstoy, he swims in the cycle of universal metamorphosis and the rigid crust of existence does not imprison him. He changes opinions in a flash; if he was an atheist, he becomes a Christian: every touch transforms him: plastic, mobile, almost without persona, he can understand others and become the others—a Russian soldier, Platon Karataev, a French officer—or a comet in the sky or the woods and fields which stretch out under the full moon all the way to the infinite horizon. His enormous body insinuates itself everywhere, like a kobold. So he never loses his natural capacity for joy: the gift that, in those years, Tolstoy prized more than any other. While Prince Andrei's mistakes turn against him, Pierre's mistakes, unbeknownst to him, prepare his future happiness. In the world of *War and Peace*, the grace of God, which is identified with the novelist's grace, elects its favorites: Pierre and not Prince Andrei, Natasha and not Sonya; it chooses them not on the basis of virtuous actions and merits but according to whether they possess or do not possess the gift of life.

Prince Andrei conquers his metaphysics in the course of sudden fulgurations, which fill his mind while the soul is abandoning the body. At equally extreme and dramatic moments, Pierre also knows not his metaphysics but his philosophy: since truth in Tolstoy is revealed only at the brink of the abyss. His long Masonic apprenticeship has not been of much help to him during the fervent years, he has known an idea of *harmonia mundi*, of the thousand invisible chains that link the earth and skies, and a symbolic science of the universe's totality which is alive in him also during his imprisonment, like the premise of future doctrines; but those symbols do not illuminate him with the light of truth. He leaves the horror of Borodino, or he is alone, ragged, barefoot, swept along by the fleeing French army, together with thousands of prisoners who fall dead around him: he spends the night in the courtyard of an inn surrounded by the stench of stables, manure and tar, or at the fire of a bivouac in a mob of French soldiers. He has two dominant dreams. In the first dream, somebody speaks to him with the same terse, enigmatic, and prophetic voice—so clear that it is obscure—in which the sybil announced her revelations, writing on leaves. We do not know to whom the voice belongs. Perhaps it is Pierre's: his long everyday experience, incapable of expressing itself, has been transformed into an oneiric experience, finding the authority of speech to which it always futilely aspired. Perhaps the speaker is really another, *the other:* the voice issues from the gates of horn, or from above the clouds; and Pierre is a seer, who communicates to us sentences that are immensely larger than himself.

In the second dream, alongside the bivouac, a mild old teacher who had taught him geography in Switzerland appears before Pierre. "Wait a moment!" the little old man says, showing Pierre a globe. "This is life!" This globe is a living, shivering sphere whose surface is formed by millions of drops of water, densely compacted. At the center there is a larger drop, which Pierre does not see, the drop of God: so God is within the sphere, the heart of life, is life itself; He is not lofty, far from us and above us, like the sky of Austerlitz. All the drops mirror God: they strive to dilate, so as to be able to reflect Him to an ever larger extent; thus egotism and the will to life, like Pierre's at this moment, are justified and consecrated. There is an incessant movement in the globe: the drops move and change places: many merge into one, or one divides into many: each strives to expand, but the others press on it from all sides, and sometimes annihilate it, sometimes fuse with it; and all this movement is nothing but the pleasure of God's self-knowledge. A drop here and there dies and is reborn: look! it is pressed and annihilated at the surface; it retreats into the depths, and then again it floats, obeying the principle of universal metamorphosis.

This nocturnal revelation of the atemporal One–All is as complete as revelations of the beyond must be. No objection can shake it: not even death, because it too is a form of the vital divine movement, which expands, contracts, is annihilated at the surface and reborn in the depths. So the scandal of death is abolished: the One–All understands, justifies, sanctifies it: like Prince Andrei at Austerlitz, Pierre triumphs over death and could apply to himself a sentence with a Gnostic flavor that he has heard during the first dream: "Man cannot have power over anything so long as he is afraid of death. But to him who is not afraid of it, everything belongs." In his dream Pierre has become master of the world. But let us observe what happens at the margins of the dream. As soon as he awakens from the revelation of the God–All, the Life–Death, Pierre refuses to understand that Platon Karataev has been killed and in fright looks away. So he is terrified by death, is unworthy of the cosmic revelation, does not see around him the flux of universal metamorphosis, and cannot become master of the world. The One–All, as Pierre conceives it in his diminished mind, does not conquer the scandal of death.

What is the task of the human drops that move, dilate, expand, are annihilated, plunge down, and then are reborn? Pierre had already learned this in his first dream, immediately after the battle of Borodino. On one hand, the universal movement reveals to him an aspect of God that at first sight overwhelms him: the love–God of incessant existence is also destiny, necessity, the inexorable horror of war itself, which at that moment sweeps millions of soldiers across the plains of Russia and covers the fields of Borodino with thousands of corpses. There is no way out: like the simple soldiers and the great Kutuzov, the human drops must accept, submit, docilely bow their heads before the God of war. The second task is much more arduous, and Pierre does not know how to accomplish it. Whereas Prince

Andrei gathers the fragments into which his life has disintegrated, Pierre's dream demands that every human drop, both the one that dissolves and the one that expands, reflecting an ever greater share of God's life, should gather, *hitch up* (as the stable master's voice repeats) all thoughts, all sensations, all revelations received while awake or dreaming: so as to hitch together all the drops, showing where their points of contact are. Neither Pierre nor any other drop could ever entirely meet this obligation. Tolstoy is speaking above all for himself. He is the one who must connect the points of the universe, the thoughts and sensations of human minds, depicting "the infinite labyrinth of concatenations in which the essence of art consists," it is he, the immense mosaicist–symphonist who is composing *War and Peace*.

Thus accompanied by dreams, Pierre is ready to meet the most perfect and compact of these human drops: a figure that is not even a character but an incarnate emblem, an oneiric image, as is only fitting that it should happen in this part of *War and Peace*, where for a moment the novel arrests its course, giving way to symbolic representations. Like the men imagined by Aristophanes in *The Symposium*, Platon Karataev is round: "His head was perfectly round: his back, chest, shoulders, even his arms, which he always held as if about to embrace some object, were round; his pleasant smile and his large, caressing, chestnut-colored eyes were round." He shares the perfection of the circle, like the sinuous, colorful nature Tolstoy contemplated on the shores of Lake Lucerne. Since he is round, he cannot understand the regular, straight line of generals, nor even Prince Andrei's tragic, broken line: he fuses together male and female qualities (when he sang, his "tones were always subtle, delicate, almost feminine"), as though he were born before the distinction between the sexes; and he can live when words, gestures, acts, human life are not separated from one another but together form a living connection, as in the request to *hitch up* during Pierre's first dream. Platon reveals to us the heart of the tender, smiling, peasant Mother Russia: the goodness, sweetness, childlike simplicity, birdlike candor, faith in providence, renunciation of all personal will, the certainty that God is scattered everywhere, the love for all appearances. After meeting Platon, Pierre carries through his definitive transformation, leaving behind forever the "straight line" of German strategists and Prince Andrei's metaphysics. He too "becomes rounded": he draws ever closer to the other circular character in the book, his double, Kutuzov—and sinks into the circular womb of nature, Natasha.

After the dreams and Karataev's revelations, an ecstatic, almost intoxicated Pierre finally understands the words that during his childhood his old nurse had said: God is here, everywhere; in the deprivations and horrors of imprisonment, and in the comforts of freedom, in the horse meat eaten in the bivouacs, in hot bouillon and clean sheets, in the shy eyes of animals, in woods and fields lit by the full moon. The fragments of life, no matter which, are connected to one another, connected to alien existences and distant worlds, and reveal to him the divine presence. Thus for Pierre God is what is closest and most accessible to him, what is at his side and before him, and what to the eyes of others appears limited, petty, and paltry. But as soon as he touches any fragment, as soon as he touches any drop which expands, disappears, or is reborn, why look! the "neighbor" immediately lengthens before his eyes, moves away, is limitless, inexhaustible, and the extremely accessible becomes eternally inaccessible. Pierre is irremediably immersed in each drop; he sees nothing but the thousands of colors, nuances, and shadows reflected in each; but his eyes have barely finished contemplating the surface than they go beyond it and pursue it in the infinite's very distant appearances. Where Prince Andrei had shown us the search for the infinite as opposed to reality, Pierre shows us that we can pursue it also in the heart of reality.

Pierre lives happily in the present. Where have the great dreams and ambitions of his life—the happiness of mankind, the salvation of Russia—gone? Like Tolstoy, he has renounced them.

For the first time in his life, ripping open the clouds of youthful dreams, during his imprisonment he becomes a realist, ready, vigilant, sticking close to things. Where at one time he had a body without knowing it, he now regains possession of it, and moves the big dirty toes of his wounded feet with the joy of a child: he loves elementary life and feels his being fuse with the All. Since they too have become divine he cultivates his pleasures, defending his natural egotism. With the usual psychological subtlety, the conclusion is left to Natasha: " 'Do you know, Marya . . .' Natasha suddenly said with an impish smile which Princess Marya had not seen on her face for a long time, 'he has become all clean, smooth, and fresh. . . . You'd say he just stepped out of a bath—morally, you understand? Isn't that true?' 'Yes . . .,' said Princess Marya. 'He's improved a lot.' And that short jacket of his, that short hair, yes, definitely, he really seems to have just taken a bath.' "

This small apologue needs no explanation: Pierre is regenerated, having descended into the revivifying waters of life.

IV

Rather than describing a character's features, or the processes of his inner life, Tolstoy preferred to render the mysterious irradiation that pours from his depths and, erupting from his eyes and his laughter, projects rays, torrents, rivers of light. Never did so many epiphanies populate the space of a novel as those that constellate *War and Peace*. Since all the drops of the terrestrial globe share the divine essence, the splendor of the characters in *War and Peace* is a part of the irradiation that, during the first days of creation, blazed out on the earth and, ever since, descends superabundantly from the skies. It is not an exclusively spiritual force. Only Marya's "deep and radiant eyes" emanate a deep, intense celestial light. Helene gives off a satisfied animal light: old Prince Bolkonsky a sparkling, ironic intellectual light: Dolokhov a lustful, violent, and brazen light: Anatol a morbid erotic light: on the young Napoleon's gaunt face appears the light of victory: on Emperor Alexander the calm, caressing light of happy and beloved regality. Only creatures without vitality, such as Vera and Sonya, do not project rays. This splendor seems to concentrate in two opposed points: the spiritual in Marya, whereas the irresistible force of the joy of existence gushes out in luminous torrents from Natasha's eyes and smile. All other sources can fade away: Napoleon and Alexander will be obscured; not Marya, nor Natasha, who even at the end of the book, when her fascination is extinguished, "spreads an exultant light from her transfigured face."

The Rostov family is a warm maternal womb: a cosmos, with its institutions, its language, its habits, its complicities, its terrible cruelties, its unimaginable uniformity and compactness; the "others" can enter it, provided they are converted to these hidden laws, as Prince Andrei is about to do and as Pierre will do. It is closed, as a novel is closed, whose form must resemble its intricate compactness. When we think of the exquisite eighteenth-century music that reigns at Lisye Gori, the noisy operatic music, the Verdian clamor of cymbals, drums, and trumpets that we hear in the Rostov home seems almost unbearable to us. There refinement of manners, here joviality, cordiality, childlike approximation: there systematic cultivation of the intelligence, here total absence of intellectual interests: style is juxtaposed to the absolute lack of style: contempt and intellectual arrogance to affectionate good spirits: the strict preservation of social distances to a patriarchal familiarity between masters and servants; silence or the music of clocks to laughter, dances, masquerades, buffooneries. Although Count Rostov gets sauce stains on his vest by poking his nose in the kitchen, Tolstoy is disposed to forgive him much graver sins. He mocks him without ferocity but loves him because he is good, because he is foolish and amiable, because of the happy, affectionate immediacy that reigns in his house, and because he has invented him. He loves him above all for *les jeunes filles* who fill the rooms: the rustle of skirts, the whisper and laughter of youthful voices, while through the crack of the door flashes something azure, ribbons, black hair, and cheerful faces.

In the family, Natasha has a friend, almost a double, her brother Nikolai, with whom understanding is perfect. " 'Do you know something,' she said suddenly, 'I am certain that I will never again be as happy and tranquil.' 'These really are absurdities, foolishness, lies,' said Nikolai; and he thought: 'What a charmer, my Natasha! I don't have and never will have another friend like her. What is she getting married for?—She and I could always go about together!' " When we go over the experiences of Nikolai's life, we must admit that he is a mediocre man: he does all the things that an ordinary man would do; and perhaps his one stroke of genius is his being enamored of Emperor Alexander, who appears to him in an apotheosis of light, like a beloved woman or a god. He always agrees with the group's ideas—family, army, society: he does not suspect that there exist values whose origin cannot be found "here": he has no doubts: he is quick to raise his voice and his hands; and even his wife's spiritual world is foreign to him. Everything for him is real, evident, defined, like the set phases of a hunt. But we can imagine what his figure would have become in the hands of Flaubert or a French naturalist: a catalogue of commonplaces and monotonous gestures, scrutinized by the eye of a ruthless entomologist. By giving him so much prominence, Tolstoy probably wanted to win a bet with himself, and the novelists of his time. There are no zones of shadow in reality: no heart is unpoetic and dead: if a great writer penetrates the most conventional of souls he will find in it treasures of freshness, vital gaiety, inspiration, fantasy, and will fall in love with it, as if he were depicting Prince Andrei or Stavrogin.

Now at last she, the queen of the *jeunes filles* of all time, Natasha, comes to meet us with her rapid, light, and impetuous step, her eyes and smile radiant with light. Natasha is the youthful joy of life: the absurd happiness that nobody could or would be able to explain with causes (you are healthy, rich, in love, something wonderful has happened to you), and it overwhelms us suddenly, without reason, and also leaves us without reason: irresponsible existence, which looks at itself in the mirror and is madly pleased with itself; the subtle and light music—neither rules, principles, ideas, nor preconceptions—which echoes in our hearts and without which living would become monotonous and burdensome. As Prince Andrei asked himself: "What is she so exultant about? What might she be thinking about? . . . And what is she so very happy about?" Natasha is *so very happy* because she's possessed by the most profound narcissism echoing in the pages of any of Tolstoy's novels or diaries. She loves herself and has the need to be loved: she admires herself and has the need to be admired; and in the soliloquies she holds with herself before falling asleep, there always is a man—naturally the most intelligent and best man in the world—who repeats: "How, how adorable she is. . . . There is everything in her, everything; she is extraordinarily intelligent and appealing, and what's more pretty, extraordinarily pretty, and she knows how to do everything—she swims, rides magnificently, and what a voice! . . . a voice, no doubt, astonishing!" As happens with every true narcissist, the spirit of her childhood has not completely abandoned her; she plays like a young girl: she sings, commands, is bored, runs, chatters, carries on, dances, hunts, falls asleep, dreams with a childlike spontaneity and discontinuity; and the adults look at her with so much love because in seeing her they remember the golden season of their own youth. Tolstoy asks us to believe that, unless we become like Natasha, we shall never be able to be happy. And yet, at times, we feel sorry for her. In her joy and her vital intoxication there is something excessive that might bring about her downfall: Natasha walks at one centimeter from the abyss and only grace prevents her from falling into it.

Whereas the world of the "false" culminates in the figure of Helene, in *War and Peace* Natasha represents the opposite pole: nature, Russian nature, such as Tolstoy imagined it. Tolstoy forces her to stay in the country for almost a year: he sends her out hunting wolves, shrieking like a savage: sets her among hunters and peasants, has her eat fritters and boiled honey, and, finally, when the "uncles' " balalaika plays "Down the Paved Way," he has her dance the peasant dance. I won't say that these last pages, where Tolstoy's hand, elsewhere so sovereignly light, bears down heavily on meanings, are the ones I prefer in *War and Peace.* Some time later he bares Natasha's shoulders and arms and accompanies her to the theater, where during those same years Eugene Onegin takes his boredom amid the luster of the boxes and buzz of the galleries. Natasha alights from her carriage, goes through the corridor of the *baignoires*, and enters her box, her slim, youthful beauty bared to the eyes of the connoisseurs: Julia Karagin displays her thick red neck dusted with powder, Helene her snow-white shoulders, her thick braid, and her almost naked breast; while, at the center of the parterre, Dolokhov in Persian costume stands erect, with his enormous mass of kinky hair combed upward.

As soon as the curtain rises, "nature" contemplates, through Natasha's eyes, the falseness, unreality, and lies of the operatic theater: those painted cardboards, that hole in the canvas which represents the moon, those men in silk trousers and a feather on the head who sing together with very fat women dressed in white, those paper castles, those raspberry-colored thrones, those dancers paid sixty thousand rubles a year, with their tripping little steps and tremendous leaps. . . . Some psychoanalyst might say that had Natasha loved opera more than Tolstoy was willing to allow her, she would have put up better resistance to the first attack of a representative of the "false"—Anatol. Besides the theater, there is another world that Natasha does not understand: the world of writing. When she is away from Andrei, she writes him dry and schoolgirlish letters, whose errors in calligraphy her mother corrects. The natural joy of life is expressed by looks, laughter, her step, running, the lively movement of her entire body: something that only the eye, and perhaps only all five amorous senses together, can grasp, and how can it be imprisoned by words, or even less by writing's abstract signs? Natasha escapes any form of literature: she is, for Tolstoy, a goal that every character pursues, that he himself pursues with words, and that betrays every verbal transcription.

When Princess Marya, jealous and suspicious of Natasha, asks Pierre: "Tell me, with a hand on your heart, the whole truth, to the bottom: what kind of girl is she, and how do you judge her? . . . Is she intelligent?" Pierre reflects: "I think not—actually, yes. She doesn't deign to be intelligent. . . . But no, she's enchanting and nothing else." We cannot blame Pierre for hesitating and contradicting himself: if it is true that Natasha does not know the intellectual understanding of thoughts and events, she possesses in a unique way a magical intuition of life. She is quick to grasp the nuances of intonation, the looks and expressions of the people she is talking to: she senses the mysteries that hide behind the surface of existence; when she listens to Pierre after his return from imprisonment, she does not miss a word, a vibration of his voice, a look, the tremor of a muscle, and understands not only what he is telling but also what cannot be expressed in words. Her psychological portraits have an incomparable metaphorical precision. She discerns the future: understands when a man must die, as though nothing that belongs to the cycle of life can conceal its secrets from her piercing eye. So robustly realistic, there is only one faculty she does not possess: the sense of the infinite; her gaze, confined to this life, does not see it. The paradox of *War and Peace* decrees that two *chercheurs d'infini* such as Andrei and Pierre stake all their desires and hopes for salvation on so marvelously limited a person.

With the help of these gifts, Natasha listens within herself to what Rousseau called "the feeling of existence stripped of all affectation." Like a very sensitive metronome or an immaterial clock, she perceives the slow flow of life: time that passes without anything filling it, neither actions nor specific thoughts, save for its own indeterminate flow. It is the third day of the Christmas holiday and Natasha is bored: she needs Prince Andrei, "right away, this minute," and she tells this to her mother with glittering eyes and unsmiling. She goes into the rooms with the sofas, then she goes to the maids' rooms where she exchanges a few words with an old woman: then to the entrance hall, where she orders the servants, just like that, purely for a whim, to bring her a rooster, some chalk, and a bit of oats. When she walks past the pantry, she calls for the samovar, although it is not yet time to have tea; and meanwhile she asks herself: "What should I do? Where should I go?" She climbs the stairs, runs to the floor above, where two governesses are discussing whether life is cheaper in Moscow or Odessa; she listens to them, then gets up and repeats, enunciating each syllable: Ma-da-gas-car. When her younger brother Petya walks by she climbs on his shoulders and makes him carry her piggyback. More and more bored, she goes into the drawing room, picks up the guitar, and tries to play a musical phrase from an opera; and meanwhile she abandons herself to remembering, her eyes hanging on a shaft of light coming from the pantry door. Sonya crosses the drawing room carrying a small glass in her hand: it seems to Natasha that already once before, from the pantry door, through that same opening, light fell in this way, and Sonya came by holding a small glass. "But yes, yes of course, this already happened point by point. . . ." And so on—in these marvelous pages, perhaps the boldest in *War and Peace*, Natasha's boredom and waiting, and that carefully enunciated Ma-da-gas-car ("No, that's no good . . . the island of Madagascar") introduce us into the very substance of time in the act of being consumed.

Some time before, in that same country house, the moon's motionless and springlike light shines down on a row of trees, black on one side and white on the other: it silvers the fresh, damp vegetation and a big leafy tree. Like Prince Andrei on the floor below, Natasha cannot sleep: she chats with Sonya: sings a musical phrase; leans out the window, so far that the rustle of her dress and even her breath can be heard below. She looks at the moon, its light on the earth, the large black shadow " 'Sonya! Sonya—' she says, 'how can you possibly sleep! Come and look, for a moment. What magic! Ah, what magic! Come, Sonya, wake up—' " and there are almost tears in her voice—" 'There has never been a magical night like this, you know? There's never been.' " Then she insists: " 'No, you've got to look at this moon! . . . Ah, what magic! Come here! Come, darling, come here. So, do you see it? Here, I could sit down here, like this, look, holding my hands tightly under my knees—tight, tight as possible— . . . the body must be all tense and then I could fly away. Here, like this. . . .' " Natasha's flight toward the lunar sky is not the flight of the disembodied soul toward its lost country. Natasha lives only on this earth, she only knows earthly joys and sensations, bound to our reality by relationships that nobody would be able to break: and yet her happiness is so great that it seems to her that she has wings and can leap up in flight, possessed by the vertigo of lightness. She flies even though remaining on the ground: she goes beyond time even while staying in time; she attains the eternal while staying among us. Perhaps Tolstoy never spoke to us so profoundly of himself, as in this scene and in the scene of Levin's engagement, which is its perfect counterpart. When he identifies with Natasha, the love he has for life is without reservations and without shadow, but provided it can leap, knees tightly clasped, beyond life. There is not a writer like him, in whom the most absolute immanence is overturned without effort and as though by an inner force and impetus becomes the lightest, most paradoxical transcendence.

So rich with happiness, so full of love for herself and existence, nourished by time and capable of wings, Natasha exerts an immense erotic attraction on the characters of *War and Peace*. Boris, Denisov, Prince Andrei, Kuragin, Pierre, and who knows how many others seeing her at balls or in the streets of Moscow "drink the wine of her charm" and are rejuvenated by contact with her. Her juvenile, lissome freshness should not deceive us. The strength embodied in Natasha is tremendous and ineluctable: it is a kind of feminine chthonic and fateful deity; the biological automatism unleashed in war finds in her mocking eyes and light, impetuous step a sweeter version. No resistance to Natasha is possible: there is no point in staying away from her, traveling to Italy, trying to forget her; one can only surrender, with beatific and ecstatic facility, drink to the dregs the wine of her fascination and be possessed by her. But to surrender is not enough. Like every great erotic temperament, Natasha carries within her destructive potentials that could make of her a potent sexual animal, much more terrifying than marmoreal Helene, with her uniformly radiant smile. So Pierre's act is twofold: while he yields to Natasha, he chains her with the bonds of matrimony, which tame her sexual violence.

Before achieving its apogee, Natasha's light runs the risk of being dimmed by the light that in the epiphanies of *War and Peace* occupies the opposite pole: the hiddenly poisonous, tenebrous light of Helene and Anatol Kuragin. According to a rumor, which accompanies them like a leitmotif, this brother and sister are bound together by an incestuous relationship: they represent the abyss of corruption, enclosed in the world of the "false," and which insidiously attacks the characters whom fate must join—Pierre, Marya, Natasha. As though to emphasize the symbolic character of the double seduction, Tolstoy has it take place in the temple in which the "false" crowns itself: the opera theater where Duport dressed in sequins takes enormous leaps and hurried little steps in exchange for sixty thousand rubles. At first Natasha does not understand the scenery, songs, and dances: then, contaminated by the artificial light, the atmosphere's warmth, and the hundreds of eyes gazing at her bare arms and neck, she enters into a state of intoxication, and is no longer "aware of what she is doing, where she is, and what is unfolding before her." The other seductress is Helene with her bare breast and the double row of pearls: or dressed in a deep purple velvet gown with its high collar, which imparts a triumphantly mournful tone to her presence. Helene tries to corrupt Natasha out of love of corruption, of which she is both daughter and mistress: she praises her beauty and her toilettes: speaks about the new gown *en gaze métallique* which she has just received from Paris; and Natasha thinks she is falling in love with that purple and marmoreal beauty.

Anatol's seduction is first of all a seduction by the gaze. At first in the parterre and then in his sister's box, Anatol stares into Natasha's eyes, "with a gaze so enraptured and caressing that it seems strange to her to stand so close to him, look at him like this, be so sure that she attracts him, and still not know each other." Then the act ends, the door to the box opens, Natasha and Anatol sit next to each other: her eyes, which were still protected by an invisible barrier, are subjugated by his eyes, who looks now at her face, now at her neck, now at her bare arms. All the sexuality that Tolstoy has removed from *War and Peace*, exorcising it because of terror and neurosis, is concentrated here: what happens in a few instants through Natasha's and Anatol's glances is perhaps more intimate than any lovers' embrace in nineteenth-century literature. Natasha knows what is most terrible in Eros: the fascination and damnation of absolute proximity, the collapse of all barriers, the feeling of unlimited intimacy. Even the scene of the kiss, which Helene opens and closes with words and the rustle of her dress, is less intense. In one of his great moments of omission, Tolstoy avoids representing it, as though he did not wish to assume its narrative responsibility. It is Natasha who observes it and tells it herself: the story does not take place in the present, as Anatol kisses her, but in an unspecified future, so that the scene is narrated in the past ("Afterward she remembered that she had asked her father . . ."); and this twofold optical shift adds uncertainty, nuance, and confusion to her intoxicated gaze.

There is no spectacle more painful than seeing the joy of life obfuscated, shadowed, obscured, as Natasha sees during the two crises of her existence: after the end of her love for Anatol and after the deaths of Prince Andrei and Petya. We see her in her room, wearing a simple black woolen dress, her braid carelessly tied into a small bun, while she tears and crumples something with her nervous fingers and stares fixedly and motionless at the first object on which her eyes fall. Or we enter with Pierre Princess Marya's mansion, and there, sitting in a corner, unrecognizable, is a person dressed in black, her attentive, good eyes sadly questioning, her face severe, gaunt, and pale, and there is not even a trace in her of the occult smile filled with the joy of life that so enchanted Prince Andrei; only after several minutes, with effort, like the opening of a rusty door, the attentive face smiles and, through the opening of that door, the happiness he had long forgotten suddenly breathes upon Pierre. So where is Natasha? Natasha is dead, sunk in her grief. Immediately afterward she is reborn like grass every spring, like the branch of a pruned tree; and with her almost demonic egotism, with her extraordinary swiftness, her invincible capacity to forget, she medicates her wounds, soothes her sorrows, overcomes the death instinct, again obeys the rhythm of existence, as no other creature in *War and Peace*. She begins to sing again: her face, her gaze, her voice change: she no longer speaks about the past: the hope for happiness wells up in her again; the gay sparkle and splendor, for a time veiled in her eyes, light up again, while her lips curl in a strange smile.

For this reason, too, Natasha is the favorite of Tolstoy and the gods of *War and Peace*. The gods and Tolstoy love her because she is full of joy and life: because she projects light and emanates Eros; because, in a word, she possesses that very rare gift which is "natural grace"; and in exchange for this grace, even though she is not especially virtuous, all possible gifts are strewn over the path of her existence. In the world of *War and Peace*, there are also persons from whom the gods avert their eyes: such as Sonya, who is full of good qualities, sacrifices herself for others, while neither the gods nor the others (not even the very good-hearted Marya) show any concern for her. With a surprising display of culture and her customary cruelty, Natasha defines her theological condition with great precision. " 'Do you know something?' " Natasha said. " 'You know the New Testament so well; well, look, there is a passage that actually deals with Sonya.' 'What?' Countess Marya asked, in surprise. 'Those who have will be given, and from those who have not will be taken away, do you remember? She is one of those who have not. Why? I don't know: perhaps she lacks all egotism. . . . —I don't know: she will never be given, and will always be taken from. . . . She is a sterile flower: like those strawberry flowers, you know?' " The gods of *War and Peace* are terribly partial and cruel. Whoever is not an egotist and so does not possess "natural grace," which is founded on egotism, can be good and disinterested: but what does it matter? If he has the one fault of not having received the precious gift of joy, the gods will take from him even the few things he does have, locking him inside the walls of desolation.

V

In his *Histoire du Consulat et de l'Empire*, Adolphe Thiers describes how, during the 1812 campaign, the French cavalry captured a Cossack. Napoleon gave orders that he be brought before him, and the Cossack conversed for some time with the king of armies, though not knowing his identity. When he was told, "stricken by a kind of stupor, he did not utter another word and walked with his eyes constantly fixed on the conqueror, whose name had reached him across the steppes of the East." In *War and Peace* Tolstoy is amused to correct and make fun of Thiers. Thiers' unnamed Cossack becomes a Cossack we know very well—Lavrushka, the servant Denisov has given to Nikolai Rostov. Lavruskha, this astute *commedia dell'arte* servant, immediately understands that he is talking to Napoleon, and, with his tipsy, merry, rascally face, tries to ingratiate himself with him, adulates him, mocks him, and plays the fool; and, when he is finally informed that he is speaking to the man who has written his name on the Pyramids, he pretends to be astounded and dumbstruck, goggles his eyes, to please his new masters. Tolstoy works with the material he has pillaged from history books and the memoirs of contemporaries; and, in his extremely ingenious game of montage, he takes many liberties, as when he attributes to the 1812 Napoleon habits he has learned from Las Cases' *Mémorial* and which therefore go back to the St. Helena period. While another writer would have emphasized his arbitrary contribution, his revisions of the historical reality, Tolstoy does exactly the opposite. The "true history" of 1812 Russia is not the one told by Thiers, working with mediocrity and honesty on the documents: it is the one he tells, with his Kutuzov, his Denisov, his Nikolai Rostov, and his Lavruskha. His is not only the poetic truth but also the historical truth, and all of historiography is simply swept aside. Never had a writer made so total a claim: never had he demanded of his readers that they believe in him as the source of everything, the narrator of real events, the narrator of imaginary events, the philosopher of what has happened and of what will happen. Someone allows him to be always present in the wings of history, like a ubiquitous and irreverent urchin at the very moment when secrets are plotted, great events are prepared, famous sentences are pronounced. Without the slightest doubt, without offering hypotheses or conjectures, or even leaving a zone of shadow, he knows exactly *everything* that has happened: nothing of what Bonaparte thought, felt, said, or did before the battle of Borodino escapes him. History is at his feet, like Egypt's forty centuries of history are at the feet of Napoleon. If then we were to ask ourselves: "How could Tolstoy be so certain?" the answer would be easy. Whereas Thiers, with his tiny mole eyes enslaved by deceptive, contradictory documents, did not see, the mysterious god of *War and Peace* had bestowed on him a visionary faculty that no one could put in doubt. He *saw;* and thus he was certain that on that day Napoleon had scratched his back or that the next day Lavruskha had mocked him.

When we read a historical novel, for example, Manzoni's *Betrothed*, we usually have the obscure sensation that the historical characters and the invented characters are cut from different cloths: that a subtle line separates them; and that, when we see Cardinal Federigo and Renzo and Lucia simultaneously on stage, two different realities are brought close, yet never amalgamated. Tolstoy's case is the direct opposite. Although he insists upon life's extraneousness in respect to the great events of history ("life, meanwhile, the real life of man, with its substantial interests of health, illness, work, rest . . . unfolding, as usual, independently from and outside of all rapprochement with or hostility for Napoleon Bonaparte"), the scene of *War and Peace* is one and undivided. No special light surrounds the historical characters (Emperor Alexander's aureole is formed above all by Nikolai's and Petya's romantic imaginations): he has with them the same familiarity and intimacy he has with Natasha and Pierre. His knowledge is minute, microscopic, and molecular, like his knowledge of all reality. If the truth about Lisa is revealed to us by the light fuzz over her curled-up lip, the truth about Napoleon and Kutuzov is given us by details of the same sort: the fat body's folds, the single eye, the small white hands, the facile tears, the running nose of a cold, the reading of novels by Madame de Genlis. The sole difference is that the historical character, unlike the imaginary characters, is rarely seen with the novelist's introspective eye.

If we scrutinize more closely the chain of historical events, we are struck by a quality that private life does not reveal or reveals with less intensity and violence. We remember, for instance, the French Revolution and the so-called Napoleonic Wars. Behind the illusions of the leaders and peoples, behind the colored banners of ideology, nestles a phenomenon now of a biological, now a mechanical type, which is impelled by the same necessity as natural and mechanical phenomena. In Paris, in 1789, a movement of peoples begins, from West to East, which comes to clash with a countermovement from East to West: until in 1812 the first movement reaches the extreme limit which is Moscow; and, with surprising symmetry, the second movement, which also sweeps along peoples caught in the middle, comes to its completion. The return movement reaches the point of departure of the first movement: Paris, and is becalmed. This process is akin to a double shifting of the sea's waves which, driven by the wind, go first in one direction and then in another, and in the end flow back and "on the calmed sea are made to form whirlpools." All of European history from 1789 to 1813 is explained by Tolstoy with analogies of this kind. The 1789 revolution is a fermentation process, which expands: the battle of Austerlitz is the movement of a huge tower clock, where one wheel slowly begins to turn, then a second, a third, and then with increasing rapidity all the other wheels, the pulley blocks, the sprockets begin to twirl and activate the escape-wheel pinion, and the carillon starts up, until the hands begin to move. The French invasion of Russia gains momentum as it approaches Moscow, just as the velocity of a weight increases the closer it gets to the ground: the Russian army, after the battle of

Borodino, draws back with the same necessity as a billiard ball hitting another which crashes into it with a greater force of impulsion. As for the French army, after the Moscow fire, it is a wounded animal that senses its end and no longer knows what it is doing: hearing the rustle of a step it flings itself in front of the hunter's shot, runs back and forth, and hastens its own destruction: whereas, on the road back, it remains bound by its own enormous mass—by the same law of attraction in accordance with which a mound of snow does not liquify instantly but is rendered compact by the heat's force.

History is thus a very dense interweave of necessities, a concatenation of infinite necessary phenomena, just as a storm consists in the concatenation of infinite waves, all driven by winds acting upon each other. That is all there is to history. And if some character wishes to perform a free act, an action that breaks the chain of events, like Pierre who wants to kill Napoleon, he will realize that he is but a mote swept along and tossed by the storm. Many might well ask themselves: why does all this happen? Why did the revolution of 1789 explode like fermenting wine? What is the meaning of the double tide of peoples, which first is driven from Paris to Moscow and then from Moscow to Paris? And why that whirlpool which continues to agitate the becalmed waters? In a word: what are the ends or aims of history? Tolstoy provides no answer. His acrid, corrosive, and grotesque sensibility prevents him from believing in the flags that, when all is accomplished, men hoist over events. Napoleon did not go to Moscow for the greatness of France or the French Revolution, nor Alexander to Paris in the name of Russia's greatness, nor did anything happen in the name of the rights of men or of sovereigns or the representative republic. History is not guided by a providence, and it has no ends: it is only the unceasing tide from West to East, from East to West, which repeats itself for centuries and leaves behind in its path millions of casualties and men frozen to death.

Everything then should lead us to believe that there is no one behind the events: only necessity, pure necessity, a clock that begins to move, a wounded animal, an avalanche of snow which melts. And yet, ever more frequently, between the lines of *War and Peace* resound deep and solemn tolls, which allude to a different force: "That dreadful work continued to be fulfilled, which is not fulfilled in accordance with the will of man, but in accordance with the will of the One who guides men and worlds." Therefore it is God who makes history, even though He has thrown away all providential plans, all designs; and it is exactly because of this that history is incomprehensible to us. But which God? Usually the appearance of God in events is seen as a matter of sudden, blazing lightning strokes with which sacred time rips open profane time. Here, there is not a trace of sacred time: God reveals Himself in the compact chain of biological–mechanical necessity, the double tide, the fermenting wine, the weight that increases in speed as it nears the ground, the wounded beast. With a theological and imaginative force such as He had never shown, God has merged the biblical "fearfulness," which He does not intend to renounce (the perennial attitude of vengeance against sinning humanity), with the "menace" of natural necessity: He has stolen from His positive adversaries all the instruments they have prepared against Him and used them *ad majorem Dei gloriam*. There never was a God so atrocious, so tyrannical, so inexorable, so ready to cut off all hope and all possibility of escape. This God is not the only one to show Himself in the pages of *War and Peace*. Marya's Christian God is a pure loving instant: Prince Andrei's God is an empty, quiet principle that stands infinitely above natural necessity: Natasha's God (granted that He exists) is nature in the spring; and Pierre's pantheistic God embraces both war and necessity in a harmonious play of drops, which are reflected in the infinite. Any attempt at synthesis among these Gods is pointless: *War and Peace* is a polytheistic book; Tolstoy has carried every theological hypothesis to the point of scandal, which they entail, and he wants us to experience the contradictions of heaven.

If we try to look at the fabric of necessity and fate from the obverse side, we see that it is formed by a series of innumerable events: what on one side is part of a necessary and mechanical *tide* is on the other side the product of a capricious act without remote intentions. Like an obedient and mocking servant, chance is there, ready to supply the knots in the net of destiny; and, with a marvelous capacity for metamorphosis, Tolstoy, this poet of the sacred and inevitable drama of history, becomes the ironic playwright of the millions of absurd and grotesque details of which it is composed. We are not spared a single chance happening in Napoleon's history: it is by chance that the English fleet permits the French fleet to pass on its way to Egypt, it is by chance that the plague does not attack him, it is chance that puts the Duke of Enghien in his hands and makes him kill him, it is chance that prevents him from launching the expedition to England which would have meant catastrophe for him, it is by chance that he caught a cold at Borodino, and finally it is by chance that someone flung out the first spark of the Moscow fire. In the battle of Borodino we also have another series of chance events: that the Russian army delays so long in attacking Napoleon (as the obscure will of history decrees) is not determined by conscious intention; Bagration avoids joining Barclay's army so as not to fall under his command: the emperor's presence in the army multiplies the uncertainties surrounding the decisions to be made: Paulucci exerts influence on Alexander and makes him set aside Pfuel's plan: Barclay is unable to make his generals obey and, feeling observed and spied upon, avoids joining battle. . . . Men aim at a goal, and history uses their little desires to construct something grandiosely different.

This multiplication of chance events carries with it a narrative consequence: the canvas of *War and Peace*, though remaining compact and grandiose, is infinitely subdivided, as though it were painted by an artist capable only of representing an officer's hat or the shoe of a horse. When he must describe an apple falling from a tree, Tolstoy is not content to mention the force of gravity: he adds all the conditions and concomitant causes—the withering stalk, the apple that grows heavier, the wind shaking it, the boy sitting below it and wanting to eat it. Thus, when he listens to the causes of events recorded by historians, he is willing to accept them all, but he multiplies them and asserts that every event is produced "by billions of causes": if the causes of the 1812 war were the offense inflicted on the Grand Duke of Oldenburg, the failure to observe the Continental system, Napoleon's thirst for domination, Alexander's firmness, the diplomats' mistakes, there was also the desire of almost any French corporal to rejoin the army. By multiplying themselves, the causes become minimal: one of the causes of the battle of Tarutino is to be found in the fact that a Cossack on patrol kills a hare with his rifle and wounds another: in chasing the wounded hare, he comes upon the left flank of Murat's army, which is camping there unconcerned, and he tells his comrades about it. Everything becomes molecular, miniscule, madly detailed, told by a man who uses the microscope to describe spaces that only a telescope can capture. *War and Peace* is a novel born from a fatal cognitive renunciation. Had he abandoned himself completely to his vocation, Tolstoy would have narrated all the human movements of the hundreds of thousands of Russians and Frenchmen who had confronted each other in battle, and those other millions who had remained at home: all their passions, desires, repentances, humiliations, sufferings, upsurges of pride, fear, and enthusiasm: all the slightest nuances of these feelings; the causes, concomitant causes, and the most minute conditions surrounding their actions.

Tolstoy furnishes us with two versions of a battle: the ideal battle, in conformity with the science of war, as the German general Pfuel imagines it; and the real battle, as *War and Peace* depicts it—Schöngraben, Austerlitz, Borodino. General Pfuel is convinced that there exists a science of war with immutable laws. Relying on this science, he prepares his strategic plan: deploys his troops under the best possible conditions: he gives the order of battle: during its course, depending on developments, he sends his messengers with orders to advance, retreat, encircle: if he has obeyed the *esprit de géométrie* he wins; and then, on the basis of the plans, deployments, and accounts of combatants, historians compile those most faithful and truthful records which are history books. So from forecast to forecast, from realization to realization, the well-oiled stagecoach which is universal history proceeds. Against this idea not so much of war as of the universe, Tolstoy raises in the first instance one objection: the nape of Pfuel's neck. This German, so honest and abstracted, so desperately sure of his ideas, is not revealed by them but rather by the nape of his neck, on which stand out the bristly tufts of hair that are the objective correlative of his nature. As always happens in Tolstoy, only our physical being does not lie: only our physical features tell, with absolute precision, what we are.

The true battles of Schöngraben and Borodino—these metaphors for what happens every day in the universe in both war and peace—are exactly the opposite of Pfuel's ideal battle. Plans and strategic forecasts are not put into effect, because human intelligence cannot foresee and dominate reality. What happens is a chaotic dust of personal and chance actions, a swarming of ants, a scrabbling of animals which can neither be understood nor narrated: at Schöngraben, Tushin's battery fires from his little hill, the regiment in the hollow retreats, two battalions descend from the higher terrain to attack the French, Zherkov is frightened and does not carry his message, the infantry regiment on the left flank escapes thanks to Timokhin's sharpshooters, Nikolai Rostov is wounded, Prince Andrei roams about trying to understand what the art of war is. . . . But men, liars and megalomaniacs, impose a fictitious order on events. At Borodino, Napoleon's adjutants gallop toward him from the battlefield, reporting on the developments of the battle. All these reports are false: either because in the middle of a battle it is impossible to say what is happening at a given moment, or because many of those adjutants do not venture into the real battlefield and confine themselves to reporting what they hear, and also because during the time in which the adjutants cover the two or three kilometers that separate them from Napoleon, circumstances change and the information becomes untrustworthy. On the basis of these misleading reports, Napoleon decides upon his orders, which either have already been carried out or it will never be possible to carry out. All this information and these orders serve as the basis for the even more lying reports by the commanders in chief; and historians use these reports to write their books, which are therefore lies to the third power.

As for Tolstoy, so as not to narrate the battles of *War and Peace* in Pfuel's manner, he must have been strongly tempted to ignore all the documents and history books he had read. He possessed an irrefutable gift: his own retrospective glance. If he wanted to tell the truth about Schöngraben, Austerlitz, and Borodino, he only had to follow Stendhal's example in the opening chapters of *The Charterhouse of Parma:* renouncing any overall reenactment of the battle and narrating what his characters—Nikolai, Prince Andrei, and Pierre—see and experience. Had he followed this method, applying it throughout the novel, Tolstoy would have given a grandiosely fragmented and chaotic representation of reality. The universe would have remained an incomprehensible enigma: a collection of fragments, a disconnected detritus. But he dared not be so consequential and reserved this privileged glance above all for the scenes of war.

Far from the battles, what we might call "the surface of history" unfolds: a thin layer, similar to a barely iced-over pond, on which pirouette the great, the kings, emperors, generals, statesmen, noble ladies, all those who imagine they drive the carriage of universal history. Tolstoy's contempt is delicious and ruthless: with outrageous familiarity, nihilist acerbity, a vulgarity worthy of Figaro, the elegance of a gentleman, the witty cynicism of his Bilibin, he derides acquired fame, destroys glories, recounts futilities, absurd displays, and idiocies. This is all the great can offer. And yet history's surface gives him some joy, which Tolstoy cannot renounce. He loves a picturesque charlatan like Murat: tall, his tricorn hat black with plumes, his black hair falling in curls on his shoulders, covered with braids and precious stones, all enveloped in a red mantle, all sparkling and flapping under the vivid sun of June: with his braids and mantles he imagines he is the King of Naples ("*Les malheureux, ils ne savent pas que je les quitte demain!*"); but, when he speaks with the envoy of Alexander I he uses the tone in which servants speak among themselves, anxious to remain good friends despite their masters' falling out. Nobody can help smiling at General Balashev's story. From a palace in Vilna, Emperor Alexander sends him on a mission to Napoleon: he waits four days in isolation and boredom before being admitted: until the French advance, enter Vilna, and Napoleon receives Balashev "in that very same Vilna palace from which Alexander had dispatched him on his mission," while in the antechamber are waiting a crowd of generals, courtiers, and Polish magnates, many of whom waited earlier in the emperor's antechamber. Balashev returns to the place he had departed from, and the circle closes upon itself. Meanwhile history too closes its circle, playing with the great: it carries first one, then another to his peak, and after their deaths will carry many others aloft: vicissitudes and unimportant changes, the gambols of air and froth, to which only the great attach importance, calling them "glory" and "power." The hero of this surface is Napoleon. Tolstoy gives us two opposed portraits of him: one at the battle of Austerlitz and the other during the Russian campaign; he executes the first like a *peintre en plein air*, the second like an acerbic and bilious court painter. On the heights of Austerlitz Napoleon mounts a small gray Arab horse and wears a bright blue overcoat, the same one he wore in the Italian campaign. Not a muscle twitches in his still, thin face while his shining eyes, motionless, stare fixedly at a distant point: he feels well, fresh, in a good mood, and in that joyful disposition of the spirit in which everything seems possible and everything succeeds; and on his cold face there is the shadow of proud and merited happiness which often shines on the faces of loved and fortunate children. When the sun comes completely out of the mist, he peels his glove off his beautiful white hand and gives the order to begin the battle. In Russia we see him in an interior: Napoleon's belly is round, his thighs are fat, his legs short, his white, soft neck overflows the collar of his uniform, his face is yellow and puffy: he gives off a smell of cologne; this impression of precocious and unhealthy obesity becomes accentuated when he bathes, and puffs, grunts, and twists under his attendant's brush. Both at Austerlitz and in Russia his hands are small and white: a trait that Tolstoy likes to associate with power, as if cruel men, with a robust, pitiless hand, disguised their strength under a feminine, delicate appearance. But the two portraits are incomparable. The general at Austerlitz, so loved and envied by Prince Andrei, is the young man favored by fortune, Machiavelli's bold prince: who looks upon history as an intertwining of chance events, seizes them with his shining eyes, and possesses an exact intuition of how to bend them to his desires.

Tolstoy, who harbors some tenderness for the first Napoleon, detests the second Napoleon, because he believes himself to be the sovereign of universal history and commits the sin of hubris: he thinks that everything on earth is dependent on him and his will; everything he does is right, not because it accords with the concept of good and evil, but because *he* is the one who does it. He sits before his imaginary chessboard: his pawns are thousands of men who at that day's end will cover the earth's fields and hills with blood; he thinks he can deploy them at his pleasure and that no resistance, obstacle, or chance event will ever be able to stand in the way of the mathematical perfection of his moves. In reality, Napoleon is not the sovereign of anything: not even of his own body, subject to colds and getting fat, like that of any of us. He is only an actor, a puppet of wood and cloth whom the Great Puppeteer has forced to assume a body, to don the uniform of a general or emperor of the French, to cover his face with the luster of makeup, to assume power, give battle, win and be defeated, because that is how the farce He has written for him unfolds, and such is the course of the tide and countertide movement obeyed by universal history. He playacts, he does not act: the only praise that can be bestowed on him is the praise of a drama critic: "Thanks to his great tact and his great war experience he played his role of apparent dominator of events with calm and dignity." What the substance of his power amounts to is revealed to us by the incomparable scene at Tilsit in which Napoleon rewards *le plus brave des soldats russes* with the Legion of Honor. He does not ask for the cross, but without speaking holds out his "small, soft hand, as if to take something": the people in his retinue move, talk, hand something to each other, until a page, bowing obsequiously before that stretched-out hand, deposits on it the cross with the red ribbon. Napoleon does not do as we do, who look at and seize what we take: without looking, he is content to bring together two fingers, and the cross—as if it too wanted to meet his wishes—"is caught in between." Nor, immediately after, does he pin the Legion of Honor to the chest of the Russian soldier Lazarev: he only rests it on his tunic and, withdrawing his fingers, he turns toward Emperor Alexander as though knowing that the cross must forever remain attached to the soldier's chest. And this in fact happens because helpful Russian and French hands immediately catch the cross and stick it into the tunic. "One might have said that Napoleon knew that, in order for that soldier to be forever happy, rewarded, and different from the rest of the world, all that was needed was his hand, Napoleon's hand, to deign to graze that soldier's chest." The allegory is transparent. Through Nikolai Rostov's eyes we see the omnipotence of materialized power: it is enough for Napoleon to hold out his soft hand, and all possible and impossible things are realized. But what is this power? Something merely theatrical: the gestures of an actor, the gestures of a witch doctor, which weightless move through the air.

During the Russian campaign, Napoleon's true failure is not a defeat on the battlefields but the colossal flop of an actor. It is ten o'clock in the morning of September 2, 1812, and, beneath the enchanted splendor of the warm autumnal light, Napoleon contemplates Moscow from the height of the Poklonnaya: like a large and beautiful woman's body the city pulses with its cupolas under the sun's rays. He dismounts from his horse and gives the order for Moscow's topographical map to be unfolded before him: "*Une ville occupée par l'ennemi ressemble à une fille qui a perdu son honneur*," he says to himself. Tolstoy gives him the first and last interior monologue of his life: Napoleon thinks, plans, raves, but we never have the impression of penetrating his true self as in the prodigious Tolstoyan monologues, probably because Napoleon does not have a "self." He would like to speak to the assembly of boyars, "in a clear, solemn and grandiose manner": sets the days for a *réunion dans le palais des Czars*, where all Russian and French magnates would convene, appoint a governor; and dedicate the welfare institutions *à ma chère mère*. But the cortege of boyars does not arrive: in Moscow's empty hive, abandoned by its inhabitants, only a bunch of drunks is left; Napoleon cannot make a speech to anyone. *Le coup de théâtre avait raté*. So, while the actor loses his audience, the man also founders: ever more vain, histrionic, incapable of any truth whatsoever either with himself or others, blinded and stupefied by the power due to which he has lost his youthful agility of mind and spirit.

Napoleon's true glory is that of a writer: he is the genius of empty and brilliant rhetoric, of the intellectual formula, the epigraphic sentence that seems to contain some mysterious profound substance and actually contains only wind. As the maker of formulas, Napoleon only sums up a general tendency: it appears that events take place, men win or die, happiness or misfortune are spread on earth, because a certain number of actors, standing on the stage of universal history, shaped and polished sentences ready to be printed in books and memorized by students. It is a dictionary of *sottises* similar to Flaubert's, which Tolstoy collects with infinite attention; and to which he juxtaposes as a cynical counterpoise Bilibin's parodistic *bons mots*, which will also be very successful in the salons of Petersburg and Moscow. Napoleon proclaims: "A large number of convents and churches is always a sign of a people's backwardness": "*Notre corps est une machine à vivre*": "You know, Rapp, what military art is? It is the art of being stronger than the enemy at a given moment," and the great of his time painfully try to compete with him. As for Tolstoy, he declares himself defeated for the first time in his life: none other than he, who sees history better than professional historians, admits that he does not have Napoleon's verbal imagination for coining celebrated sentences. So he gathers together those he finds in the books of Napoleonic history with the patience of a mosaicist: save for the fact that sometimes he improves on his sources, condenses, abbreviates, adds a sharpness and, in his small Yasnaya Polyana laboratory, amuses himself by producing "some Napoleons" better than Napoleon.

Whereas Napoleon is the master of surfaces, Kutuzov is the humble, submissive servant of history's depths. As soon as we see him, an eighteenth-century aroma assails us: the same scent of wigs, tobacco, lathes that envelops Prince Bolkonsky; but Kutuzov is not a man of the Enlightenment, and he venerates old Russia's religious wisdom that Peter the Great wanted to destroy. When he is not taken up by the occupations of war, he is amiably sociable: we like to imagine him encircled by a group of ladies: he is an obsequious courtier as in Catherine's time: he is tender and libertine: his motto—"Patience and Time"—comes from a fable by La Fontaine, *Patience et longueur de temps/Font plus que force ni que rage;* and his literary tastes are also less up-to-date than Prince Andrei's and Pierre's. If Napoleon, especially at Austerlitz, emanates youthful vitality, Kutuzov's flaccid obesity, the weariness of his face and gait, his deep yawns are only too indicative of his old age. He is the victim of his old, senile body, but old age, laziness, worldliness, indolence, and wanton behavior are signs of the vital experience that has become concentrated in his limbs.

Napoleon is a great actor: Kutuzov detests the lights, poses, rhetoric, and smoke of the stage. Like a true son of Romanticism, Napoleon flaunts the inspired traits of his persona: Kutuzov disappears behind his function, content with being a soldier, a general, a Russian, and a bureaucrat. Napoleon is gifted to the highest degree in deductive intelligence, while Kutuzov has no knowledge of it. In exchange for this renunciation, history's God has bestowed on him a mind in many of its aspects similar to that of Tolstoy's, who nevertheless discerned in him the symbol of qualities he never possessed. Like Tolstoy, Kutuzov has a very strong sense of possibility; and confronted by any situation, lying sleepless on his cot, he strives to foresee all the possible eventualities—not two, as doctrinaires do, but two thousand. Just as Tolstoy can intuit behind bodies or on bodies the feelings of men, so Kutuzov can sense from negligible clues, from the fugitive winds of chance, the course of the events being prepared by history's God. The youthful Napoleon at Austerlitz also understands the course of reality: but he immediately aims at doing violence to it, subjecting it to his desire for domination. On the contrary, Kutuzov possesses the rare quality of statesmen and generals: the contemplative intuition that distinguishes poets and mystics. His very attentive ear listens to all of reality's voices and whispers: his one eye, which (as the Greeks thought) has gained in visual perception, sees all the signs that appear on the horizon; and he reproduces both voices and signs in the immaculate space of his mind. If he could, he would renounce action: he would never raise his glove to give the order for battle; immobile on the plain amid his troops like a wise Taoist emperor.

History forces him to give battle. As his motto says ("Patience and Time: these are my invincible knights!"), he puts off the action of war as long as possible: his generals threaten rebellion, his soldiers tremble with belligerent ardor; but he understands that a thing must be done only when it is absolutely ripe. The appointed day arrives: unlike the Napoleons and Pfuels, Kutuzov knows that strategic plans rationally calculated while sitting at a desk, wise deployments, are good for nothing: the battlefield is not a chessboard, he is not a chess player: a science of war does not exist, just as a science of life does not exist; he lets his soldiers fight, and supports and tries to guide the elusive force that is their morale. Chance surrounds him on all sides: enemy actions he has not foreseen, decisions made by subalterns under the violence of enemy fire, here an attack, there a retreat; the only thing he can do is accept chance, arrange it in his mind so as to give it an appearance of order and bring it into harmony. If history is a fatal event, which takes place beyond our thoughts and desires, he cannot pretend that he is guiding it as Napoleon does, with his wretched pride as an actor and modern man: he must obey it, let the will of destiny be done. We do not know what his feelings are when faced by history's atrocious God. Will he always serve Him? Will he always venerate Him? Will he always worship biological necessity—the tide that without visible cause carries men from West to East and from East to West? Will he never have the slightest impulse of rebellion, confronted by so much waste and so many castastrophes? Until the end, Kutuzov behaves as God's most humble servant, as he does with Emperor Alexander. If we could infer his feelings from those of Pierre, his double, we would have to imagine that in that necessity, which to us seems only mechanical, he finds a hidden, feminine tenderness.

VI

Turgenev said that there is not a trace of freedom in *War and Peace.* If we think of the tide that sweeps men from West to East and from East to West, Turgenev was right: men are bits of straw tossed about by the storm and nothing is left them but to surrender and worship, as Kutuzov and Platon Karataev do. Also in private life the marks of necessity are innumerable: Lisa and Sonya are the victims of destiny: the act that impels Pierre to marry Helene is not free: the love of Prince Andrei and Natasha is not approved by destiny, which has other plans for them; and the minor characters, with their physical codes, are perhaps the prisoners of their bodies. When one examines the novelistic machine, with its play of chance events, providential encounters and correspondences, one notices an analogous weight of fate. As an often ironically repeated sentence says, "*Les mariages se font dans les cieux*": it seems that the immense narrative structure, the representation of an entire society, the story of a war that drenches Europe in blood, the vicissitudes of innumerable minor characters have the sole purpose of allowing Pierre to marry Natasha and Marya to marry Nikolai, uniting somehow the *côté Rostov* with the *côté Bolkonsky* twice over. Chance is always there, helpful, ready to prepare the threads so that the providential woof of the plot can be woven: Andrei's journey, the business with Anatol, Andrei's death, Helene's death: Sonya's letter giving Nikolai his freedom, the meeting between Marya and Nikolai, first at Bogucharovo, then at Voronezh, and old Prince Bolkonsky's death. Rarely has a novel's god engineered two marriages with greater tenacity. And in what book did we meet such worshipers of fate as Pierre, Kutuzov, and Platon Karataev?

And yet, *War and Peace* is not a true novel of destiny. In *Tess of the D'Urbervilles* and *Anna Karenina* we discover a twofold sense of fate: on the one hand the characters continuously collide with a chain of small, absurd facts, miraculous coincidences, uniformly negative signs, which someone, like a devious, malign blacksmith, has shaped, while on the other hand they are possessed by their passions which grow, flare up, become unshakable, and kill, in just as fatal a fashion. Neither Pierre nor Natasha, nor Marya, nor Nikolai, and not even Prince Andrei have anything in common with these figures. They eat, sleep, think, dream, love, make war, laugh, repent, suffer, and make impossible projects: and they are never abandoned by the consciousness that they can move freely on the path of life which is open, without obstacles, and leads them in all the directions prepared by their desires. Nobody could ever compare Andrei's and Pierre's joyful, luminous passion for Natasha with Anna's tremendously fatal passion. When the curtain descends upon the epilogue, we discover that this freedom was apparent: death was the inner necessity that Prince Andrei carried within himself: all of Pierre's thoughts on existence were but allusions to his future worship of life through Natasha's body: Marya and Nikolai must mutually complete each other by meeting their opposite; while Natasha must wait to be overtaken by immense, bitter passivity. What does it matter? Human freedom is always apparent: but some among us, those most gifted with vitality, imagination, or *amor fati*, live this appearance as though it were the most profound of substances.

The epilogue of *War and Peace*, so beautiful and so misunderstood, is one of the most superb movements of concentration and unification to appear at the end of a novel. In the final chapters of his books, Dickens likes to make all his characters reappear in a kind of fantastic ballet: some lucky, some wretched, some virtuous, some in prison, some married, some bachelors, some drinking an English beer, some in far-off Australia. Tolstoy instead seems to forget the entire multitude he evoked from nothing; and with a sovereign gesture of annoyance has it disappear behind the wings, like a Great Puppeteer when he no longer needs his actors. His characters have been reduced to the Bolkonsky and Rostov families, plus Pierre, who has assumed the part of a Bolkonsky, and old Denisov: all the places that, as E. M. Forster says, have until now resounded like "great chords"—rivers, forests, streets, fields, gardens, and battlefields—have become Lisye Gori, which reveals it is the place where the book was born; the antitheses, which supported the scaffolding of the entire novel, have vanished. The world of the "false" seems forever swept away with Helene (although someone still remembers Prince Vasily): war is cancelled by peace: the French have returned to Paris, Napoleon is dying at St. Helena, while Kutuzov is already dead: Petersburg and Moscow, the enemy capitals, are just shadows in the background, from which rare news arrives; and the primary antithesis between the Rostovs and Bolkonskys is healed by marriage.

This reduction to unity has a moral meaning. The youth of the four main characters becomes maturity: desires are realized; and those ecstatic fulgurations of light, happiness, and intuition of the universe, which had possessed Pierre, Natasha, and even the modest and unassuming Nikolai, give way to the prose of everyday life. The principle of reality triumphs, embodied in family life, over the disquietudes of the spirit. Much is lost: very much is always lost, in Tolstoy's novels, when we live in time; and yet something of those youthful dreams, those desires, those lights, those disquietudes is preserved in the hearts of the four survivors. And the person who reminds us of this is precisely Natasha, who seems to have lost more than anyone else. When we scrutinize her with the eyes of her old suitor Denisov, we experience the melancholy disappointment that seizes us when looking at a portrait, which is not a very good likeness, of a person who was dear to us. Where did they go—the slim, restless figure, the flame burning perpetually with animation, the radiant joy of life, the beatific narcissism, the capacity to fly, with knees held close together, beyond time? A shadow has been cast on Natasha. Florid, buxom, fecund, disheveled, wearing a dressing gown, holding in her hands the diapers of her last-born, her face's features firmer, she has become a demonic priestess of the family and the conjugal Eros, a jealous tyrant of her meek husband. But an interruption of the everyday rhythm is enough: after two months of absence at Petersburg, Pierre returns home; Natasha once again has her light step and—vivid, resplendent—"a light of exaltation emanates in floods from her transfigured face." The shadow that weighed on her has been removed.

Nor does Pierre live any longer on the peak of life. Who could compare this quiet family existence of his to the moments of intoxication during his imprisonment, when, in his dreams, as though possessed by God, he discovered the meaning of the universe, venerated its sacredness, saw the human drops merge, die, and be reborn, and discovered the necessity of "connecting"? Now Pierre has again been seized by passionate belief in the ideologies of his youth: he is setting up a mediocre society of conservative gentlemen* in opposition to the government, on which Tolstoy lets fall an amiable irony; and he has once again purposes, aims, projects—those aims whose folly he had understood during the first days of his freedom. But, on the other hand, his good humor, his joyfulness, his ability to cheer up and enliven others make him as enchanting as in the past. As for Nikolai, who has become a limited, irascible, and conservative landowner, he has not even a shadow of the charm of the young hussar who was enamored of Alexander. Now another emotion lifts him above himself: the admiration for his wife's spirituality, who, by contrast, makes him feel his own mediocrity and nullity.

But it is hard to believe that a novel like *War and Peace*, born from an infinite movement of expansion, can end with the exaltation of the principles of reality and isolation. The real winner in the epilogue of *War and Peace* is precisely the one defeated, Prince Andrei, the one who did not know how to love the flesh. The "infinite, sublime, and indefinable" impulse that animated him is not concluded with his death. He is now a memory: silent for Pierre and Natasha: a "divinity" of which it is impossible for his son to create a human image: beyond all limited family religion, every victory of bare facts, he lays claims to the right of that which is not accomplished, not embodied, and not realized, to that which can never be accomplished, embodied, and realized—the spirit's aspiration, dissatisfaction, restlessness, and insatiability. The sky of Austerlitz continues to be a goal that *War and Peace* has never reached, and in its emptiness is hidden the Archimedean point of this novel so teeming

*English in original—TRANS.

with events. If the colorful and fulfilled realm of the present is the right of Natasha and Pierre, Nikolai and Marya, the realm of the future is Prince Andrei's. His son Nikolai inherits it: the lean, pallid, sickly fifteen-year-old boy, with his curly blond hair over his frail neck, who listens in silence to the political conversations of the adults, is startled and whispers something to himself, as though he were experiencing who knows what new violent emotions, and meanwhile, with a nervous movement of his fidgeting fingers, breaks the goose quills and sealing wax lying on his uncle's desk.

The great novel, which has celebrated life's plenitude and reality, ends with young Nikolai's dream of glory: a dream—the space of the void, of shadows, of the indefinite, presentiments, and divine revelations. Nikolenka dreams he is with Pierre, the helmets of Plutarch's heroes on their heads, and marching at the head of an immense army, formed by many whitish, slanting lines which fill the air like those spider threads the French call *le fil de la Vierge*. Glory stands before him. When he turns around, Pierre is no longer there: his father is in his place, Prince Andrei, without a face, without form—none other than he who had cultivated the rigid perfection of the closed line and now perhaps reveals himself in his true essence. But this dream is a return to the past: because Nikolai's dream of glory is the same desire that had stirred his young father, when he hoped to become a general like Napoleon. "I ask only one thing of God," the boy thinks, "that the same things that happened to Plutarch's men happen to me; and I too will act as they did. I will perform even better deeds. Everybody shall know about them, everybody shall love and admire me." While *Madame Bovary* begins and ends by inexorably killing past and future, *War and Peace* does not have a beginning, and could very well start all over again here, recounting the thoughts and experiences of young Nikolai, similar to and different from those of his father and Pierre. At moments we are seized by another impulse: to go back, as Nikolai does by identifying with his father, and try to imagine another *War and Peace*, where the same characters combine in different relationships and perform different deeds. Perhaps Tolstoy thought of this. *War and Peace* is one possible representation in that game of infinite possibility which is the world, where we succeeded in knowing only one form suspended from the nail of the void.

PART THREE

Anna Karenina

I

Many other writers after finishing *War and Peace* would have lived in the shadow of this immense edifice, with its sturdy main house, its innumerable peasant huts, its fields and woods extending to the line of the horizon, its echoes of our entire world and presentiments of other worlds. Dozens of figures were left barely sketched: philosophic or intellectual themes barely hinted at; and if Tolstoy had been a more prudent author, less prodigal with his strength or less tragic, he would have developed those themes and those figures, writing brief novels or stories and raising in the shadow of *War and Peace*'s principal edifice hunting pavilions in which to amiably spend the rest of his life. But, like every great dilettante, Tolstoy had to start from the beginning with every book of his, as though he did not have an existence behind him. A few years later he confessed to his cousin Alexandra that he found *War and Peace* repugnant. "I had a feeling similar to that experienced by a man when seeing the traces of the orgy in which he has participated." Everything must have left him with this impression: the attempt to give a complete image of the universe, the philosophical ambition, the multitude of places and figures, the presence of two languages, the optimistic feeling that the ending, albeit so problematic, could arouse. *War and Peace* was a cosmos: with his ferocious nihilistic spirit, Tolstoy needed to destroy his cosmos, to lacerate and shatter it, and then search among the shards that now lay spread on the ground before him for glimmers of truth that might allow him to attempt a new architecture, with no trace of the orgy in which he had participated.

The first impression that Tolstoy arouses immediately after finishing *War and Peace* is that of a man deserted by the lucid imaginative intoxication in which he had lived for years, and without which, as he later said, "it is impossible to live." The letters of this period allow us to see two very acute crises. In August 1869, while he was staying for the night at an inn at Arzamas, he was assailed by a sensation of terror so violent as to verge on madness, and on that sensation, for the time being unnamed, eleven years later he wrote the admirable story "Notes of a Madman." Two years later, while he was taking his usual kumiss* cure in the steppes, among those Bashkir populations which reminded him of Herodotus' Scythians, every day, at six in the evening, he was overcome by boredom, *Sorge*,† and it seemed to him that in the most painful way his soul separated from his body. Any modern psychiatrist could diagnose in these anxiety attacks the aggressive beginning of a period of depression, which in subsequent years became stabilized, now with more intense curves, now with periods of remission. As happens in every depression, Tolstoy felt that life "had come to a halt." In the happy moments of his youth and maturity, he had lived immersed in the continuous music of life: during the years of *War and Peace* he had listened to and reproduced this music; and now, suddenly, he found himself projected outside existence, while it stopped before his eyes, fixed, immobile, sclerotic, funereal. Movement had ended, the colorful, enchanting rhythm seemed gone forever.

If life had stopped so suddenly, how could he fail to stop too? He looked at all things like a dead man among the dead: he no longer saw what there was to see, with those eyes that at one time had contemplated the entire universe: no longer heard what others heard; every intellectual and poetic pleasure was gone. The world's phenomena no longer held any fascination, and it seemed to him he knew everything that men can know. He no longer desired anything. "If a sorceress came to me and asked what I wish, I would be unable to express a single desire. If I had any desires, such as, for instance, raising a particular breed of horses, as I dream of doing,

*Fermented mare's milk, believed to have health-giving effects —Trans.
†Care—Trans.

killing ten foxes in a single field, and so on, having an enormous success with a book of mine, which would earn a million rubles, learning Arabic or Mongolian, and so on, I still know that these desires . . . are only the residues of habitual desires. In these moments, when such desires come to me, my inner voice already tells me that they will not satisfy me." This is how he lived, apathetic, indifferent to everything and everyone, sad, despondent, without energy, and without joy, for days and entire weeks on end: all flames seemed extinguished in his soul: he felt like weeping: he was afraid of being sick; it seemed to him that everything was over and all that was left for him was to die. The contagion of his "moral death" spread throughout the house, and Sonya, with her acute hysteria, wrote in her *Diary*, as though her husband's hand had dictated the lines: "Country life, too isolated, ends by becoming unbearable to me. Grim apathy, indifference to everything. Today, tomorrow, for months and years, everything will be eternally the same. I wake in the morning and do not have the courage to get up. What awaits me? Yes, I know, the cook will come, then Nanya with her usual complaints: the servants grouse about the food, there is no more sugar, we have to send for some. Then, even though my right shoulder aches, I will silently embroider some little holes, then there will be the children's grammar and piano lessons. . . . When evening comes it will be the same English embroidery and Aunt Pelageya's and Lev's eternal and detestable games of solitaire."

From time to time this opaque blanket of indifference and torpor which oppressed and protected him would lift, and then anguish again attacked him terribly. As at Arzamas, he felt that he was going mad: at night he roamed the house without matches, losing his way amid those unknown walls, climbing steps that took him who knows where, calling for help, as though he were in some unknown place of terror and desolation. When he would reflect it seemed to him that life was a stupid and malicious hoax that someone or Someone had played on him: while he was struggling up there, who knows where, someone or Someone rubbed his hands at the spectacle of him who, having reached the pinnacle of his time, stood there like a fool, clearly seeing that there was nothing in life, there had been nothing in the past and there would be nothing in the future. Where could he turn for help? Although he searched for Him and interrogated Him desperately, God had gone into hiding: books of philosophy were of no use: family life no longer had meaning; and if he thought about art, the stupendous illusion he had inhabited for so many years, it no longer attracted him. Art was, for him, the mirror of life, in which is reflected everything, comedy, tragedy, the deeply emotional, the beautiful and the terrible, all lights, colors, and nuances: but now that life had become absurd and atrocious, how could the mirror still cast its spell? It only sent back to him the horror multiplied. He thrashed about, searched for a road without finding it. He was like a man lost in a wood, who, gripped by the fear of being lost, dashed about in all directions in the hope of finding the road, knowing that every step takes him farther away from it. So, wrapped in the coils of depression, he morbidly cultivated the pleasures of suicide: he looked at a board suspended between two wardrobe closets in his room and thought that there, right there, he could hang himself; he went hunting with his gun and thought that it would be so simple to point it against his temple.

If we ask ourselves the reason for these attacks of depression, if we ask ourselves why the confidence that had supported him during the writing of *War and Peace* had abandoned him, we would probably have to look for an explanation in the very structure of Tolstoy's personality. He was possessed by the most tremendous narcissistic spirit that ever dominated a novelist's personality. By writing *War and Peace* he had projected his "self" outside himself, transforming his intoxicated narcissistic energy into an objective universe: for several years, without a moment's lapse or doubt, he had made his self coincide with everyday reality. That self had poured forth currents of intelligence and love: through a transformation which never ceases to astonish us, it had become distance, perspective, and sovereign architectural harmony. But a great narcissist such as Tolstoy can never be certain how long his vital equilibrium will last. A subterranean wound, or simply weariness after the long sustained effort, was enough for the self projected into the world to abandon the forms of reality with which it had imbued itself. It was a slash, a pain, a dreadful laceration. How could he now still desire and embrace the universe? Bereft of the colors diffused by his spirit, the world had become a petrified and monstrous reality which stared at him with hostile eyes, a squalid castle in ruins which cast spectral shadows over him, a living death which also wanted his death—and which sent toward his heart those sudden, piercing attacks of anxiety.

Between one crisis and the next, more or less lengthy periods of remission opened up: anxiety left him: he forgot the horror from which he issued; and it seemed to him he was happy and that his existence, like that of all happy people, had no history. During the winter he skated on the frozen snow, now on two feet, now on only one, now backward, with a boy's merriment. When summer came, he passed his time riding, strolling through the forest, caressing with his hands the polished trunks of the birch trees, hunting otters and wild ducks, together with the steppes' nomads, swimming with his children in the Voronka's waters, playing croquet and ball with them. In the evening, before the sunset light deserted the house at Yasnaya Polyana and that noisy, happy existence was enveloped by the shroud of night, he told his children stories about horses, woodcocks, and dogs. He read to them *Twenty Thousand Leagues under the Sea*, *The Sons of Captain Grant*, and *The Three Musketeers;* and with his clumsy and inexperienced hand he drew sketches for *Around the World in Eighty Days*.

During these games and readings, he scrutinized his children, trying to penetrate the present and future of those lives that were growing mysteriously alongside his. The oldest, Serezha, had about him something patient, mild, and submissive. "When he laughs, he does not impel you to laugh along with him, but when he cries I can hardly keep from crying": and Tolstoy thought that perhaps when he grew up he would become like his own older brother, who had rejoiced and suffered only inside himself. Ilya was white, red, luminous, impulsive, and violent: he had big bones, did not study well, and never got sick. "When he cries, he gets angry and becomes disagreeable. But when he laughs, everybody laughs with him." He loved to do things forbidden by the grown-ups and he immediately understood what was forbidden. He was sensual: he liked to sleep late; and when he ate currant jelly he smacked his lips with voracious gluttony. Tanya loved the smaller children: her greatest satisfaction was to hold and touch a small body, to give gifts to her brothers, to sacrifice for them. But the father's eyes rested above all on Masha. She was a weak, sickly little girl, not pretty, with skin white as milk and large, strange, bright blue eyes. The father imagined she would become a mysterious creature. "She will suffer, seek and not find anything: but all her life she will try to reach the inaccessible."

At the end of 1871, Tolstoy began to study Greek. With his incredible capacity for learning, after a few weeks he read Xenophon straight from the text; whereas for Homer he required a dictionary and some effort. But it seemed to him that he had finally discovered the fount of beauty: Homer was like "the water welling from the spring which cracks your teeth with the reflection and the sun and even the motes and grains of dust that make it even purer and fresher." The Greeks, Homer, Plato, Xenophon, made him dream again of a pure, elegant, concentrated art, in which words stood by themselves in marvelous equilibrium on the brink of the abyss that threatens human works from all sides. That art, so refined and calculated, made him think of life which is "so beautiful, so light, so brief," whereas human representations usually are "so ugly, so heavy, so long." He too wanted to write in this manner: a dance, a brief linear design, an embroidery, as he had sometimes done during his youth. His anguish needed levity and wings. What use did he have now for "insipid prolixities" such as *War and Peace?* To avenge art, which he thought he had offended, he prepared a new edition of his novel, from which he expurgated all the philosophical divagations and, to obtain unity of style, translated the French dialogues.

With a leap that does not surprise us, Xenophon led him back to Pushkin, who had been the inspiration for several stories and some "allegros" in *War and Peace.* One morning in March 1873, after breakfast, he by chance leafed through a collection of prose pieces which his wife had left in the drawing room on the windowsill. A beginning struck him: "The guests arrived at Countess G.'s *dacha.** The room filled with women and men arriving together from the theater, where a new Italian opera was being performed. . . ." He liked that way of entering directly into the story: the swift, gay prose seduced him and reawakened his inspiration, which for months had

*Country house—TRANS.

languished discouraged, exhausted, and uncertain. Together with the fate of Pushkin's character, a female image flashed through his mind, which had risen before him as he struggled with drowsiness: first the naked elbow of an elegant, aristocratic arm, then the shoulder, the neck, and finally the entire figure of a beautiful woman in an evening gown who stared at him imploringly, with sad eyes, as though begging him for help—and another memory, more tragic, the terribly lacerated body of a woman who had thrown herself under the train at a station near Yasnaya Polyana. Everything crystallized with great speed in his imagination; and Tolstoy immediately began to write something that was supposed to be only a novella—not an interminable chronical like *War and Peace*—with the lightness, wit, and amusment, that in Pushkin were the superior form of art. He must have discovered in himself the dizzying speed that makes novelists so gay, for in a letter to Strakhov on March 25, 1873, he said he had already finished the first draft of a very lively and passionate novel which had completely captured his soul.

Then the élan came to a halt. When winter returned he holed up every morning in his study, far from the family's noise, and he stayed there until three in the afternoon, silent and unapproachable like a scowling divinity. The novel proceeded with difficulty. In the quiet of his study he felt that he was in the dark, and he tried in vain to capture the minutest sounds and flickers of light that might dispel the darkness. No matter how attentively he looked, he was unable to see the faces and hear the words of his characters: or he assigned to them the wrong faces and gestures. Thus Anna Karenina—his beautiful, beloved Anna Karenina—was in the beginning a vulgar woman, with a low forehead, a short nose, and so fat as to appear monstrous, while Karenin clasped his hands behind his back instead of cracking the joints of his fingers. Of all people, he, the most infallible eye in nineteenth-century narrative, was unable to focus the image, the physique of his characters, the "objective correlative" of the soul was for him blurred and obscure; and only little by little, slowly, laboriously, did he sharply define his vision. Nor were relations among the characters more evident at the beginning: he did not know with what marriages he ought to link them, whether to have Levin marry Kitty or Anna, as though his narrative game was purely a matter of combinations. The most arduous problem was another: the light "long story" by now held him captive. He was supposed to develop only one theme, the fate of Anna Karenina: whereas his variegated, complex, polycentric, contradiction-loving mind needed to express its truth at least through a binocular vision in which two themes are reflected, counterposed, mutually integrated, and lead to a conclusion that no one would ever be able to sum up in intellectual terms.

When he wrote *War and Peace*, he was much more immersed in his imagination: now he worked from the outside, with crystalline coldness and the sovereign lack of interest that only a master can achieve. He often took his mind off it, busied himself with other things, deserted his desk for months on end, and announced to friends that his novel bored him: "I take up again the boring, trivial *Anna Karenina*, and I only pray God to give me the strength to get her out of the way as soon as possible"; "My Anna has become a bore, I have her up to my eyebrows"; "Oh, if only someone could finish *Anna Karenina* for me." Some mornings he woke up well disposed, with the alacrity and intellectual lucidity that should always arouse doubt in any writer: everything ran swiftly; and the next morning he had to throw everything away, because he had worked only with his intelligence. Or he woke with his nerves on edge: and from that irritation a strange wealth of inventions and images seemed to be born; and the next morning he once more had to strike out everything, because imagination without intelligence generates empty phantoms of mist. But, during the last month of 1876, the structure of *Anna Karenina* revealed its richness to him. The novel began to move at a feverish pace. Concentrated and overexcited, Tolstoy wrote without interruption, drawing from the darkness the last sparks and sounds that still were hidden in it. Just as a painter needs light to put the final touches to his painting, he needed the light of winter—the inner light, which failed him in autumn—to finish his book. Every day he completed a chapter: in the evening, after putting the children to bed, his wife sat at the small mahogany desk and until late into the night copied in her clear, fine handwriting the pages her husband had written during the day.

As epigraph to his novel, he chose the biblical sentence—"Vengeance, is mine; and I shall repay"—which recurs at three places in the Old and New Testaments with different meanings. In Deuteronomy 32, a moment before dying Moses proclaims the name of Yahweh and His Being—the only one existing in the world: "See now that I, even I, am He, and there is no other God beside Me: it is I who make death and make life, I wound and heal, no one excapes My hand!" He proclaims Yahweh who chooses Israel, guides it through the mountains of the earth, makes it suck honey from the cliff and oil from the rock. He proclaims Yahweh's law and revenge against the children of Israel who abandoned Him and against the impious enemies of His people—"their grapes are grapes of gall, their clusters are bitter. Their wine is the poison of vipers." "To Me belongeth revenge and recompense, their foot shall waver in due time: for the day of their calamity is at hand, and the things that come upon them make haste." In the Epistle to the Hebrews 10:30, the roar of vengeance against those who have trampled the Son of God, profaned the blood of the Covenant, and outraged the spirit of grace continues to resound. But, in the Epistle to the Romans 12:19–21, the memory of revenge only hovers in the background to remind men that they must not judge but love. "Dearly beloved, avenge not yourselves, but rather give place to the wrath of God; for it is written: 'Vengeance is Mine, I will make retribution,' saith the Lord. Therefore if thine enemy hunger, feed him; if he thirst, give him drink. . . . Be not overcome by evil, but overcome evil with good."

Everything leads us to believe that Tolstoy, who so loved ambivalences, knew his epigraph's double meaning very well. Those few words stand at the beginning of *Anna Karenina* to signify that only God is, that God's Being translates into law and vengeance, that those who break the law, like Anna Karenina, can only know poisonous grapes from bitter clusters while all others—the Russian society of Petersburg and Moscow which has known Anna, the anguished and indifferent writer who told the story, and we readers who share her story—neither can nor must judge. But the ultimate meaning of this acute, obscure sentence lies in the fact that it refuses to illuminate the book. In *War and Peace* God was present everywhere: in the empty sky of Austerlitz from which He looked down upon the vanity of life and death, in Pierre's dreams where all the drops were reflected, and in the horrors of war as Kutuzov comtemplated it. In *Anna Karenina*, there is not the slightest trace of Him: God has disappeared from the sky, from the dreams of men, from the events which do not reflect Him, even from the thoughts of Levin, who thinks he draws inspiration from Him, and from the profound heart of Tolstoy who believed in those years that he was thinking about Him. Instead of being the only one who can say *I*, instead of being the only figure which *is*, instead of being the only inhabitant of the skies, instead of doing vengeance upon those who break the law, God has departed, and the novel depicts the emptiness and desolation His disappearance has left in the world.

If God is dead, Natasha also dies, nature's erotic divinity, who cannot live without resting in the arms of God (whom she does not know). Her figure is split: on one side Kitty's mild conjugal image and, on the other, Anna's luminous force. But in Anna, Natasha's Eros, which gathered up and included all of life, the whole expanse of time, has become terribly exclusive: Anna wants a body, the possession of a body: all the rest is unknown to her; and those who live like this know Eros as destiny and plunge toward destruction. No Pierre can contemplate her, worship her, and recognize in her the symbol of life: no one can even understand her. As for Kitty, the happiness she assures Levin is delightful, but it does not save him from the anguish of existence. Everything becomes degraded, and bruised. In *War and Peace*, Prince Andrei had triumphed at Austerlitz over the idea of death: Pierre, at least in his dreams, overcame his terror ("To those who are not afraid of death, everything belongs"). In *Anna Karenina*, this terror appears again, naked, chilling, paralyzing, screaming, inhuman: no intellectual mediation can ward it off; and then living is like walking around a bearskin. In *War and Peace*, for those who wished to abandon themselves to it, the realm of the unconscious was a mild and liquid maternal womb, from which poured consolation, tenderness, and sudden flashes of prophetic wisdom. The dreams in *Anna Karenina* are nightmares, containing the presentiment of disaster.

II

Anna Karenina, this novel of desertion, emptiness, and death, opens under the effervescent sign of Stepan Arkadyevich Oblonsky, called Stiva by his friends. We could not encounter a better guide: because Stepan offers a meeting point for the two novels that intertwine in this book: he is Anna Karenina's brother and the brother-in-law of Kitty Sherbatsky, whom Levin ardently loves. In Petersburg and Moscow, in every stratum or corner of good society, he knows everybody; and fate offers him the possibility of protecting the birth of the two loves narrated in the book: he is at the station when Vronsky meets Anna; and he invites Levin and Kitty to dinner at his house on the day of their unspoken declaration of love—and everything goes off beautifully, the hors d'oeuvres, six brands of vodka, cheeses, caviar, herring, French breads, the soup *à la Marie Louise*, the flaky pastries which melt in your mouth, and the guests' conversation. But to treat him like this, as a simple structural prop, would be an insult to Stepan and to us readers. Tolstoy had an intuition here as inspired as Dostoevsky's at the beginning of *The Possessed*: to reach the lowest depths by starting from scintillating surfaces; to strike up a gay and frivolous, luminous and happy music as the overture to an immeasurably tragic opera. Stepan is a "common" man: the Nikolai of *Anna Karenina*, although much more attractive. In science, art, politics, general conception of life, his ideas are those of the majority; and he changes them when the majority changes them, like a hat or a no-longer-fashionable overcoat. He cannot stand—and they actually make his legs ache—even the smallest *Te*

Deum, and he cannot understand the significance of all those dreadful, high-sounding words about another world, when it is so pleasant to live in this one! He likes to read "his" newspaper, moderately progressive, and smokes a cigar after dinner, both for the light mist they generate in his head. But Tolstoy loves him with an exorbitant passion, as he loves almost all fatuous, light-minded men—perhaps because of the fatuousness he knew in himself; and he depicts his gestures with great grace, wit, frivolity, perfidy, sometimes with a touch worthy of the grand theater of the boulevards. He loves his physique: the good-humored, brightly shining face, the eyes that sparkle gaily, the involuntary, sometimes slightly stupid smile, his roundish, well-cared-for body, the springy gait of his nimble legs, and even the fragrance that emanates from his sideburns, his gray robe with its bright blue silk lining, his wallet, his watch with its double chains and pendants, the cigarettes he distributes in all of his pockets. He loves Stepan's lack of conscience and irresponsibility (only he, coming back from the theater, could make his wife, to whom he has just been unfaithful, the present of an enormous pear); his almost feminine tenderness, his indulgence, his cordiality to everyone; his joy and his talent for giving joy, his ability to fuse all separate musics into a single music: his deep forgetfulness of his own past; his optimism without uncertainties.

Stepan Oblonsky lives his supreme moment at the restaurant, where the essence of life is revealed to him, for he too has his moments of ecstasy. As soon as he enters the England with Levin, he is transfigured, because these temples of food and falsity, luxury and artifice are made to measure for his spirit and body. He immediately shows a "restrained vivacity," gives orders to the Tatar waiters in frock coats and with napkins over their arms who follow him, bows left and right to friends who greet him with delight, goes to the counter, has vodka and salted fish for appetizers; then he says something "to the Frenchwoman who sits behind the cash register, all painted and covered with ribbons, laces, and braids, and she too begins laughing wholeheartedly." And with what gaiety he studies the menu: he chooses from it with the attention of a violinist studying the program of the concert that will make him famous, or a general dictating to his adjutant the battle plan that will make his name immortal in the history of strategy. We know his hesitations, his doubts, the definitive and peremptory assurance of his choice: first two—no, better three—dozen Flensburg oysters, a clear vegetable soup, turbot with a thick sauce, roast beef,* a capon, fruit salad, and champagne and Chablis. How irritated we are with Levin, with his Rousseauan tastes, cabbage soups and grits, so gnarled and tangled, unable to enjoy the surfaces of existence! But Levin also relaxes for a moment, attains our identical contemplative beatitude, and happily looks at Stepan as he slips the starched napkin into his vest, tears the oysters from their mother-of-pearl shells with his silver fork, and, with wet, glistening eyes, swallows them down one after the other.

Like the most expert of guides, Stepan accompanies us through the bourgeois patrician society of Petersburg and Moscow. Despite appearances, Tolstoy is fascinated by this world: the elegance and corruption, the intelligence and vulgarity, wealth and cynicism, cruelty and foolishness captivate him much more subtly than in *War and Peace*. Now he describes the thick woolen carpets, the brightly lit tables, the samovar's silver, the French tapestries, the mirrored sconces where human figures leave their ephemeral reflection; now he depicts the women's gestures and gowns, with a spare stylization and a deformation almost in Pope's manner. Now he is in a corner, like an unknown guest; he listens to the chatter, the froth, the gossip of the conversation: he collects the platitudes with a ferocious Flaubertian precision and transforms the words' insubstantiality into a crystalline and perfidious mosaic. Almost in jest, Tolstoy lets us meet again an old acquaintance from *War and Peace*: Countess Apraksin, the symbol of inexhaustible, empty conversation. There Prince Andrei's wife informed us that her husband had died, and she had cried *les larmes de ses yeux*. Here somebody, we don't know exactly who, informs us of her sudden death, the death of that Countess Apraksin whom we thought as immortal as gossip. With this minute hint, Tolstoy tells that he has forever buried under the tombstone of his novel also the spirit of futile conversation.

Barely announced by Stepan's tenderness, emerging from the so-

*English in original—TRANS.

ciety whose purest flower she is, Anna Karenina comes to meet us with her light, firm step. Tolstoy never loved any of his characters so deeply, not even Natasha: for her he violates the principle of *War and Peace*, where he did away with the description of the main characters; and to her he dedicates a gallery of portraits with the touch and the *souplesse* of a great fashionable portrait painter. Here she is at the ball: "Anna wore a very low-cut, black velvet gown which bared her full, well-turned shoulders the color of old ivory, her bosom and her rounded arms with their tiny wrists. The gown was richly trimmed with Venetian guipure. On her head, in her black hair, which was all hers, she wore a little wreath of pansies, and another like it winding through the white lace" at her waist. And here is the first portrait in oils: "Alexei Alexandrovich looked at it. The impenetrable eyes stared at him with irony and impudence . . . intolerably impudent and provoking for him was the sight of the black lace arranged on her head, her black hair, and the beautiful white hand with its ring finger covered with rings." When she lives with Vronsky, she appears before us "dressed in a light silken velvet gown, ordered from Paris, her breast uncovered and on her head a precious white lace which framed her face and enhanced her beauty." Dolly sees her on horseback, her black hair escaping from under the tall hat, her thin waist in the black riding habit, a calm and graceful seat on the saddle. Like a regal and lacerating gift, her beauty never leaves her, not even when close to death. When Levin looks at the portrait that Mikhailov has made of her, lit by a reflector lamp, he cannot tear his eyes away from it: "It was not a painting, but an enchanting living women, with dark ringlets of hair, the shoulders and arms bared, and the hint of a pensive smile on lips covered by a soft down, who looked at him tenderly and triumphant, with eyes that disturbed him." From the dusk surrounding the portrait she herself comes toward us, Anna Karenina, in a dark gown of metallic blue, and with a seductiveness that no portrait will ever be able to express.

So who is this woman covered with lace, in her black velvet or silk gowns and her impudent or tender eyes? Anna Karenina is the supreme luminous epiphany that Tolstoy has ever tried to capture in words: her light is so intense and penetrating that it bedazzles night and death; when Karenin sees her from a distance, he feels the rays that emanate from her and reach him as the sun's rays reach a butterfly.* We know what the fate of light is in the world: "and the darkness comprehended it not" (John, 1:5). Anna meets with the same fate: she is rejected, offended, and humiliated by the darkness; and what is most atrocious, invaded and overcome by the black night she carries in her own heart. When Tolstoy presents her to us for the first time, as she alights from the Petersburg train, Anna's exuberant, vital happiness erupts in the joyful scintillation of her gray eyes: as though afraid to reveal herself, she tries to muffle this vital splendor; but it comes through against her will, in the barely perceptible smile, though more affectionate than a caress, that flickers at the corners of her mouth. Her fate seems to be that of giving to others, to a degree immensely greater than that of her brother, the gift of life and happiness, of ringing, joyous laughter.

This resplendent happiness springs from the fact that Anna lives every moment passionately: the prey at times of the fugitive and changeable excitement of the moment. Natasha has the same devotion to the moment: but she also has a solidity, a tenacity, an ability to forget, an ignorance of any sphere superior to everyday reality, which Anna does not know. Anna's music is lighter and more vulnerable, and subject to deep flaws. In order to hear its first sounds, we must remember the details that Tolstoy so enjoys repeating. Anna has small, agile hands, a firm, light step, a strong neck, a full body, light, nimble movements: a unique mixture of weakness, levity, and chthonic vitality, like the mare Frou-Frou. We know how she bends her head, how she looks out from behind her long lashes, how she half closes her eyes when gazing at something in the distance, how her step is assured and straight, how she rests her small beautiful hand on the white of the tablecloth, or energetically clasps the hands that are offered her. Whatever she does, she does with naturalness, simplicity, and grace: with the aristocratic nonchalance that seems to leave the world together with her.

When she appears on stage, she seems happy with her existence. She has a son she loves; and some hints let us sense a relationship not

*In a variant text.

of love but of affectionate trust with her husband. Why then the "serious, at times sad" expression that Kitty catches in her eyes? Despite her exuberance, life is not giving her the dreamed-of joys and lights: she has left behind the bluish mist of her youth, and after that immense, fortunate, and gay circle, her path is becoming ever more restricted—and now she is about to enter the tunnel of maturity, where cold walls will imprison her on all sides. Even though she barely senses the deep impulses of her heart, she has a desperate hunger, a nervous anxiety for life. On the train that is supposed to take her back to Petersburg, she reads an English novel; and she is unable to read it with detached eyes, obtaining a contemplative pleasure from the plot. The "reflected" pleasure is not enough for her: she wants to live through those existences. She reads how the novel's heroine sits by a sickbed and she has the desire to walk on tiptoe in the sick man's room: she reads that a member of Parliament makes a speech and she has the desire to be the one to deliver that speech; she reads that Lady Mary hunts on horseback—and she has the desire to go riding.

When speaking to Dolly, who says to her: "How happy you are, Anna! Everything is limpid and beautiful in your soul," Anna replies that we all have skeletons in our souls, and that hers are very dark. We wonder what they might be. Simply her desire for life and love? Or does Anna know that her light conceals a shadow, which until now we have not perceived? On the train that takes her to Petersburg Anna has a hysterical fit which ends with an attack of drowsiness. She feels her nerves like strings strained to the breaking point: her eyes dilate, her fingers and toes twitch nervously, something inside stifles her breath, while a kind of unaccountable merriment takes possession of her. During this hysterical attack, like someone hallucinating or inspired, she "sees" in the shifting twilight: images and sounds strike her with extraordinary clarity: she tries to abandon herself to the vision; and reality becomes the form before her eyes. Perhaps the maid sitting next to her is a stranger: her fur is an animal: the fireman, who has come to look at the thermometer, nibbles at something while leaning against the side of the compartment: the old woman stretches her legs the length of the carriage and fills it with a black steam; meanwhile her "self" splits in two, and leads her to think she is someone else. How far we are from the Anna of the joyous eyes and smile, whom we met a few days earlier at the station! In this Anna who dreams and "sees" like a romantic heroine in the train's twilight gloom, the authoress of the hallucinatory monologue that precedes her death is already announced: the tragic greatness of her destiny is fed by the possibility of delirium, by the madness she always carries locked within herself. Before its gates her author stands guard—Tolstoy, who attributes to his character something of the delirium that had torn him apart during those years: the delirium that perhaps always threatened his extremely labile consciousness; and which led him to intuit what healthy, righteous men will never know.

As soon as Anna and Vronsky meet at Moscow's station, they abandon forever their everyday existence: a commonplace existence composed of small conjugal and maternal joys, small loves, small satisfactions of the ego—and they enter the fated life that the demon Eros prepares for his happy and unfortunate servants. A sign warns us of this: the railroad guard crushed by the train; an event that contains in itself the entire future story of their love, until Anna's death under the train. In erotic passion there is neither a shadow nor trace of freedom: "Everything that has happened could not fail to happen." Whoever enters the world of Eros knows passion as a mechanical, ineluctable game of drives and counterdrives, of reactions and counterreactions: like an objective force that seizes the self from the outside, enters into it, and reigns terribly over it, and does not tolerate the slightest diversion and the slightest resistance. Whoever loves, discovers the *other*, the stranger within himself. As at the point of death, Anna says to her husband: "There is another woman in me, and I am afraid of her: it is she who began to love another." If lovers do not know what they want, Eros knows its goals perfectly: every great erotic passion is tragic, and demands disaster, destruction, ruin, death, the lovers' shame. There is no escape. Is it possible to love such a destiny? While Pierre and Kutuzov experience the contemplative joys of *amor fati*, Anna does not know them: but Pierre's and Kutuzov's fate is a woman or a war, which can be looked at with the free eyes of the mind; and Anna's fate is something at once too close and inscrutable, external and horribly internal, which one can only run to meet, plunging into the abyss it has prepared for us. There is no nineteenth-century novelist (only, perhaps, a poet) who has been able like Tolstoy to create around Eros this dreadful, sacred, and venerable climate. He does not kill Anna in the name of the "Law of the Father," as D. H. Lawrence accused him of doing; he does not have her killed by the God of vengeance, who has completely vanished from the novel's stage; nor does Anna kill herself, as some claim, because of her moral scruples. With sovereign justice and delicate compassion, Tolstoy allows Anna to be destroyed by the force of Eros, who has taken complete possession of her.

Anna is not an ideologist or an intellectual of love: she has no relationship with the heroines D. H. Lawrence patterned after her; she is a fearless explorer of an exclusively terrestrial experience for which the earth can offer no answers. There is in her a frightful desire for the absolute: just as, for others, life has meaning only if it is concentrated in the search for God, or the writing of a book, or a dream of power, for her life must be absorbed by the search for love. The powerful drive for knowledge that guides her is no less intense than the one that drives Prince Andrei to investigate God and death; and it is more disinterested than that which animates Levin. This amorous search unfolds through several stages. The first is a rediscovery of her inner light: the tremulous, flaring gleam that shines in her eyes, the laughter of happiness that curls her lips: her face's heightened color, her more even voice, her softer figure, her swifter movements, as she looks down at us from her portrait, "tender and triumphant, with troubling eyes." Even from the very beginning, Eros reveals to us the shadow of this light. Anna is *Vénus toute entière à sa proie attachée*—she wants to dominate, swallow, devour Vronsky lying at her feet, his head bent, with the submissive, frightened eyes of "an intelligent dog who feels guilty." Eros is a possessive fury: Anna is subjugated by Vronsky's subjection; she makes him her prey, and in turn becomes Vronsky's prey. For her, enclosed as she is in this fateful circle, love becomes something frightful and cruel. Anna's face "gives off a lively gleam: but this gleam is no longer gay, it resembles the sinister glow of a fire on a dark night." Anna's light and laughter are already lost: this glow is the dark splendor of Eros, the atrocious desire to take possession of a body, the presage of a candle about to be doused, the definitive revelation that will accompany her under the wheels of the train.

When the union of the bodies is consummated, Eros reveals his face: Crime, Sacrilege. He who loves in this way throws himself on the beloved's body; and while appearing only to caress, kiss, embrace, and penetrate it, kills it, hacks it to pieces, drags it in the dust, dismembers it with persistence and fury, and hides the dismembered body within himself. The killing of Frou-Frou by Vronsky—the mare so similar to Anna, feminine and frail as a bird—is only a repetition of the crime. The horror of propinquity in *War and Peace* never attained this diapason. After the culmination, the two lovers seem to become accustomed to crime: Eros imbues the bodies, glances, gestures, ambience, and atmospheres with its fragrance of honey; Anna and Vronsky do not communicate with words, as Merezhkovsky observes, but with glances and smiles, the sounds of the voice, with postures and movements. Anna wants to transform Vronsky into a radiant body of love. Nothing could prevent them from achieving total identification, by melting into a single figure: so much trust does Tolstoy have in the physical language. But, in reality, full identification—like that, for instance, which bound Pierre and Natasha—never takes place. Even when love is at its fullest, the wills are identical, yet the inner times are not the same, the thoughts and sensations do not coincide, words cannot fully express feelings.

Before meeting Vronsky, and knowing Crime, Anna has a recurrent dream which burdens her existence. In the dream it seems to her she must run to her room—to get something, to find out something. There is somebody in a corner. When she turns, Anna sees a small peasant with tousled beard who bends over a sack and rummages in it, saying, "*Il faut le battre, le fer, le broyer, le pétrir.*" The small peasant with his tousled beard is a mute symbol that does not allude to any other reality: he is not the biblical God of vengeance, who prepares for those who break the law "grapes of gall with bitter clusters," a grape whose wine is "the poison of vipers": he is not the devil, as in the first notes for the novel. In his repugnant gnome's figure, which arises from folkloristic memories, is concentrated the malignant force at work in the universe, persecuting the few creatures of light. The old gnome is as distant and inexorable as destiny, because he acts "without paying any attention" to Anna. After her union with Vronsky, something unheard-of occurs. Anna's nightmare passes to Vronsky, who dreams it with some variations: the peasant becomes a tax collector, the French words are now incomprehensible. Even though language still separates them, the bond between Anna and Vronsky is therefore so close and deep-going that it reaches the unconscious. The two wounded souls meet in horror: they dream the same dreams; as always, Vronsky is the passive and feminine place were Anna pours the hallucinated wealth of her inner life. Now the gnome with the tousled beard is no longer a presage of destiny: from the moment he is dreamed by both he becomes—even if Tolstoy did not want him to—the horrible god who dominates their erotic life, the sinister archetype of their love.

Anna's two "husbands" occupy two identical and opposed places in the book's architecture. Let us imagine that Karenin was always old: that he always had those large, tired eyes, those white hands with swollen veins, that head leaning to one side, that weary appearance; and always envied the strong, healthy, and sanguine men with red necks, robust calves, and perfumed sideburns, like Stepan Oblonsky and Vronsky. Life for him is an "absurd and incomprehensible" mystery: the feelings, passions, sensations, the entire inflamed, hot, and colorful world into which the others seem to sink with so much joy arouses fear in him; and human pain with its gaudiest flower—tears—sweeps him into terror. So, in order to survive, not to let himself be engulfed by the maelstrom, he can only pretend he is dead. He suppresses his feelings, ignores those of others, erases all traces of his unconscious, does not see, does not want to see real things. With a kind of grandiose heroism and quixotic folly, he transforms existence into a monstrous, bureaucratic dossier, living in the place where lie extinguished the "reflexes of life." The very ones that do not satisfy Anna's insatiable heart.

He constructs for himself a system, in its own way perfect, like the raving system of a paranoid. When he pushes the folder of ongoing business to the center of his desk, he has an imperceptible smile of satisfaction: now that he is in contact with graphs and dead things, a lively color spreads over his habitually dull face, and he handles emotions and ministerial reports with the selfsame delight. He adores order and precision, the well-arranged objects on his desk, the excellent writing materials, the sharply pronounced words, time compartmentalized with rigid punctuality in accordance with the tick of clocks—those clocks that bring obsession and death to this earth. But his masterpiece is perhaps the construction of his body, almost as though he wished to show the men "with red necks" that he is of a different substance. He likes to clasp his hands and crack the joints of his fingers, like a wooden automaton. He habitually speaks a bureaucratic language and his thin, reedy voice takes on a mocking tone: a mask to repress every human feeling. The joy with which Tolstoy derides him is incomparable: there is no irony, perfidy, farcical taunt that he does not inflict on him, as in the scene with the lawyer who, with festive enthusiasm and an irrepressible glitter of mockery in his eyes, catches the moths flying past his nose.

Precisely at this moment, rendered ridiculous and grotesque, Karenin achieves the supreme metamorphosis: like many Tolstoyan characters, he oscillates between very distant psychological extremes, and his range of possibilities is so vast that he could become another man.* His instinct for contradiction is aroused by Anna, who throughout the novel acts as the force that awakens the living from sleep and dramatically impels them toward the far latitudes of their existence. Anna is dying of puerperal fever, she looks at her husband with moved and enchanted tenderness and in her delirum declares that none other than he, that boring, bureaucratic, dessicated man with pointed ears and crackling hands, is a good man, who has an obcure presentiment of love and sorrow. At that touch, Karenin awakens from his death: he who has killed life rediscovers life: a joyful feeling of absolute love and forgiveness fills his soul:

*The extreme case of psychological contradiction in Tolstoy is that of Dolokhov, cruel adventurer and most loving son. But we notice similar oscillations in Prince Vasily; in Boris who, almost without transition, is transformed into a parvenu snob; in Bagration, great general and clumsy automaton at the English Club. One must remember how much the habit of seeing one character with the eyes of the other characters contributes to this impression of contradiction.

laying his head on Anna's arm, he sobs like a child; and every day for hours on end he goes to the room of the daughter who is not his and, sadly smiling, contemplates that small, puckered face. Tolstoy has placed the novel's peak here: Anna, Karenin, Vronsky go beyond the psychological barriers that imprison them; and what would happen if everything continued like this—that existence in three, which Anna has dreamed of in her guilty dreams? But, as alway happens in Tolstoy's novels, nobody can remain at his peak: neither Prince Andrei at Austerlitz, nor Pierre during his imprisonment, nor Levin on the day of his engagement; all are sucked back into the quotidian. Anna rediscovers her repugnance for her husband: the world's vulgar and savage force crucifies Karenin, pitilessly persecutes his lacerated heart: he is alone, covered with shame, derided and despised by everyone; and to save himself, he clings to a spiritual hypocrisy that soon will become repugnant.

In accordance with one of the correspondences that pleases his mind in love with architectonic precision, Tolstoy makes Vronsky Karenin's exact opposite. It is with great joy that we leave Karenin's sclerotic and dusty world for the elegance, naturalness, worldly savoir-faire, enchanting aristocratic candor that Vronsky diffuses like a perfume from his harmonious person. Some devotee of Levin might maintain that he cares too much about orderly, customary things: but Vronsky's order is so human, and it makes him a good administrator, an excellent host, a refined master of his own life. While Karenin does not have a body, Vronsky joyfully lives in his body and together with his body: with pleasure he puts his red, hairy body under the sink's stream of water, massages his head with a bath towel; and it is with pleasure that his white, regular teeth sink into the meat of a steak. Even his light baldness, which bares his head, is an additional sign of physicality. In a scene that has an almost outrageous intensity, he experiences the joyful sensation of his body. He rests one leg on the knee of the other, palps his flexible calf, feels his breath moving in his chest, and smells the brilliantine in his mustache; he tastes in advance the joy of the amorous encounter: everything he sees from the carriage's window in the clear, fresh air of the August evening seems to reflect and increase his physical well-being.

Like Levin, Vronsky has a close relationship with animals. He loves Frou-Frou his mare—which bears the name of a loose girl—like a woman: he calls her "dear," "my darling"; and with feminine delicacy he shares the mare's femininely elegant hysteria—she, nervous, mobile, agitated, inhaling deeply, rests now on one foot, now on the other, twitches her nostrils, dilated and thin like the wings of a bat, shivers, perks her pointed ear, protrudes her strong dark lip, and then shifts one after the other her shapely legs. But, in *Anna Karenina*, both the love of women and love for animals are destined not to save one from the horror of existence. During the race at Krasnoe Selo, Vronsky breaks Frou-Frou's back, who like a mortally wounded bird writhes at his feet. With a precise correspondence, Tolstoy makes us understand that Vronsky's crime is an erotic crime; and that Eros' sacrilegious horror can also insinuate itself into our relationship with nature.

This average, well-balanced, and orderly man, who does not know the dramatic essence of reality, is attracted by amorous passion as by an unknown and desired universe. At first glance, he is lost: Anna's joyfully sparkling eyes and affectionate laughter enchain him. His passion for Anna carries him beyond the confines of his self, to a place that he cannot control with the simple code of savoir-faire. There are no laws here, but only destiny, unpredictability. As happened to Karenin, Anna pushes him where he, by himself, would never have gone. When Anna is ill, overcome by love, despair, and grief at having lost her, the lack of meaning in life away from her, he picks up his revolver, rests it against his heart, and almost beside himself pulls the trigger. Thus, without meaning to, he enters the tragic dimension of existence. What would have happened if, saved from the wound, he had remained in this sphere? Would Anna's and Vronsky's paths have joined? Would they have explored together, like sacrificial victims, the territory of love? But Vronsky's fate is identical with Karenin's. Just as the husband rejects his Christian impulse, so Vronsky condemns his suicide attempt ("it is too foolish"): he cancels it from his mind, resumes his habits; and tries to transform tragic Eros into a tranquil, normal conjugal relationship. Someone will punish him terribly: not being able to understand Anna's tragic nature, he will cause her death and will remain alone, faced by her suicide.

When Anna and Vronsky lived together, they did not create the family life that Vronsky so much desired. No one is guilty: tragic Eros does not tolerate being transformed into a fact of everyday life. But Tolstoy enumerates the list of culpabilities: just as Vronsky is the dilettante painter, so Anna does things that according to him are equally amateurish: she reads, writes children's books, philanthropically raises an English trainer's daughter—all actions performed to alleviate anguish. None other than she who desperately loved truth organizes around Vronsky a small false theatrical unreal court; and she speaks French and English as though to validate her sin. Unlike Kitty, she cannnot and does not want to become a wife, a mother, a mistress of the house: she connects her maternity to the recollection of her first son: she ignores the daughter she had by Vronsky; she wants to be sterile, hating the generation and continuity of life and breaking every tie that makes her similar to Natasha. By now she is just a lover, a very beautiful courtesan, amorous and aware of her arts, who seduces Vronsky and unconsciously tries to attract young men to prove to herself that Vronsky can still love her. But all these open or subterranean accusations, which Tolstoy directs at his heroine, are in vain. Anna has never been so beautiful and enchanting, so light and luminous as when she is devoured by the darkness of her decline: artificiality and falseness, as always happens in Tolstoy, give her a new naturalness; and we never stop falling in love with this woman dressed in metallic blue, who lives in the shadow of the portrait made of her long before.

By now Anna and Vronsky are prey to the mechanics of eroticism, which reveal a strange affinity with the mechanics of history: the most intimate impulses and desires of the heart seem dictated by an external force that imposes a predetermined form on every gesture. The heart's existence is one great battle. On the one hand, Anna wants all of Vronsky's thoughts and emotions to be concentrated on her: she wants to absorb him and swallow him in her womb, annul him in her amorous spider's web; and she knows only the life dedicated to Eros. On the other hand, Vronsky, his desires satisfied, knows the "desire of desires": melancholy. This flylike absorption repels him. Little by little, he moves away from a love that has become too burdensome, and tries to rebuild around himself the old everyday life: his club, the races, business, politics, agriculture—all activities that Anna sees as only *pis-allers*. At one time they had reached so deep a union of their bodies as to share the same dreams: now the horror of proximity, the excess of identification arouse repulsion. Physical hatred is born. When she drinks a cup of coffee, Anna understands (or thinks she understands) that Vronsky finds her hand which holds the cup, her small finger, and the sound she makes with her lips disgusting.

Subjected to this tension, fragile and delicate like Frou-Frou, Anna breaks. She now has the habit of half closing her eyes, as if she were observing something in the distance, but in reality not to see what is close to her: the loss of her son, perhaps the future loss of Vronsky; she tries to be blind, so as not to destroy the precarious happiness that is left her. But being blind is not enough: all the expunged thoughts rise up again in her dreams and keep her awake; so then she has to turn to morphine and opium, to beg a brief remission during the nocturnal hours. She is afraid of herself: she feels neurasthenia stifling her: she fears the instinct of self-destruction, and the madness that brutally ransacks her soul; like all great tragic heroines, instead of mitigating her passions, she instigates, provokes, builds them up, deliberately poisons her heart, just as during the first train trip she had deliberately exploited her hysteria in order "to see." "I feel I'm plunging head-first into an abyss, but that I must not save myself, and that I cannot!" she has already said to her brother, with a tenacity and a will for knowledge that will stay with her until death. She is alone now: everybody has deserted her, and not even her brother, who has mediated among so many people and conciliated so many causes, can do anything for her. All mediation and conciliation are impossible by now: everything must be taken to the extreme point of laceration.

Having gotten into the carriage, which under the May sun sweeps her toward death, Anna has a vision. Everything she sees is reflected in her eyes: the signs of the shops, two girls who smile, who knows why, two coachmen who insult each other viciously, a fat gentleman who greets her by mistake, two boys eating ice cream, a merchant who crosses himself, a party of people who are going on an outing in a cart, a drunken worker, strange streets, and the endless houses of men. . . . All she sees seems to her dirty, deformed, disgusting, like in the nightmare from which even opium and morphine did not save her. Right there, some malformed, insolent, and hurried young people: her servant, with his obtuse, bestial, and moronic smile: a clumsy lady with a dress ridiculously wide at the back: a spoiled little girl who laughs unnaturally: a repulsive husband and wife, who are bored and hate each other, and attentively examine her dress; a youth who will not take his eyes off her—poor, piteous, deformed individuals. Who is Anna Karenina at this moment? Just a hysterical woman who paints the world with the colors of her nightmares? A person enveloped by darkness? Just a woman about to throw herself under the train to punish her lover? Certainly Anna is delirious: but her delirium, like a kind of Platonic clairvoyance, allows her to discover in that "clear, penetrating" May light the truth about the world and mankind.

This truth is simple. Our life is nothing but low appetites: "If not bonbons, at least dirty ice cream," like those boys who are buying it from the sweaty ice-cream vendor. Our life is hatred: Kitty hates Anna, Anna hates Kitty, Anna hates Vronsky, Vronsky hates Anna, husbands hate wives, wives hate husbands, endlessly men hate each other in the houses without end; and the lies of the bells that toll vespers try in vain to conceal these truths. So Anna has reached the culmination, the Eros to whom she has consecrated her existence now reveals the flaming, devouring charge of hatred it bears within itself. We do not imagine that in these pages Tolstoy is far away, shut up to write in his comfortable winter room. Never as at this moment has he mingled his breath with Anna's, shared her feelings and glances, become a candle that is consumed and doused, a small red bag one throws away, and now he is even about to throw himself with her under the wheels of the train, performing the suicide Levin has never dared to carry out. For the first time he unleashes through the delirium of his most beloved creature, his own monstrous hatred of the world, which was to triumph darkly in "The Kreutzer Sonata." Perhaps, without knowing it, he was always full of hatred: like Anna's Eros he has his peak in hatred, his immense love—that love which impelled him to embrace the whole universe as born from a dream of God and even adopt as sacred the horrors of war—found its summit in the most profound aversion. The enchanting skin and the amorous glitter were gone: depression had killed them in one part of him; and now hatred began to blaze up sinisterly.

When one understands these things, it is time to die. Anna had already had a presentiment of her own death the night before: she lay in bed, with her eyes open, looking at the light of a candle just guttering out, at the molded ceiling's frame and the shadow of a screen that invaded it; and suddenly the screen's shadow swayed, invaded the entire frame, the entire ceiling, other shadows from the other side rushed to it, for an instant they fled, then advanced with renewed swiftness, swayed a little, merged, and in the room and inside herself darkness prevailed. In the morning, the sinister signs had multiplied: despite the opium, toward dawn she had again dreamed of the gnome with the tousled beard who repeated his French words and did "something frightful with an iron above her." At the station, Anna projects her nightmare into the deformed, misshapen, and vacillating space of reality: she sees a dirty peasant, with a cap from which his disheveled hair straggles, pass below the little window and bend over the wheels of the carriage; and soon after she remembers the man crushed by the train on the day of her first encounter with Vronsky. By now everything is accomplished: the candle and the two men have prepared her path, and all that remains for her to do is throw away her small red bag and fling herself under the train at the small Obiralovka station. At the very last instant, while something huge and inexorable drags her down on her back, Anna Karenina has her definitive vision. "The candle in whose light she had read the book filled with trouble and deception, sorrow and evil, flared up with a brighter light than ever, illuminated for her everything that before had been in darkness, sputtered, and went out forever." What does this last, sputtering glimmer of the candle reveal? The truth, which the entire book desperately investigated concerning the essence or absence of God? The truth about life and death? About this world or other worlds? The last word on love or hatred? As happens in *War and Peace*, when a "great light" descends into Prince Andrei's inner core and before the eyes of his mind the curtain that has hidden the unknown from him is lifted, Tolstoy does not know what this light contains. The revelation remains obscure for everyone, except Anna Karenina. Whereas in *War and Peace* another light descended from the sky or the divine continuity of life, here the sole gleam shoots out when life and death, existence and preexistence meet: Levin's son is born, Anna and Nikolai are dying, and in this moment of transition between two worlds the tiniest crack, an invisible fissure opens in the wall of darkness. It is the briefest opening glimpsed only by the dying or the just born, on which we cannot built a theology and philosophy, much less a literature. On this fissure alone, through which the gaze ventures into the night, Tolstoy built—he tells us this three times—the architecture of *Anna Karenina*.

Then it is night again. We hear talk about Anna, once again at a railroad station, while some amateurish volunteers leave for a stupid war—like old ladies' gossip in a casual conversation. In his long overcoat, his hat pulled down and his hands in his pockets, Vronsky is a wreck, and the toothache he suffers from casts a grotesque light on his grief. Less than two months have passed. Stepan, whose "joyful smile" suddenly appears sinister to us, has already forgotten how desperately he sobbed over his sister's body: Vronsky's mother curses her; and Vronsky can no longer remember the mysterious and triumphant creature of light whom he had met at another railroad station. Every trace of Anna, every memory of a great love that had brightened the world, has vanished.

III

Thomas Mann advised us to think that Levin had written *Anna Karenina*. I believe one cannot imagine worse advice. Levin could never write *Anna Karenina;* nor any of Tolstoy's stories. He does not know the demonic levity with which Tolstoy passed through every sorrow, and the no less demonic levity with which his hand filled sheets of paper. The author of a great novel is at the same time present and absent in every line of his book: in the characters, the landscapes, a galloping mare, a bird that flies away, the colors of a woman's dress, a conversation about mushrooms or jams. The space he inhabits is the totality of the book, and the labyrinthine complexity of its internal concatenations. Levin gathers in himself many experiences of Tolstoy's youth and maturity: he is shy, spiteful, hostile, litigious, arrogant, proud, clumsy, jealous, as was Tolstoy. For stretches he walks alongside him; but not even for an instant, while going down Levin's road, can we forget that Tolstoy is objectivizing and distancing his youthful life and often casts a derisory light on the young, insufferable moralist he had been. In the beginning Levin had been introduced in the novel as a kind of buffoonish athlete; and also in the final draft he represents the voice of disharmony and grotesque fracture when compared to Anna's tragic harmony.

Levin does not love himself. When he thinks of himself, he has a scornful smile: he finds himself repugnant: " 'Yes, there is something disagreeable and repulsive in me,' he repeats, 'Who am I? What am I? A man of no account, who is not necessary for anything or to anyone.' " His weakness, uncertainty, and lack of assurance sink into such deep, tumultuous layers of his being that they are reversed and become an acrid, continuous aggressiveness, hatred, and rancor toward the world that seems to him an immense lie, purposely concocted to offend him. He is jarring, fragmentary, tortuous, incoherent, restless, doubting, fickle, and neurasthenic. To protect himself, he constructs between himself and reality a wall spiked with moralisms. He suffers from an acute sense of guilt, and ends by accusing his neighbor. Incapable of possessing himself, he wants to possess others and tortures them with a systematic jealousy in which he expresses his abstract logical spirit. While Anna Karenina has a natural instinct for happiness, his jagged character prevents him from being happy—save for very brief, very intense flashes. But in the end his lacerated and contradictory nature is his true source of strength, for it allows him to sense dramatically the lacerations and contradictions in Russian life and in any human life, which escape average, well-balanced natures such as Vronsky's.

We are at the height of summer: the green-gray rye, with its still light ear, sways in the wind: the green oats, with tufts of yellow grass scattered here and there, stand out amid the late crops: the corn is already ripening, covering the earth, piles of dried manure in the open exhale sharply in the dawn together with the herbs, and on the flat plains , waiting for the scythe, extend the meadows surrounded by the blackish clumps of uprooted wood sorrel. One morning Levin goes with his scythe to cut grass along with his peasants. At first he scythes badly, laboriously; with violence and effort: then, little by little, he forgets about himself; he scythes as if he were playing, as if it were not his hands guiding the scythe but the scythe itself dragging his whole body along with it; and the work accomplishes itself, regular and precise. As we follow Levin's movements, we have before our eyes one of the great symbols of *War and Peace*: natural action, spontaneous, without intention, without memories, without effort, which wells up from the passive depths of our being: Kutuzov's and Pierre's involuntary action. But Levin's is a brief beatitude. Only by exception does his life experience this naturalness, this liberation of the entire being through action: he is too aggressive and purposeful to abandon himself to nature.

Perhaps Levin would have been lost if he hadn't remained a boy incapable of growing up. When we most detest him, his candor ends by disarming us. As young boys do, he lives a profoundly physical life: his very thoughts are psycho-physical irradiations, invasions, explosions. So he is whole, body and spirit, in what he feels: his sensations are immediate and violent, everything is intense, ardent, exalted, and exasperated; a single fire of passion, a total commitment of the self, an energy that now concentrates, now disperses in all directions. In these moments of exaltation, identical to those that assailed the young Tolstoy, he experiences the intermittent blessing of happiness: ardent blood courses through his veins, his mind is absolutely lucid, his heart joyful and ecstatic, he feels that he can leap beyond time with the wings of the body, as on the morning of his engagement. The world of everyday habit and the insignificant does not exist for him. Like Tolstoy, he lives to grasp a series of epiphanies in reality.

At a time when the immediate relationship with nature is in shreds, Levin is almost the only one to preserve the old vital rhythms. With every pore of his skin, every nerve of his body, every impulse of his intelligence, he senses the arrival of spring. Here suddenly a tepid wind rises, then a warm, tempestuous rain falls, and as though to hide the mystery of change, a thick fog advances: waters melt, ice crackles and moves, turbid and frothy the torrents run more swiftly, the resplendent sun hastily devours the last thin layer of ice, the air trepidates with vapors released by the revivified earth: old grass and new grass grow green, the buds on the viburnum, currant, and birch swell: and then a bee begins to hum, the hare lets out a prolonged screech, and we hear a distant whistle, a second, a third whistle, the ever closer trill of a woodcock, like thick canvas being ripped at regular intervals. . . . Levin does not like to hear the beauty of nature spoken about in the religious and ecstatic tones of dilettantes. His bond with the earth is more direct and immediate: that of both an exploiter and a lover. When he enters the meadow's immense gray-green sea, unstirred by the wind, and the grass, soft as silk, colored here and there by bunches of stock, reaches almost to his waist—Tolstoy makes it clear that an erotic relationship binds him to the earth. Levin acts like Vronsky with Frou-Frou: only he does not know the horror of a crime committed upon nature.

He is never so happy as when he goes hunting. Then his ear picks up the most subtle sounds that pierce the transparent early morning silence—that of a bee which, with the hiss of a bullet, comes out of the hive, or the soft sway of the broom and bushes of reeds in the early mist: while his sense of smell captures the redolence of the roots, swamp grass, rust, and the manure of horses and birds, so intense amid the swamp moss. At the most dramatic moment of the hunt, sounds lose their habitual distance and begin to strike him chaotically but with great clarity. Stepan's approaching steps seem to him the distant pounding of horses' hooves, while the crumbling of a hillock which he has climbed seems to him the flight of a woodcock. The relationship with the animal world, so profound in the natural epic of *War and Peace*, becomes even more intense, acute, and subtle. Never did the animal world seem so close to ours, so close as to lend us its sensations and learn our human ones: as though at the last moment, at the point of separating himself forever from nature, Tolstoy wanted nervously to exalt the lost paradise. Through Frou-Frou's nostrils, ears, and legs he penetrates among horses as though he were one of them: or he adopts the thoughts, sensations, intuitions, looks, and language of the bitch Laska hunting woodcock.

When he was preparing the novel, Tolstoy planned to make Levin fall in love with Anna Karenina; and at least a shadow of this remains, the meeting between the two in Moscow, when Anna unconsciously tries to awaken in Levin a feeling of love. We can try to imagine what might have happened. A terrible clash between impassioned and dramatic temperaments? Or would the tragicomic Levin understand Anna's tragic nature better than Vronsky? And would death under the wheels have been avoided? But Tolstoy soon realized that no relationship between the two was possible: Levin's amorous search leads him in a direction opposed to that taken by Anna. Like the young Tolstoy, he is possessed by an Oedipal obsession: he dreams of renewing in marriage the family life of his father and mother: his future wife must repeat the "delicate and saintly ideal of womanhood his mother represented": he merges the maternal image with that of the desired wife; and, around this obsession, everything becomes fixed and immobilized. As a result, Levin shuns the erotic potential which Anna nevertheless sees in him when she compares him to Vronsky. Apparently without tension or a sense of renunciation, letting himself be invaded by his dream, he turns his back on the world of Eros: fate, the possessive predatory instinct, tragedy, crime, and death.*

The first, provisory crystallization of Levin's love is collective. Like a child, he falls in love with the whole Sherbatsky family: the house, father, mother, servants, and the three daughters: everything that happens in the family is enveloped in a poetic and mysterious veil of mist; the teachers of French literature, music, drawing, and dancing, the sounds of the piano, the girls' strange habit of speaking English one day and French the next, the carriage rides, Dolly's long fur coat, Kitty's red stockings, the servant with the gold cockade on his hat. . . . Then, almost by chance, Levin's emotion crystallizes around Kitty. One winter afternoon, while the rays of the sun pierce the luminous shell of icy air, he walks toward the skating ground. She is there, wearing her little dainty boots. He dare not approach her, so sacred and impenetrable the place where she is appears to him. Everything happens as in a religious revelation: Kitty is at the center, the sun that illuminates all things: but, like the sun, she dazzles one's eyes or becomes obscured if Levin dares come too close to her; and the heart is prey to the same shudder that overcomes the initiate—joy, anxiousness, fear, the sight's dimming, the inability to see, a sense of one's wretchedness. In its first apparition, Kitty's sun burns Levin: then the light lessens, approaches, smiles at him, speaks to him; the love that fills Levin's heart is absolute passion, which transforms itself into an inebriated, enthusiastic feeling of love for others. Kitty's gaze reaches what he wants: it carries him back, moved and placated, to the day of his early childhood; but, in this regression, the incestuous shadow, which could accompany the Oedipal emotion, is nullified.

While Anna is the enthusiastic and outpouring light of Eros, Kitty is the "calm light" that illuminates family existence. Tolstoy dedicates to her his most delicate bourgeois pastel. When she goes to the ball, her gown is a perfect fit, the shoulder strap does not slip down

*All this was even clearer in one of the first drafts: "His love was so far removed from sensuality that he often feared he would not have children."

at all, the rosebuds are neither crushed nor dangling: the small pink shoes with their curved heels do not press but rather delight the foot. The dense *bandeaux* of blond hair are solidly attached to her little head as if they were part of her: the small velvet ribbon of her medallion tenderly encircles her neck. "This little velvet ribbon was enchanting, and at home, looking at her neck in the pier glass, Kitty had felt that that little ribbon spoke. There might still be some doubt about all the rest, but the little velvet ribbon was enchanting." In the slight tremor of her lips, and the wet glisten that veils her eyes, there is something irreparably fragile: if Kitty were to walk alone in life, she would most likely lose her way; but she chooses to shut herself up in the well-protected, well-defined family idyll. Like a bird, she prepares her nest: her lazy, smiling happiness; she becomes wife, mother, mistress of the house—and acquires an unsuspected solidity. She wields the keys of the housewife: arranges the furniture, hangs curtains, decorates the rooms, takes care of the tablecloths, sheets, mattresses, organizes the pantry, gives the cook her menu for dinner, bathes her son.

After a difficult period, "family happiness" begins. It is not the ecstatic moment Levin experienced on the morning before his marriage proposal—the ecstatic moment cannot last in time—but it is a full, rich happiness which buoys up all of existence. Whereas at one time Levin wrote and worked because without that his life would have been too dark, now these occupations are indispensable so that "life should not become too uniformly radiant." One afternoon everybody goes searching for mushrooms, and Levin and Kitty walk ahead of the others, on the dusty road strewn with ears and grains of rye. Kitty is pregnant and leans on Levin's arm. During the conversation nothing happens—nothing, save for the fact that Levin makes sure that his wife does not tire herself, and scolds her when she makes too abrupt a movement jumping over a branch. The two of them talk: talk about everything, pass from subject to subject, the conversation changes like the clouds chasing across the sky, like the ever mutable shape of things—the way to cook jam, how to declare one's love, Sergei Ivanovich and Varenka, Levin who is not satisfied with himself, Kitty's father; and then they stop to pluck a flower's petals to see whether Varenka will marry Sergei Ivanovich. These disconnected, indirect words, to which we would like to listen longer, reveal to us better than any intellectual analysis what Levin's and Kitty's love is. It is not Anna's and Vronsky's passion that fuses two bodies and two unconsciousnesses in a fire without words. It is a tenderness that has forgotten Eros, a profound belonging to each other of souls, so that it is never quite clear where one ends and the other begins: something so light and fragile that it must be sheltered and protected with every care; something that can always have recourse to confession and the impetus of words, even if the words seem to speak of other things.

Around Levin's and Kitty's conjugal idyll unfolds Europe's last rural idyll. Tolstoy knows everything about a country house: the persons who inhabit it, the guests who visit it, the servants, the children's rackets, the atmosphere of every room, the shadows in the hallways, the spaciousness of the kitchen, the noises, murmurs, and lights. In Dolly's house, rain drips in the hallway, the closets don't shut, there are no cast-iron pans, tureens, or ironing board: the children are sick or in danger of getting sick: but on the day of communion their clothes are darned, refashioned, and washed, buttons are sewn on and ribbons prepared; in church, Alesha keeps twisting about to look at her back, Tanya watches over the little ones, Lily, when she receives communion, says, in English: Please, some more. On Kitty and Levin's estate there is a less precarious orderliness. The big house is packed full: Dolly's family, Kitty's mother, Levin's brother, Varenka, and other occasional guests. Chickens, turkeys, and ducks must be purchased to feed so many people: small vests and knitted swaddling clothes must be made: an expedition to hunt for mushrooms in the woods must be organized; and strawberry and raspberry jam must be prepared according to a new method, without adding water to it, although Agafya, the old guardian of Levin's spirit, is convinced that the raspberries will clot. While the jam cooks and a sparrow comes to rest on the balustrade, the women chat about servants and marriages, loves and marinades: the petulant, gossipy, exuberant realm of women for an instant occupies the world's stage. Everything is enchanting: we too smell the fragrance of the jams and marinades; but everything is threatened, much more than the Rostovs' rural existence. How long will the rich, populous, tumultuous happy life in the country houses last? Forever, without ever ending? We know that is impossible: this beauty is consumed as it is being described; and that is why its representation is so touching.

Whereas Prince Andrei and Pierre dominated death with intelligence, Levin is overwhelmed by the thought of death. He feels its dark shadow spreading over everyday life. He sees it everywhere: in the living and loved bodies that surround him, in the old peasant woman who fans out the wheat with her rake, in the young peasant whose curly beard is full of chaff, in the dappled horse that laboriously drags its belly, in the girl with the red jacket who removes the grain from the chaff with such a nimble gesture, and in himself. But, if death exists, what is the meaning of life? Our thoughts, our feelings, our acts during the day, the tomes that vanity or inspiration impel us to write, the exploits that will be inscribed in golden letters in the book of universal history—all our existence "is taking a turn around the bearskin." Levin comes into direct contact with death when his brother Nikolai dies in a provincial town. In that unnamed place, everything has a Dostoevskian air. The hotel is shady: a soldier in a dirty uniform and with a cigarette hanging from his lips acts as porter, the waiter is in greasy tails, the cast-iron stairway is gloomy and unpleasant, on the table in the main salon stands a bunch of dusty wax flowers, dirt, disorder, and dust everywhere, while an officious bustle and industriousness remind us that there is a railroad station nearby—the sign of evil. The room in which Nikolai lies is small, dirty, covered with spittle, a suffocating stench: the dying man stretches an enormous hand out on the bed, like a rake, incomprehensibly attached to a frail arm, thin, and even like a spindle. This simple physical detail, in which Tolstoyan sobriety gives way to the violence of unimaginable deformity, carries us into the heart of life's horror.

When he is about to be routed by death, at the very brink, an instant before *she* crashes in—Levin has a twofold consolation. First it is Kitty, the little family bird, who has just begun to build her nest, and seems not to know the mysteries that her husband vainly investigates. With her sweet, very delicate hands, full of scruple, affection, and attention, she cleans the room, makes the bed, changes the pillowcase and the dying man's shirt, washes him, scatters about perfume, fluffs up the pillow, transforms the anonymous, dirty hotel room into a room like hers, with tidy beds, brushes, combs, and little mirrors in place, arranged properly, the towels set out. What in appearance could be more useless in the face of death? Kitty has the same gift as Natasha: the feminine science of mitigating it; the science Anna cannot possess, because Eros leads to death, does not placate it. This caring, cleaning, mitigating introduce life's order into the anteroom of death; and, at the same time, perhaps they contain a more important spark—for, with the movements of her hands, Kitty shows that she understands what death is and what is beyond it, although she cannot tell it to any of us. Meanwhile the dying man lies with his eyes closed: muscles quiver on his forehead, as though he were thinking profoundly and intensely; and from the expression of the severe face and the movement of the eyebrow's muscle, Levin understands that something is becoming clear to his brother which still remains obscure to him. It is the same fissure that illuminated Anna Karenina's suicide. The dying know what there is beyond: but this wisdom is still forbidden to us. Death, which threatens life's every instant, offers us one of the lights that go beyond its confines.

Some time later, Kitty and Levin's son is born. And it is horror again: Kitty's terrible cries and moans, her face which has become monstrous and shapeless. There is a rustle, an anxious breathing, a different voice, the bold, rash cry which refuses to consider anything, the cry of a new human being. It is the other fissure: preexistence encounters existence. In this instant, when two worlds touch and we hear the bold voice of a child, an unearthly light touches our earth. By insisting three times on the same theme, making cautious allusions, Tolstoy repeats that this gleam is the only metaphysical truth—the most dubious and uncertain truth—that *Anna Karenina* can offer.

The stories of Anna and Levin correspond perfectly. While Anna's erotic exploration ends in a tragic checkmate, Levin reads Plato and Spinoza, Kant and Schelling, Hegel and Schopenhauer and A.S. Khomyakov*, and his answer to the greatest intellectual

*A Russian writer, poet and Slavophile (1804-60)—TRANS.

problems ("What am I and why am I here?") also ends in a checkmate. To him life seems the vicious derision of some demon: just as Anna threw herself under the train, Levin is tortured by the thought of suicide. He does not talk about this with Kitty, as Pierre would have done with Natasha if such dreadful thoughts had tortured him. The intimacy between him and Kitty is not as complete; and, although he expresses himself with words, he halts when words verge on the inexpressible. Perhaps the absence of Eros keeps them apart, as, on the other hand, Eros puts distance between lovers. The only thing that saves Levin from despair is the existence he leads, even if it does not answer his intellectual questions. The farm, the relations with peasants and neighbors, his sisters' and brothers' affairs, the relations with his wife and relatives, his preoccupation about his son, his new bee-raising take up all his time.

One day, almost by chance, he overhears a peasant speaking: "Fokanich is a truthful old man. He lives for his soul. He remembers God." Hearing these words, confused thoughts, dense with meaning, burst in a swarm inside him, as if they were coming from who knows what remote place and, all straining toward a single goal, began to whirl about in his head, blinding him with their light. What did Levin understand with the words "He remembers God"? In the night of his soul, is God suddenly revealed to him, like the sky of Austerlitz and dreams had revealed Him to Prince Andrei and Pierre? Perhaps an incomprehensible, absurd God, but no less present in the heart? Levin's revelation is much poorer: in the absolute absence of God, the religious desolation that continues to envelop him, he recognizes Him as the principle of Christian morality. For him God is an ethical absurdity to which he clings with all his strength: a dry, arid, limited faith, like that which thereafter will inspire Tolstoy and the hero of *Resurrection*. The true climax of *Anna Karenina* still resides in the very brief flashes, the paradoxical fissures that three times have allowed us to glimpse something unearthly. Tolstoy's artistic justice has decreed that Anna's life must sink into night and horror and that Levin must be granted some light. But her quest, during which Anna has learned all that we may know about Eros, was infinitely richer, more grandiose and dramatic than Levin's modest religious investigation.

When Levin's family is dispersed in the countryside, the summer clouds mass together in a large dark cloud, which rapidly advances toward the house and hides the sun as in an eclipse. The wind persists, tears leaves from the linden trees, twists the birches' white branches, bends the acacias, flowers, grass, and the tops of the trees: the white curtain of rain swoops down swiftly; and suddenly everything is inflamed, the earth catches fire, the celestial vault overhead splits open, lightning strikes the green crown of the big oak, under which Levin thinks Kitty and the child have sought shelter, and it crashes to the ground. But his anguish lasts but an instant, and from now on only favorable signs multiply. Kitty, the nurse, and child are safe at the other end of the wood under an old linden tree. The child, as in Virgil, recognizes its mother. Evening falls. Now a flash of lightning which hides the stars lights up Kitty's calm and joyous face: now the flash fades, and the Milky Way and the stars again appear in the sky; until Kitty, for the last time renouncing to touch the inexpressible with words, entrusts her husband with a small domestic chore: "Listen, Kostya! Do me a favor. Go into the corner room and see if they've prepared everything properly for Sergei Ivanovich. I can't go, I'm embarrassed. See if they've put in the new washstand." We could not imagine a more enchanting conclusion: with this light play of symbols, this discretion, and this touch in a minor key, with the assurance that the "new washstand" is well worth any discussion about the major world systems. Life continues, and all tragedies dissolve in its music. There is the light of the stars, the light of Kitty's face; and for the time being this twofold light seems to be enough. But there is no doubt—so frail is Levin's and Tolstoy's new faith—that other clouds, other storms, and other lightning bolts will crash to the ground the crowns of the very tall oak trees.

IV

Tolstoy was justly proud of the structure of *Anna Karenina*, which today seems to us the supremely balanced and elegant flower of the European novel. When S. A. Rachinsky pointed out to him that there was no architecture in the book, but two somewhat disconnected themes developed alongside each other, he answered: "Your opinion of *Anna Karenina* seems unjust to me. On the contrary, I am proud of the architecture—the vaults are built in such a way that it isn't even possible to discover where their keystones are. This is what I mainly tried to achieve. The cohesiveness of the structure is not founded on the plot or the relationship (of mutual acquaintance) among the characters, but on an inner bond." The two novels of Anna and Levin meet in a number of fundamental scenes: Kitty loves or thinks she loves Vronsky; Anna, Kitty, and Vronsky attend the same ball; Stepan, Karenin, Levin, and Kitty dine together on the day of the declaration of love. Dolly visits the two lovers in their rich country house, and for a few hours Levin loves Anna who is about to kill herself. So at times the two novels are mirrored in each other: the motif of one finds its true meaning only when it hears its own echo in a motif of the other. At other times they are counterposed, as though representing absolute antitheses of the same theme: Anna's erotic life is the opposite of Levin's family life. Then the play of antitheses moves into each character's inner life: the tension between tragic and antitragic attitudes separates in one and the same way Anna and Vronsky, Levin and Kitty. Finally, as in *War and Peace*, a dense series of family relationships, friendships, and loves links all the characters tightly together, as though to signify that a novel is a compact space, hedged in by a thousand inner relationships.

Although they correspond to and mirror each other, the two novels of Anna and Levin are constructed in accordance with opposed narrative principles. Anna's novel is a closed book; it opens at the Moscow railroad station where Anna meets Vronsky and closes in on itself at the Obiralovka station where Anna throws herself under the train, and a presage in the first scene already anticipates the last. It teems with objective symbols, which pursue each other throughout the book. The names of all the characters begin with *A*, as though Tolstoy meant to brand them with an indelible sign: Alexei Karenin, Alexei Vronsky, Anna Karenina, the maid Annushka, Vronsky's daughter Annie, besides Hanna, the little adopted English girl; and we involuntarily think of *A*, the "scarlet letter," the mark of adultery that Hester Prynne wore on the bodice of her dress surrounded by elaborate embroideries and adorned by fantastic golden flourishes. Train and station are sinisterly repeated symbols: the station in Moscow where the worker is crushed, the train in which Anna and Vronsky travel together through the storm, the Petersburg station where Anna sees her husband again, Anna's suicide under the train at the Obiralovka station, Vronsky's stop at the station during his suicidal journey to the Serbian front; and it is quite possible that the complex railroad symbology (used again in *Resurrection*) was planted in Tolstoy's mind when reading Dickens' *Dombey and Son*. The dream about the old man, which Anna's unconscious transmits to or imposes on Vronsky's unconscious, has a different function during the course of the story: now it presages Anna's death in childbirth, now her death under the train; while the image of the candle that accompanies her last day hints now at Anna's demise, now at an unearthly revelation.

This network of symbolic coincidences woven with an at once vigorous and delicate hand replaces the network of novelistic coincidences that multiplies particularly in the last part of *War and Peace*. The novelistic coincidences of *War and Peace* were the signs of the triumphant and picturesque intertwining of events that life is: these symbolic patterns show that we have entered the ironclad construction of special events and omens that destiny prepares for its favorite victims. If anyone had asked Tolstoy what was the meaning of each of these signs, he probably would not have been able to answer. He distributed them throughout the book, at intervals, in the first place to delimit his construction, giving the impression of a world terribly enclosed within itself. And so the letter *A*, for example, is a silent symbol, which we will never be able to translate into an explicit allegory like Hawthorne's. With this use of signs, Tolstoy develops one of the supreme forms of the European novel: the symbolic–symphonic novel which reaches its peak in Goethe's *Elective Affinities* and in *Madame Bovary*. In both cases, as in *Anna Karenina*, we have an admirably closed form, which departs from a determined point and ends at another, which corresponds to the first point like the conclusive move in a chess game. In both cases, the closing of the book is made visible by the return of a number of symbolic objects: the chemical game, the hands on the chest, the miniature, the handwriting, Ottilie's glass and small trinket box, the tombstones in the cemetery, the child's eyes in *Elective Affinities;* Emma's eyes, the bridal bouquet, the green silk cigarette case, Binet's lathe, and the blind man on the road to Rouen in *Madame Bovary*. While the mind plays with these small signs, it silently summons destiny—which seems to be able to appear among us only in this beautiful closed form furrowed by a thousand presentiments.

As John Bayley has written, Anna's novel is as tragic and contracted as Levin's is expansive and relaxed. His is an open book, like *War and Peace*: it begins at any point whatsoever in the plot, which we could replace at will, and ends with Levin on his way to see about his brother's new washstand, a minimal event, to which we could indefinitely add another series of events of the same kind. It knows no sign, presage, or symbolic object.* The reason for this is clear: Levin's novel is not the book of destiny, which is completely uninterested in him, Kitty, his agricultural projects, and his religious ideas. The extraordinary beauty of *Anna Karenina*'s architecture requires that a compact form be placed and, so to speak, dissolved in a form as continuous and labile as life itself.

*There may be a slight contagion of the railroad symbology: it is at the station that Levin tells Kitty's cousin that, for him, it is now time to die; and the hotel in which Nikolai dies is near the station.

PART FOUR

What a Novel Is

I

With the incomprehensible ease of someone who feels at home everywhere, Tolstoy penetrates into every body and every soul. While Balzac and Proust strive to become their creatures, but halt a moment before dissolving in them, caught in the actor's and mime's grandiose gesture—Tolstoy *is* all the rest of the world, with the same naturalness with which he lives his own life. If he wishes, he is a young girl who looks at herself smiling in the mirror and admires her pink tulle gown with its pink petticoat: he senses with her the gown that is a perfect fit, the thick *bandeaux* of blond hair that lie firmly on her small head as if they were her own, and "the small velvet ribbon of the medallion which tenderly encircles her neck." If he wishes, Tolstoy is a hunting bitch, sniffing the air with dilated nostrils; or a racing mare that extends her long neck and a leg. He identifies with his characters to such a point that we often have the impression that he lets himself become their succubus: falls in love together with them, suffers with them, dies with them. His senses, "marvelously obedient, clairvoyant, acutely auditive, robustly tactile," seize all the sights, colors, sounds, and smells that fill the universe. His senses do not have our limits; they dive to the depths, leap into the distance; and the last microscopic tremor of a blade of grass or the azure distance of the infinite also fall prey to them. The lightest molecules of existence, the atoms of feeling, the unconscious thoughts that flash through the mind, the relationships between distant sensations and feelings, invisible, casual, almost absurd details—this minutely detailed dust of minutes is the place that Tolstoy prefers to inhabit. He knows that this dust forms the very substance of reality: the precious substance that he alone knows.

No matter to what extent this world reaches toward the double infinite, Tolstoy's well-organized mind never loses its precision. In the scene of the race in *Anna Karenina*, another writer would perhaps have merged in a single impasto the three points of view of Vronsky (and his mare), Anna, and Karenin, and the events that take place simultaneously on the track and in the stands. Tolstoy's first impulse, however, is to separate the simultaneous, distinguishing the three points of view in three scenes and in three different chapters. Every object is sharply fixed by the mind and, if necessary, broken down into its parts. A crystalline light surrounds it as in the nocturnal sleigh ride in *War and Peace*: all around the atmosphere shines brightly, picks out trees, people, clothes, the roofs of houses, stones on the road, giving them an unnatural transparency and vividness, an extraordinary delicacy of contour, while occasionally a light mist which dissipates and becomes diaphanous before our eyes veils all things. This process of fixing reality allows Tolstoy his very light and ruthless detachment. We were without reserve a girl at her mirror, a hunting bitch, a mare: it seemed to us that our life coincided completely with their sensations; and now we are the falcon, hovering high in the sky, the eye of God who looks at all things without participating in any of them.

While he narrates, Tolstoy reduces to zero the character and role of the narrator, who always had such prominence in the novel's history. *War and Peace* and *Anna Karenina* are not written by an ego, which exhibits its storytelling or histrionic abilities, at every moment insists upon its relationship with the audience, chatters volubly and comments on events as the narrator does in Fielding, Stendhal, or Dickens. If we leave aside the essayistic sections in *War and Peace*, Tolstoy tends to avoid any comment whatsoever: the reader must draw his own conclusions from the narrative elements and connections that were put under his eyes, without relying on the writer's help. He does not entrust the story to a character that says "I," as Dostoevsky does so willingly, or even to a multitude of narrators, who supplement each other or narrate one inside the other, as in Dickens and Conrad. Nor does he have recourse to the invention of *Madame Bovary*, where the role of the narrator is eroded by an unnamed *voice*, an extenuated and exhausting modulation in which are reflected thoughts, dreams, hopes, disappointments, frustrations, regrets, Emma's spoken and unspoken words. According to Tolstoy, all these forms risk weakening the transparency and immediacy needed to narrate. Any mediation at all is abolished: the narrator is simply an "I" fixed at the same time on things and high in the sky, which looks at things, chooses, builds, orders, and represents them; and attributes to them the same degree of vitality (or, more precisely: an augmented degree of vitality) that they have in the world. No bookish smell, no narrative gimmick must remind us, John Bayley writes, that "we are reading a novel" and are living in the realm of illusion. So Tolstoy uses the most classical narrative form; the third person; which he always uses, except in the case of "The Kreutzer Sonata." A commonplace makes him the classical representative of this form, and sees in him the emblem of the all-seeing narrator, who knows everything that happens, depicts present, past, and future, penetrates without meeting resistance into the characters' souls, and does not know the art of reticence. No legend ever had less foundation. Especially in *War and Peace* Tolstoy possesses as E. M. Forster says, an "intermittent knowledge" of events, which passes from all-seeingness to total ignorance, and exploits the systematic restrictions of point of view. His case is not as extreme as Dickens' in *Bleak House*, where the narrator does not know or does not tell what he knows: so that all the principal scenes are systematically avoided and narrating becomes the art of omitting in such a way as to produce the impression of an impending and threatening mystery. In no case does Tolstoy wish to arouse such a sensation of mystery. Like the most discreet and reticent of guides, he simply avoids telling us, even in the most allusive way, what Pierre Bezukhov's youth in Paris was like, or why Prince Andrei married Lisa, with whom he is already disappointed at the beginning of *War and Peace*. These reticences may derive from Tolstoy's habit of not narrating his characters' "prehistory"; but there are more intentional omissions. During the battle of Schöngraben, a French shell falls in the center of a column, killing an unspecified number of soldiers: Tolstoy does not linger to represent the carnage;

we are only told that "the soldiers, describing a semicircle, gave a wide berth to *something*, there at the spot where the shell had fallen." The love between Natasha and Prince Andrei climaxes in the long conversations that take place during the engagement period or in the *isba**: but absolutely nothing of these conversations is told us. So, at times, it can happen that certain events remain obscure.

Rather than in the omission of events, the most typical instance of Tolstoyan reticence consists in transforming the narrator's figure, abolishing in it any gift for intuition and penetration, and reducing it to a gaze that fixedly contemplates the pure surface of things. Let me mention only a few examples. When Natasha, in love with Anatol, is locked up in the house by the energetic Marya Dmitrievna, a less sober writer than Tolstoy would have told us her passions and torments. Tolstoy confines himself to describing Natasha's pale face, her dry, wide-open, and petrified eyes which stare straight ahead and minutely scrutinize the street, her cracked lips, and the gelid expression, rancorous and full of dignity, with which she receives Pierre. That is all we know. In a parallel scene, when Prince Andrei knows he has been abandoned by Natasha, our knowledge is again limited to a face: here is Andrei, with a new, deep crease between his eyebrows, a cold, mean, disagreeable laugh like his father's, his voice more animated than usual, which becomes heated in discussion, accompanied by an energetic gesticulation of his hands. This metamorphosis of the narrator reaches the extreme in the case of Petya's death: reduced to a pure gaze, unaware of any interior event, the narrator does not know that the boy is dead and confines himself to taking note of strange gestures: "Some of the French, amid the dense swaying smoke, threw away their arms, coming out from the bushes around the Cossacks, others fled down the slope toward the pond. Petya galloped on his horse along the manor house's courtyard and, instead of holding the reins, groped strangely, rapidly clawed the air with his hands, and, at the same time, ever more obviously, slipped to one side of the saddle." Only a few lines later, reacquiring an awareness he had lost before, the narrator informs us that "a bullet had struck him in the head." Such a novelistic attitude seems

*A small log cabin—TRANS.

especially appropriate in the case of *War and Peace*, where the writer wishes to underline his impotence in the face of an immense and incomprehensible reality. In *Anna Karenina*, the restriction of the field of vision is less systematic, and Tolstoy recovers at least a part of his omniscience.

When Tolstoy imagined that he was God (something which happened to him very often), he had to think about how to infuse his presence into the novels he was writing. God could be the supreme and immoble eye above terrestrial events: the distant, quiet, and gray sky of Austerlitz. But Tolstoy was a pantheist: he knew that God was incarnated in all human beings: something eternal, infinite, and omnipotent had made itself mortal, weak, and limited; and therefore if he wanted to portray God's gaze in his novels, he had to reproduce *all* the points of view of the characters: he had to be Pierre, Natasha, Prince Andrei, Count Rostov, Prince Vasily, Helene, Denisov, and Dolokhov, each of them a refraction of God . . . It was a grandiose project, which once struck him in his *Diaries*: Tolstoy never accomplished it, perhaps overcome by the solipsistic vertigo to which it would have led him; but its debris is somehow left behind in the narrations based on the characters' points of view, strewn about chiefly in *War and Peace*. When he composed them, he had famous precedents, *The Charterhouse of Parma*, where the action is seen in turn through the eyes of Fabrizio, Gina, Clelia, Count Mosca; and some of Dickens' prodigious examples, when the death of Quilp (in *The Old Curiosity Shop*) and that of little Dombey (in *Dombey and Son*) are told through the eyes of the dying characters. While he sees through the eyes of Pierre, Nikolai, and Vronsky, Tolstoy on the one hand narrows the narrator's focus to the minimum, and on the other abolishes any screen between reality and representation. In the space of a page, he *is* the wounded Nikolai, Natasha at the theater, or Pierre witnessing the execution of his fellow prisoners.

The most common effect of these optics is to render reality incomprehensible and absurd. When Pierre witnesses his father's death and the quarrel over his inheritance, he understands nothing of what is happening to him. When he participates in the battle of Borodino as a spectator, his eyes see on the battery redoubt the commander's corpse and the soldier taken prisoner; but they do not recognize anything. When Nikolai Rostov is wounded at Schöngraben, all of reality, seen through his eyes which do not understand, cracks, disconnects, falls apart, becomes confused and fragmentary—a flickering of appearances. "Suddenly, it was as though a broad fan of birch switches whipped the squadron. Rostov raised his saber ready to slash out, but, at that moment, the soldier Nikitenko, who galloped in front of him, outdistanced him, and Rostov had the sensation, as in a dream, of continuing to race with unnatural speed and at the same time remain fastened to the spot. Behind him, the well-known hussar Bandarchuk caught up with him at a gallop, throwing him an angry glance. Bandarchuk's horse veered and he continued galloping, going past Rostov. 'What does this mean? I've fallen, I'm dead . . .' Rostov asked and answered himself at the same time. He was alone by now amid the fields." But the most extraordinary effect is obtained in the scene of the prisoners' execution. Even though he sees and hears, Pierre refuses to see and hear: he removes the scene from the perception of his consciousness: in turn he does not hear the officers' commands, the burst of rifle fire, the screams of the condemned men, the French throwing the bodies into a ditch; thus the character's viewpoint leads to the cancellation of reality. Of the whole terrible scene, there remains only a shapeless *something*. We only know that "there was smoke, and some Frenchmen who, their faces pale, with trembling hands, did *something* around the ditch": "He saw smoke, blood, and the pale faces of Frenchmen, who again were doing *something* there near the column, with trembling hands, jostling each other": "The worker was unable to walk, they dragged him by the armpits, while he shouted *something*": "Around the worker, frightened, pale men did *something*."

II

A novelist has one quality in common with an actor: he is obsessed by gestures. If he closes his eyes, if he tries to forget himself and the world, withdrawing into the empty, pure core of his soul, all flight is closed to him: even in there, a crowd of people pursues him, opening and half closing their eyes, smiling, relaxing and contracting the creases on their foreheads, lifting the upper lip, walking on heels or tiptoes. Amid this multitude of gestures Tolstoy likes to seize the microscopic, almost invisible ones which elude the attention of the intellectual observer and say nothing to those who compose syntheses of reality. He knows that every man has a code of invisible signs; and that the novelist must understand which belong to each character and fix them with almost maniacal precision. If a character performs a single mistaken gesture, the whole novel runs the risk of failing. But to fix the gestures lightly and almost without attention as Pushkin did is not enough for him. Tolstoy must repeat them throughout the entire book, with a reiterating procedure of extraordinary delicacy, until they become the equivalent of the characters: a transparent symbolic signature which we shall never forget, like things contemplated at a moment of revelation.

Without realizing it, Tolstoy seems divided between two contrasting tensions. As he opens his narrator's eye, on the one hand the world of gestures reveals to him that it is a book in itself, which obeys its own laws, like any structure of signs, and cannot be transcribed in any other language, least of all in that of psychology. Tolstoy has almost erected a monument to the autonomous character of gestures: Bilibin's face in *War and Peace*, now his wrinkles, which "seem washed as neatly and scrupulously as fingertips after a bath," crease on his forehead in large pleats while his eyebrows descend and deep lines are etched in his cheeks. This laborious play of folds and wrinkles means nothing: it is the automatic movement of the face's muscles, which accompanies the laborious play of *bons mots*. We are in the realm of pure surface, of which Bilibin is the absolute sovereign. Everywhere in the novels we are struck by this inexplicable arbitrariness of gesture. When after her attempt to elope with Anatol, Natasha's heart is full of despair and shame, her face is calm, cold, dignified: when Karenin's heart is tormented, his raised eyebrows give his face an air of indifference: and with a grimace that is habitual to him old Bolkonsky's grief over his son's presumed death is expressed by the shadows of a choleric, rabid, and mean face and a "somewhat unnatural" voice.

On the other hand, Tolstoy is possessed by the opposite conviction. While he believes that men's words systematically lie, he is persuaded that looks, laughter, wrinkles, the tremor of muscles, the body's movement are custodians of the hidden truth. Instead of being pure and autonomous, every sign of the body thus becomes a psychological revelation. Sometimes we surprise in Tolstoy the follower of Lavater's or Balzac's physiognomics: as when from the springy step of a general he deduces his interest in women and society life, or when he affirms that men with a sanguine complexion, having reached a certain age, all weep in the same way, or when on the face of one of Vronsky's friends he sees "the calm, continued splendor" that is on the faces of successful people.* With this Lavaterian persuasion, the novelist must interrogate and plumb the surfaces, going back from the gestures to the soul they reveal. The examples are engraved in everyone's memory: Anna Karenina "half closes" her eyes when she wants to hide her desperate situation from herself; Karenin clasps his hands and cracks his knuckles, revealing his nature as an unhappy automaton.

*Physiognomics leaves even deeper traces in the *Diaries*. "For me the back is an important indication of physiognomy and above all the way it is joined to the neck: nowhere else can one see so well the lack of assurance and the falsification of a feeling" (June 9, 1856): "A rigid back is the sign of a passionate character" (June 21, 1856).

Percy Lubbock remarked regretfully that *War and Peace* and *Anna Karenina* do not contain the descriptive vistas so dear to Balzac and which are again found in *Madame Bovary* and Turgenev: those prodigious representations of exteriors and interiors in which we are not spared the shape and tone of a single piece of furniture, the cracks in a single wall, the smell of a single room, the curve of a single landscape, and at the various seasons of the year; those meticulous prehistories by which we are informed about every character's father, mother, youth, bank account, features of face and personality. We can still find a few descriptive passages in *Childhood* and in *The Sevastopol Tales*. In *War and Peace*, under the conjoined influence of Pushkin's and Stendhal's swift hands, the portraits of objects and characters, some admirable for their precision and subtlety, like those of Prince Andrei, Tushin, and Denisov, were almost all expunged in the course of the long elaborative process. Lubbock and many of Tolstoy's contemporaries did not understand what Chekhov understood immediately: Tolstoy's is a radical reform of narrative art. He, of all people, whose mind was so crowded with gestures, wanted to thin down the novel's substance, making it less dense and congested with objects—the Balzacian objects "so charged with distilled life," as Henry James said, "that we find ourselves dropping [them], in certain states of sensibility, as we drop an object unguardedly touched that startles us by being animate." The novel needs air, space, atmosphere around characters and events. The great Balzacian portraits subdivided the novel's execution between two different figures: the narrator and the essayist-describer who sometimes had difficulty collaborating, breaking up the continuity of novelistic time. The Tolstoyan reform is born from the absolute necessity of saving the novel's unity: except in the philosophic-historic digressions of *War and Peace*, the figure who narrates and describes must be the same, the description must melt into the narration as salts in water, time must continue its implacable, slow-fast rhythm. While we know everything about the Pension Vauquer, we do not know even one detail about the great houses in *War and Peace*, Lisye Gori and Otradnoe: and yet we live in them, breathe their atmosphere, as if they were the summer houses of our childhood and youth. As for the characters, having abolished all the prehistory of their lives, Tolstoy has recourse to a series of small touches, strewn throughout the novel, which often tend to have a symbolic value; or he looks at them through the eyes of other characters.*

Like Dickens, Tolstoy divided the crowd of his characters into two groups; those who are entitled to a physical portrait and those about whom we know only the atmosphere. According to this Dickensian paradox, the former are the minor characters. The first time we meet Lisa, Tolstoy writes: "Her pretty little upper lip, shadowed by a light fuzz, was a bit short in relation to the row of her teeth, but all the more charming when she lifted it and even more attractive when at times it jutted out and covered her lower lip. As always happens with truly attractive women her defects—the shortness of that lip and her half-open mouth—gave the impression of a beauty peculiar to her and to her alone." Again and again, Tolstoy goes back to that too-short lip, that charming shadow of fuzz; now he compares her face to that of a squirrel: now he dwells on the resplendent smile; and he takes the time to repeat these minute details even when the little princess is rigidified by death.

With these repeated touches, he creates a signature that accompanies Lisa and all other minor figures every time they appear on the stage: like a leitmotif, which in opera announces a character's appearance and reappearance. Thus, with a sovereign gesture of appropriation, he firmly takes possession of them: he does not tolerate their leaving his control, sentences them to being static, because the signature cannot be changed but only varied; and at the same time, he forbids himself and his readers to penetrate their souls, to know what they think and feel, forcing himself to see them only with the eye of the "external" narrator. In the end, our knowledge of Lisa is minimal; and we ask ourselves what might be hidden behind the little princess' short lip and light fuzz—she who is so soon carried off by death. I believe that Tolstoy got the cue for this iterative technique from Dickens' minor characters: Rosa Dartle with the scar on her face and Uriah Heep with his red eyes (*David Copperfield*) or Karker with his feline teeth (*Dombey and Son*). Nevertheless, the difference is great, for where Dickens plays on the signatures with a

*Tolstoy is not the prisoner of his own method. In *War and Peace* there are several ample physical portraits, such as those of Bilibin and Speransky.

fantastic power of grotesque variation and visionary intuition, Tolstoy hints at one of the thousand human mysteries that his discreet hand is content to touch on lightly.

Tolstoy has not left us any description of the principal characters of *War and Peace*. We just know that Prince Andrei is a not very tall young man, with an elegant and harmonious aspect and brusque manners: that Pierre is big, clumsy, and has two enormous red hands; and that Natasha as a young girl has a wide mouth, slim arms, black eyes and hair. Tolstoy wants his principal characters to live in the boundless freedom of their psychological abundance, able to move, develop, and change without being prisoners of a signature or a portrait. Our imagination must be free to body them forth as it pleases, starting from the few elements he offers it.*

This love for narrative objects leads Tolstoy to the same conclusion reached by Flaubert: restrict the role that the intellectual analysis of emotions had reserved for itself in the novel and dissolve it in the uninterrupted process of objective narration. Prince Andrei has dedicated several months of his life to Speransky's projects for reform. The day after the ball with Natasha, when Bitsky comes to tell him about the session of the State Council, a thought flits into his mind. "What does all this have to do with me and Bitsky, what does it matter to us here what the emperor chose to tell the State Council? Is this stuff going to make me any happier or better?" Then he goes to dinner in Speransky's small apartment, scrupulously clean like certain monastic quarters. As soon as he hears his acute ringing theatrical laughter, shakes his white hand, and sees from up close his glassy, impenetrable eyes, all the fascination that had tied him to Speransky vanishes, and he leaves the house. Another writer would have described the slow cooling of Prince Andrei's passion for reform by minutely analyzing the reasons for this estrangement. Tolstoy, on the contrary, completely eliminates the description of

*The characters' division into two groups is not repeated in *Anna Karenina*, where Tolstoy recurs less systematically to the iterative procedures of *War and Peace*. In *Resurrection*, however, Tolstoy applies his iterative procedures precisely to the two main characters. As for "Hadji Murad," he fashions a kind of epic formula: with the mountain people he indicates the shape of the eye, while with the Russian soldiers he describes the voices.

the psychological process that takes place in Andrei's mind: he replaces it by a number of physical sensations, which unfold with surprising rapidity and are its transparent objective correlative, and lets us ignore what had moved and profoundly agitated the life of the heart.

The most famous example of this tendency is in *Anna Karenina*. Anna has been in Moscow where she met Vronsky: she saw him again during her return journey, while the snowstorm enveloped the train: with joyful pride, frightened and happy, she listened to his passionate words; and now she returns to Petersburg. As soon as she gets off the train, the first face that attracts her attention is her husband's: "Oh, my goodness, why does he have ears like that?" she thinks, looking at his cold, representative figure and the cartilages of his ears which support the brim of his round hat. In the evening, back in her room, the same detail strikes her again: "But why do his ears stick out so strangely? Maybe he had his hair cut." We will never know whether Karenin really had a haircut; or whether, as is more likely, he always had such protruding ears. The aversion that Anna has always unconsciously felt for her husband, the amorous desire that is about to take possession of her—symbolically concentrate in this visual detail which strikes us with the violence of all gratuitous Tolstoyan objects.

Toward the end of *Anna Karenina*, Sergei Ivanovich, Levin's half-brother, falls in love with a friend of Kitty's, Varenka, and would like to marry her: but, at the same time, he would like to remain faithful to the memory of a juvenile love. One afternoon the two go to gather mushrooms in the woods. Sergei walks away among the birch trees and hazel-nut bushes, lights a cigar, and repeats to himself the rational motives that make marriage advisable. He comes to the edge of the wood, walks toward Varenka's pretty figure who, dressed in yellow, and lit by the vivid light from the sun's slanting rays, is walking with a light step toward the trunk of an old birch tree. Sergei thinks he has made his decision and is about to speak to her. Between the two falls a silence, which seems propitious to the declaration of love. Suddenly, against her will and as if by chance, Varenka begins to talk about mushrooms, and Sergei, he too against his will, answers: "I've heard it said that the whitecaps like to grow along the edges of the wood, although I can't tell a whitecap." Sergei feels that he must explain himself: he repeats in his mind all the arguments in favor of marriage, he tells himself again the words he has prepared: but instead of these words, because of a sudden thought that flashes through his mind, he asks: "And what's the difference between a whitecap and a birch mushroom?" Varenka's lips tremble with agitation as she replies: "There's no difference in the cap, but there is in the stalk." As soon as these words are uttered, they both understand that what was supposed to be said will never ever be said. Everything has taken place at the surface, a surface that a psychological novelist would have shattered to reveal the heart's secrets: the involuntary words, those that inhabit and stroll about by chance in our minds, decided Sergei's and Varenka's fate. Precisely the futile, insignificant conversation reveals the deep unconscious forces that roam in our soul, as many of our century's novelists will learn from Tolstoy.

Everything seems to reveal the presence in Tolstoy of a systematic procedure: the reticences and restrictions of the narrator's field, the recourse to the "external" narrator and to the characters' eyes, the love of gestures as symbols of the psyche, the minor characters' signatures, the choice of conversation in place of analysis—these instruments seem to make him the sovereign master of narrative surfaces. But as soon as we say something about Tolstoy, we must reverse it. Having reached the peak of his power, Tolstoy renounces the limited knowledge of gestures which has pleased him so much. Then it seems that no detail is able to convey the life of the soul; and that no physiognomy can help him. In the principal scenes of his books, Prince Andrei's and Anna Karenina's deaths or Pierre's imprisonment, only the novelist's divine omniscience penetrates the secrets of the "I," illuminates its dreams, its visions, its presentiments, its colloquy with death and heaven.

After his very bold attempt in the second of *The Sevastopol Tales*, Tolstoy ventures with ever greater passion into the part of the "I" that escapes the control of consciousness: casual, intermittent thoughts, states of semiwakefulness, the first and last flickers of sleep, deliriums, dreams. In *War and Peace* and *Anna Karenina*, he studies its states and functions with a breadth of vision that seems to conceal a general theory of the subconscious. The first stage is that of the consciousness abandoned to the freedom of associations, as in Anna Karenina's interior monologues. Here the mind appears to us like a vast and shapeless receptacle without the divisions that usually separate and channel impressions. Everything sinks into it confusedly: the shop signs seen from the carriage ("office and warehouse, dentist . . . fashions and dresses"): the casual thoughts aroused by the signs ("Filippov, doughnuts. They say they bring the dough to Petersburg. The water in Moscow is so good. And the wells and Mitishi's blini"): the fragmentary thoughts tied to the quarrel with Vronsky and the meeting with Dolly and Kitty ("Yes, I'll tell Dolly everything. She doesn't like Vronsky. I'll feel ashamed, I'll suffer, but I'll tell her everything"): the thoughts awakened by what Anna sees in the street ("At that moment she began to wonder what those two girls might be smiling so much about. About love, most likely? They don't know how troublesome it is, how petty it is . . ."): the immediate sensations that seize her ("What an awful smell this varnish has! Why don't they do anything but build and paint so much?"); plays on words ("*Tiutkin, coiffeur . . . Je me fais coiffeur par Tiutkin . . .*").

Anna's is not the monologue of the pure mind closed on itself, which works with the materials deposited there for some time: here the surface of the mind speaks, wholly open to the outside, almost lost in the outside environment, which works only from what daily reality offers to it. Gradually, this dissipation is attenuated: the mind concentrates itself, the shop signs and the passersby are forgotten; and Anna thinks again about Vronsky and Karenin, and the love and hatred that rage in men's hearts.

Prince Andrei's last delirium also takes place at the surfaces of the self. He lies in the silent half-darkness of the *isba*, his feverishly dilated eyes staring fixedly before him. A fly buzzes around his face: the buzz is transformed into music: a tenuous whispering voice which without ceasing, remorselessly, with always the same rhythm, repeats: "*Pee . . . tee. . . pee . . . tee . . . pee . . .*" and then *tee tee* and then again: *Pee . . . tee . . . tee, pee . . . tee*, and *tee tee*. This music becomes an invisible vision: it seems to him that precisely in the middle of his face, someone is erecting an aerial construction of very thin needles and motes, and that he must maintain his balance with great care so that the construction does not collapse: nevertheless, the construction does collapse, and then again, slowly, it rises at the sound of the voice's cadenced whisper. Finally, Timokhin, who is lying on the bench in his shirt, and Natasha, who opens the door and enters the *isba* in her nightgown, are in his eyes transformed into two white sphinxes. Prince Andrei's condition is the opposite of Anna's aggressive one: his mind is passive and ecstatic, the vulnerable victim of external representations and images that are born in it beyond all control of will and reason. Wakeful passivity is his visionary gift: he sees because he does not want, does not choose, does not order his impressions; the sovereign power of metamorphosis has risen in him and transforms the fly's buzz into the music of an aerial construction, Timokhin's shirt and Natasha's nightgown into white sphinxes, just as hashish provoked the uninterrupted play of analogies in Baudelaire's mind. But his is not a disconnected vision like Anna's monologue: Andrei's delirium contains an organization and an incipient harmony of motifs, which in reality are absent.

While a Cossack is sharpening his saber, Petya begins to close his eyes and nod his head. *Ozig zig, zig, Ozig, zig* . . . the saber hisses, against the whetstone, and while Petya enters sleep in a quiet, relaxed, passive spirit, the power of metamorphosis seizes him, as it seized the dying Prince Andrei. The hissing of the saber becomes an unknown hymn played by a hundred-piece orchestra: each instrument—like a violin or a trumpet, but more beautiful and limpid than violins and trumpets—performs its part and, bringing the motif to its end, is fused with another motif which it begins in an almost identical way, and then with a third, and a fourth, until they all blend together and then again scatter and again blend, now in a kind of liturgical solemnity, now into something airy, luminous, and triumphant. But then suddenly Petya's oneiric passivity is transformed into creative activity: instead of a pure passive receptacle, like Prince Andrei, he becomes an orchestra conductor, who tones down some sounds, then gives them greater vigor, *brio*, and joy, and finally makes the male and the female voices sing, commencing a rhythmic, solemn crescendo. This time, Tolstoy proposes to us an obvious antithesis. Everyday reality, which stands at the doors of sleep, is formed by fragmentary and disconnected details: the buzzes of flies, the hisses of a saber. On the other hand, the dream forms a complex and complicated order: a harmonious and symphonic construction of motifs, like that of the novels Tolstoy was writing.

So until now Tolstoy has appeared to us as a most lucid theoretician of the oneiric "form": gradually, as we venture into its innermost core, it reveals that it is organized and active like a work of art, rather than a pure random aggregation of images. But what is the "substance" of these dreams? The same as that of our waking life? Or another, radically different? Tolstoy takes a final step in two places of *War and Peace* and *Anna Karenina*. The heart of Pierre's two dreams during his imprisonment is a prophetic revelation: sentences like those of Delphi, or Gnostic texts, illuminate his mind, and, with the same margin of shadow and enigmatic solemnity, Tolstoy goes back to the origins of the oneiric world when it was the supreme means by which the deity revealed to men its ambivalent truths. As for the nightmare dreamed by Anna and Vronsky—the small peasant with the unkempt beard, rummaging in the sack and mumbling French words—it has a double character. On the one hand, it has a prophetic function, like Pierre's visions: the various details allude, each time, to what will happen or could happen to Anna—death in childbirth or her suicide under the train. But, on the other hand, it is immersed in the depths of the unconscious as no other passage in Tolstoy: one shudders because of the dreadful and sinister aura it still carries with it, even though it has reached the light. It reveals to us what the essential function of the dream is: to bring to the surface the great archetypes that live menacingly submerged in the abysses of our "I" and determine our life.

In the first part of *Madame Bovary*, Flaubert tried to deal a death blow to dialogue. Emma belongs to the visual realm, not that of words: in homage to his heroine, Flaubert imagined a novelistic pattern in which dialogue is abolished. In the first part of *Madame Bovary*, he salvaged some remnants of the spoken word, separated by quotes or in italics: or fragments of her voice transferred (by means of "free and direct speech," as the scholars say) into the narrator's voice. Thus he killed the role of the theatrical, which seemingly cannot be eliminated from any novel. Everything becomes narrative; and the novel—this varied, composite genre—is unified in the absolute figure of the narrator, who performs every possible function. At least in this matter, Tolstoy could not be further from Flaubert's attempt, for instead of abolishing dialogue, he strives to give it the greatest prominence, and increases his distance from the narrator's voice. And yet something vaguely Flaubertian marks his practice as an artist of the word. Especially in *War and Peace*, he has an appetite for *bons mots*, memorable remarks, famous sentences, or ones that could become famous: he hears a sentence in military or fashionable society, repeats it in a letter to his family, preserves it for years in his memory, or tracks it down to its historical sources; he uses it the first time in a partial form, then retouches it, reelaborates it, improves it, transforming it into one of those gems of idiocy or impertinence which every so often shine out in the life of words.

In the greater part of Tolstoy's novels, dialogue has another function. It does not reveal to us anything that we must entrust to memory: it is the voice of what passes and changes, it is fluid, inconsistent, and without structure. Several people are seated around a table in a beautiful country house: they talk about an outing in a boat, the regattas in Petersburg, work at the nearby hospital, the new American harvesters, the abuses of power in the United States and in the district councils; and we could stay there for hours listening to the hum of life, which Tolstoy has gathered in the sound box of his ears and now fixes on paper with incomparable elegance. Sometimes, as in Sergei Ivanovich and Varenka's case, we only listen to an apparent conversation: the true conversation is what unfolds beneath the spoken words; and we try to divine the sound of the real words that the characters are exchanging. Sometimes the dialogue is mendacious. The characters lie systematically, as happens in Proust: but, unlike Proust, where the implacable narrator-commentator intervenes each time that the apparent meaning of the words strays from their inner significance; Tolstoy leaves this task to us, his readers, his supreme collaborators.

III

There exists an original shape, a mental pattern by which every writer perceives the existence of reality. There are those who, like Balzac, see the world as a pile of massive tatters of torn flesh: those who see things being dissolved and annihilated in time's impasto; and those who see only geometric shapes—straight lines, circles, labyrinths, spirals. When Tolstoy looks at the world with his dilated eye, he sees atoms placed one next to the other: minimal, almost invisible details, which mysteriously fit into each other like the pieces of a puzzle; and the lines that join each piece are singularly evident. Where another writer sees the One, he sees the multiplex: in the place of time that flows without the slightest solution of continuity, he hears the minutes and seconds ticked off by the clock; instead of a compact cluster of sensations, he senses infinitely tiny sensations which in turn tend to break up into even tinier sensations; the causes of historical events subdivided into billions of subcauses, while each event loses itself in a mist of events. How can one write a novel; that is, a fictitious organization of events, when one is possessed by a mind like this? We never cease being amazed that Tolstoy has built such superb architectures as *War and Peace* and *Anna Karenina*, instead of losing himself in the infinite multiplication of existences, the indeterminate, the shapeless. While we admire the walls, vaults, buttresses, correspondences, connections, and relationships in these architectures, we must not forget the centrifugal force that animates them: they stand immobile before our eyes, despite the explosive force that, hidden, subterraneously undermines them.

If we were to ask ourselves how Tolstoy was able to introduce Time and Unity into this disconnected accumulation of atoms, we could only advance inadequate hypotheses. Not everything in the formation of a prodigious narrative capacity can be explained. Here, for what they are worth, are two hypotheses. Tolstoy's "small sensations," which in one way are unforeseeable, casual, and absolutely free, in another sense tend to come together in an iron chain of necessity. Old Bolkonsky's unnatural laughter, Lisa's lifted, fuzz-covered lip, and Marya's heavy step are the sign of the causality of existence as well as an iron cipher, which makes these characters prisoners of themselves, and therefore willing to be characters and become part of the story. In the second place, when Tolstoy looks at his atoms, he sees them immersed in a kind of impalpable fluid, a mysterious connective impasto, a secret music, like fish gliding wavily in their maternal marine element. This nameless fluid is something that certain writers perceive, others don't; and that Tolstoy, for the sake of being understood, calls "life." Thus, to evoke time in his books, he only has to render this musical fluid: he immerses events and characters in it: and single fragments lose their separateness, no longer show their point of suture, and dissolve in the breath of time.

Alongside this atomistic line, an opposite tendency lives in Tolstoy, which could have made him into a mystic of Being. In a late *Diary* notation, he writes that for God "the entire world is always the same." I as a child and I as an old man, my parents and their parents, and so on ad infinitum—all this has existed since always, immobile before God's eye. Our life, the life of the planet earth and everything that preceded it, the sun and what preceded it, and the end of the planet earth, and of the sun which will be extinguished, and so on ad infinitum—God is conscious of all this, without the restrictions of space and time. In this sense, Tolstoy also is like God. Natasha the little girl and Natasha the mother, Prince Andrei's dreams, his disappointments, and his death, Pierre's first dreams and their realization in the marriage with Natasha, Napoleon's youth and defeat, the Russia of 1805, and the Russia of 1820 are immobile and co-present, at an identical distance from his novelist's eye. All of *War and Peace* is like the globe of drops that appears to Pierre, where even the uninterrupted movement is seen at one glance, which reduces it to an atemporal phenomenon: the immense One–All dear to the gaze of mystics.

Tolstoy never represents the One–All, the immense chain of beings outside the reactions of space and time: or he represents it only once, in Pierre's dream, which constitutes a kind of novel inside the novel, at once the essence and negation of *War and Peace*. If he did represent it, every distinction between persons and forms of life, every inner limitation, and all resistance to reality, the very form of contraction that causes the birth of single beings, would dissolve; and Tolstoy would contemplate the Drop in which all drops are reflected and merged—God. But he is a man: a novelist. Just as men do not know the One–All in one glance, but see it in parts, distribute it in time and space, so Tolstoy can represent the immense Drop, the innumerable drops only divided and separated by time. With the deepest proclivities of his mind, both the atomistic and the mystical, he rejects time: and yet, every time, he immerses the "small sensations" and the One–All in the uninterrupted flow. The metaphor that best expresses his attitude is the image of God as the circle's center and circumference. Tolstoy occupies that same position: he is at every point of the circumference, in the small black velvet ribbon that encircles the girl's neck, in the hunting bitch that points, the mare that races, and such is his involvement that he seems to forget the rest of the universe; but, at the same time, he lives in the circle's motionless heart, where the world's pulse is gathered, and from which he contemplates with one glance the places of the circumference.

Thus time, accepted with a heavy heart, unfolds in the plenitude of its forces. It runs ahead, always further ahead: it never looks back, like one of those flashbacks* so dear to Dostoevsky, because by now Tolstoy has embraced the *chronos*, and the *chronos*' logic is that of never halting to reflect upon itself. Flaubert also embraces *chronos* and becomes its prisoner, much more so than Tolstoy: but he adopts the "eternal imperfect." He narrates the things that repeat themselves: the things that accumulate one upon the other: the consue-

*English in original—TRANS.

tudes and habits: life always the same, in which every morning Emma wakes up, arises, eats, comes, goes, consumes the same series of actions: life in which every day the schoolteacher, the hairdresser, the stagecoach horses appear at the same hour: the life in which the Rieule's water always flows with the same rhythm, noiselessly, with the tall thin grasses which bend like green hair: everything is like this forever, without end; and "time is a sleeping pond, so tranquil that the slightest event falling into it causes innumerable circles." Tolstoy does not love repeated time: he sets forth as seldom as possible the foreshortened views, the "summaries" as Genette calls them, the scenes in which a great quantity of time is deposited. He cultivates *chronos*, because every morning it is different and presents to us unrepeatable, absolutely singular actions, which will never again be reproduced. Not a single second resembles its neighbor: not a minute anticipates the next. Like Stevenson, he transfers the narration to the ideal plane of the present, as if everything took place at that very moment before his desirous eyes: he narrates events that cannot be repeated, passing from one present time to another present time, running from one new event to another equally new and absolutely fresh.

While he lets us discover the essence and enchantment of the present, Tolstoy awakens in us vaster feelings. Sometimes, he fixes the current scene so clearly and sharply that it halts before us, like a dried-up drop, while in the background time continues to flow. Sometimes, our impression is the opposite: such rapid reversals and changes occur in the scene—the great inner crises require but an instant in his novels—that they summon up the sound of a vertiginous allegro, a diabolical rush of minutes, while in the background the other aspect of *chronos* does not change its slow and even step.

At certain moments of the narration, the *chronos* becomes something that we can only define as sacred time. When the Rostovs spend the winter in the country at Otradnoe the plot comes to a halt: no novelistic action takes place: during the afternoon, Natasha is bored, then people in costume arrive, and there is the sleigh ride under the moon. Together with Natasha, we have come to the place where the rhythm of pure time beats and bare existence is revealed. Let us take one more step: Prince Andrei sees the quiet sky of

Austerlitz, Natasha wants to leap into the sky, Pierre dreams of the globe of drops, Levin roams the streets of Moscow before asking for Kitty's hand—"and what he saw then he never saw again." In these moments of ecstatic beatitude and the revelation of supreme truths, in these instants of epiphany, the characters of *War and Peace* and *Anna Karenina* experience a paradoxical transcendence in time. Immersed and sheathed in time, Tolstoy flees from time: if we gathered together the moments of epiphany in *War and Peace* and *Anna Karenina*, we could imagine what the representation of the One-All might have been for him. Any reader will immediately recall the analogous privileged minutes in *Remembrance of Things Past*: the madeleine and the stone in the Guermantes' courtyard. But there are two differences. The first is that Proust's protagonist experiences transcendence outside of time. The second is that for Proust the privileged minutes are the keystones and justification of *Remembrance*: whereas for Tolstoy they are only peaks that rise up out of the continuity of time. Characters and readers must leave them behind and immerse themselves again in the *chronos*.

When imagining *War and Peace* and *Anna Karenina* as an immobile One–All, Tolstoy's eye immediately perceives the relationships that hold together characters and motives. While Pierre dreams of the globe of drops, what strikes us is the complexity of their relationships. All the drops move, change place, expand, squeeze together, withdraw, and return to the surface: many fuse into a single drop, one subdivides into many; and all of them reflect God. But, when he narrates, Tolstoy must entrust the One–All to the conditions of time and space. Now for Tolstoy the essential property of time and space is to *separate*: Natasha's adolescence is separated from her childhood, Prince Andrei's love from his death: some live in Petersburg, some in Moscow, some at Otradnoe, some at Lisye Gori; while they perform a given act, the characters are prisoners of the moment in which they perform it, and are distanced from the characters who, at other moments, perform thousands of other acts. How can one obviate this fatal separation? With his both robust and wholly flexible mind, capable of flashing syntheses and infinite divarications, Tolstoy connects, brings into contact, ventures into the "infinite labyrinth of concatenations in which the essence of art consists." Now he delicately repeats the same motif to underline the unity in the same character's life: now, and it does not matter whether he does it consciously or unconsciously, he arranges that every motif is reflected in the mirror of all other possible motifs. If in his great novels Dickens multiplied the narrative centers, Tolstoy seems to want to emulate him: *War and Peace* has many novelistic centers, while *Anna Karenina* has at least two. But there is a capital difference: in order to unify these narrative centers, Dickens fashions dramatic intrigues, marvelously incredible plots that allow him to tie together all the narrative centers and characters. Instead, Tolstoy reduces dramatic structure, novelistic incredibilities, the play of coincidences (at least in *War and Peace* and in "Levin's novel") to the pure art of the linking of motifs. The result is that we encounter such great freedom and autonomy of scenes, at times structurally irrelevant, as perhaps in no other nineteenth-century novel. Any narrator of pure existence finds his model in the episodes about the Rostovs' country life, in the scene of the jams in *Anna Karenina*, or the story of Levin's shirt, for which in fact he was reproached by such a Balzacian and Jamesian critic as Percy Lubbock. On the other hand, Tolstoy never forgets to establish the narrative hierarchies: there are the foregrounds, the middle distances, and the backgrounds; the principal characters, whose every thought we know, and the secondary characters, about whom we know only the fuzzy lifted lip. We thus have the impression of walking in the only place in the universe where somehow the freedom, airiness, and levity of spaces are reconciled with the mind's invisible order.

PART FIVE

Old Age

I

Then came the terrible years: 1877, 1878, 1879. . . . While Tolstoy's heart was shrouded in clouds of anguish, while life, having come to a halt, turned against him and he saw not even a glimmer of hope on the horizon—his hand did not allow the slightest sign to escape. He was again keeping his *Diary*. On those pages, which from then on would become so numerous, filling up with the throng of his thoughts, he studied time: followed the colors and shadows of spring, of early and late summer, autumn, and incipient winter. Perhaps the thought flashed through his mind of renouncing everything—literature, doubts, thoughts, and anxieties—and remaining only the scrupulous and patient meteorologist of what the god in the sky made happen on the strip of earth around him.

In 1877, spring announced itself at the beginning of May, when, over a puddle about to dry up, appeared small, just-born butterflies—blue and mauve. Then the weather became fine, the water brown, the hemlock was covered with small white blossoms, the entire undergrowth of the old forest became a too-vivid green, evoking a strange sense of mystery and apprehension. If one walked on the meadows, invisible water lapped under one's feet. Absinthe sprouted. Coltsfoot swelled with buds, the walnut tree blossomed. The willow tree was laden with fragrance. The cuckoo sang. Grass grew, the rye paled: the tall flowers waited for the heat in order to lift their heads and bloom. The sun blossomed in the sky like the yolk of a hard egg. The oak tree was covered with new leaves. At four in the morning, on the meadow darkened by dew, wild wood sorrel gleamed with a dark splendor. At seven, under the sun's oblique rays, drops glistened on the tips of the blades of grass. The path through the undergrowth, black from being trampled, was covered by bunches of petals from the wild cherry trees which looked like snow. A little farther on in the forest a dark hare appeared: two doves came to rest on an oak tree and then flew off with a whir of wings, their reddish-white tails opened up like fans.

Then, suddenly, summer submerged the fragile spring which had barely blossomed. The wind agitated the boundless sea of rye; the dividing furrows could no longer be seen—but rather valleys, mountains, always the same undulant rye, alongside the other, gayer sea of oats with its yellow flowers. The heat became suffocating: midday was torrid; and in the afternoon flashes of heat-lightning began to appear. Rain fell thickly against the backdrop of the dark green forest, covered by a shadow. Dawn again, day came up again, a red and lilac sunset reappeared. At two o'clock, Tolstoy walked across the tall, rich pastures. There was silence, and a sweet enveloping fragrance—field mustard, with clover—predominated and stunned. The corn spread like milk: everywhere milky waves, wet rows extended confusedly and, alongside the white and scarlet corn, white butterflies fluttered. Among the trees, a bee sucked, one after the other, the flowers on a yellow umbrella. At the thirteenth flower, it flew off buzzing.

At the height of the summer, the nights grew dark. No birds: only crickets and dragonflies; while heat crushed the horizon. The sumptuous thistles began to blossom, the yellowing oats gleamed like precious stones: peasants sowed rye and bent over to cover it. A pigeon noisily flapped its wings, then flew off with a diffused noise. In the middle of August the nights were cold, the water frozen, the days clear, calm, and silent. Something moved in the shadow: an isolated leaf, cradled by a current of air—while the immobile water became transparent. The colors changed once more: the corn was the color of myrtle; the flax looked greenish from afar, reddish from the side, and brown close up. After the cold spells came moonlit nights: young saplings appeared around the oak trees, bright against the black, in the radiant light. In the *Diary*'s pages, for many months no sign revealed the storms in the heart. Then, on August 11, suddenly, an outburst. Three phrases underlined: "*Keep quiet*, *keep quiet*, and *keep quiet*." What did Tolstoy mean to say? Didn't he want to communicate, even to his *Diary*, the anguish that devoured him, the unspeakable thoughts, the nameless terrors? As he wrote later, Tolstoy could not accept the absurdity of life: to exist tragically and stoically in the nonsensical. He could not live tranquilly in a forest from which there was no exit. He had to search, question, knock at all doors, desperately pursue the meaning of things, wrap himself in his thoughts, travel the roads of the mind, and lose himself in them. He was a man lost in the forest, who is seized by the fear of being lost and thrashes about in all directions in the hope of finding the road again, knowing that every step takes him farther and farther away from it. He asked himself: "Did I perhaps neglect something, did I not understand something? Such despair cannot be the lot of all men." He searched for a long time, in torment, hastily, searched for answers to his questions in all the knowledge that men had acquired, as a dying man asks for his salvation from medicine. He found nothing. He begged, demanded, knocked, pounded: no one answered him—also because he was in such a hurry and had no time to listen to the answers.

His heart was besieged by a vexed, irksome feeling that he could only call the "search for God." It was a feeling of fear, solitude: he felt like an orphan in the midst of an alien world and hoped to receive some help from someone. He was absolutely convinced of the impossibility of demonstrating God's existence: Kant had declared this once and for all; and yet he searched for God, hoped to find Him, and out of old habit turned in prayer to the one he thought he looked for without being able to find. He asked himself: "What is this cause? This force? What should I think of it? What must be my relationship with the one I call God?" Only the already known answers came to his mind—"He is the creator, providence"—but they did not satisfy him. He was gripped by terror and began to pray to the one he had gone in search of so that He would help him. The more he prayed, the more obvious it was that He did not hear him and that there was no one to whom he could turn. With his heart full of anguish because God was not there, he continued to repeat: "Lord, have pity, save me! Teach me,

Lord!" He asked: "If You exist, then reveal to me what purpose have I, what am I?" He bowed to the ground, said all the prayers he knew, composed his own, and then added: "So reveal it to me!" He fell silent, waiting for an answer. There was no answer. And there was no one who could answer.

He was not saved by a divine revelation: the dazzling light on the road, the slight, very painful pang in the heart, a shock of the spirit, the body's trembling of which mystics speak. God remained closed in silence, and did not answer implorations and prayers. With an extreme act of intelligence, Tolstoy decided that God existed because he believed in Him. "It is enough for me to know that God is there and I live: it is enough for me to forget Him or not believe in Him, and then I die. . . . I live—really live—only when I feel Him in me and search for Him. So what more am I searching for?—A voice suddenly cried in me. Here He is, it is He. He is the one without whom one cannot live. To know God and to live is the same thing. God is life. You live searching for God, and so there will be no life without God."

This was a desperate solution, which gave him peace for a few years. But he sensed that, by itself, this very frail and intellectual faith could not be enough for him. He had the need to feel surrounded by the great family of believers, and to repeat the same gestures that, since time immemorial, all of Russia's faithful performed. Thus he recited his prayers morning and evening, rose early on Sunday to go to mass, bowed before the icons, went to confession, to communion, did not eat meat on Wednesday and Friday, talked with the pilgrims on the highway, visited the Optina Pustyn and Kiev monasteries.

11

What dismaying impressions are aroused in anyone who comes from reading *War and Peace* and *Anna Karenina* by the stories Tolstoy wrote in the 1880s! In those novels, even when destiny assaulted the creatures of light with the greatest ferocity, we had an impression of the freedom, richness, variety, and multiplicity of life's connections; and with what joy we traveled through the labyrinths. "Memoirs of a Madman," "The Death of Ivan Ilyich," "The Devil," and "The Kreutzer Sonata" are stories of an obsession: the obsession of psychological illness, of death, Eros, and hatred. As though he had forgotten the colors of springtime and summer, Tolstoy now lives penned up, the prisoner of reclusion, grimly triumphant about his claustromania. There is no freedom but instead constriction: we do not breathe but suffocate; the only journey we are allowed to take is the interminable train journey the hero takes in "The Kreutzer Sonata"—talking, blathering, smoking, cursing, without ever getting off. If in *War and Peace* and *Anna Karenina* Tolstoy intertwined all the different dimensions and tones, causing one to echo in the other—now he chooses a single dimension, a single tone, in masterpieces of gloomy monotony. Kafka liked some of these stories very much. In them there is a judge–defendant, who is preparing the briefs for an interminable trial. The defendant sits and rises, the witnesses for the prosecution (and there are no others) make their despositions, a frightening prosecuter declaims and points his finger, sinister officers of the court bustle about, the judge–defendant locks himself in chambers, very rarely is there a glimpse of even feeble light; and the entire trial is absolute and meticulous, abstract and mechanical, totally motivated and totally unmotivated, like the one Kafka set up thirty years later.

The obsession described in "Memoirs of a Madman" is without a cause. Nothing external determines it; and, although Tolstoy believes the contrary, there is no memory, no old or new psychological condition. The protagonist is attacked by one of those gloomy, nameless terrors that we find described in clinical texts on depression: in him every desire has suddenly become extinguished, every impulse, every force of life: all that is funereal and spectral erupting in his soul is transformed into the anguish of death; until, when he reaches the final stage, he discovers that life and death flow together to form a single thing. As happens in profound despressive states, this inner sensation assumes a physical form and is projected outside. Everything arouses his terror: the small white hotel seems sad to him and fills him with revulsion: the thought of the steps of the servant carrying the luggage gives him a feeling of acute anxiety: the spot on the hotel owner's cheek seems frightening to him; the small, clean, square, whitewashed room, with only one window and a red curtain, seems to him the most dreadful embodiment of existential horror. Through his anonymous character, Tolstoy for the first time makes a foray into the "square world": precisely he who had represented existence as something compact, sinuous, enfolding, circular, feminine. At one time, the square was for him the sign of abstract intelligence, of programs and purposes: now it becomes the embodiment of the horrors that burgeon within the walls of our mind.

In "The Death of Ivan Illyich," Tolstoy is the public prosecutor and the chief witness for the prosecution in the trial that death day in and day out brings against life. Some might contend that Tolstoy chose too facile a proceeding, putting in the dock a common man whose only dream is to resemble the mass of other human beings. But is the trial really so facile and its outcome so certain?

The charge that death brings against life is the most radical imaginable. Save for a brief gleam lost in a very distant childhood, existence does not exist. Man—or at least common man—does not live. Ivan Ilyich's only dream is amiability, the correctness and distinction of external forms. When he does something evil—a liaison with a milliner or a married woman, a bout of drinking, patronizing a *maison de passe*—it is the evil done by everyone; and his perfectly clean hands, his clean shirts, his graceful French words dispel all disagreeable shadows. When he should have political passions, no passion animates Ivan Ilyich: he is moderately liberal, in the same way that he knows how to play whist and grow a beard. When love and jealousy threaten to torture him, the circle traced by his clean hands and French words once more prevents him from experiencing the traumas of real life. So Ivan Ilyich rises at nine o'clock, drinks his coffee, reads his newspaper, dons his half-uniform, agreeably gliding over the surfaces of existence, without suspecting that down there, *behind there*, is something threatening and dark. As soon as he reaches the court, among colleagues and postulants, between public session and chambers, between tea, conversations, and card games, his formal existence triumphs: all the dreadful vital questions, all the sorrows and anxieties that come to his desk are emptied of all substance, transformed into abstract juridical matters. But Ivan Ilyich has yet to accomplish his masterpiece. He realizes it when he chooses his new apartment: he furnishes it in accordance with his taste, which is the taste of everyone else. The ample, high-ceilinged, old-style reception rooms, the comfortable study, the rooms for wife and daughter, the boy's study, the fireplace, *l'écran*, *l'étagère*, the dainty chairs scattered here and there, the large and small dishes hanging on the walls, the bronzes, tapestries, furniture, draperies—everything enchants him with its *comme il faut* character.

Now we understand why, through Tolstoy's mouth, death has chosen a common man as its defendant: precisely the "common" life, which seems so naive and defenseless, is the one that raises the most impenetrable barriers against death. Common life possesses a terrible suprapersonal strength, an almost anonymous compactness and assurance: made as it is of habits, formalisms, dismissals, and levity. When you question it about death, it answers that death is far away, one mustn't think about it, in a word, that it doesn't exist: when the corpse is laid out before your eyes—it answers that, yes, this is a dead man, but he is a minimal incident compared to the inexhaustible totality of existence, and meanwhile, as indeed happens in the first part of "Ivan Ilyich," it surrounds him with farce and mockery, like the cover fringed with tassels and braids, or the *pouf* with broken springs and covered in pink cretonne, on which faithful Peter Ivanovich sits down. So everything seems to be turned upside down: life, which death has wanted to convince of nonexistence, slips through death's fingers, flees, and proclaims that it is death that does not exist. For some time, the verdict remains undecided. But in the end, death is helped by chance. One day, when he is at the peak of his formal existence, Ivan Ilyich wants to show an upholsterer how the folds of a certain drape should fall: he climbs up on a small ladder, loses his balance, hits his side against the handle of the window, inflicting on himself—just for the sake of appearance—the contusion that will bring about his death.

In *War and Peace* Tolstoy tried to contemplate the realm of death, to understand what the metaphysical Other is. Here, however, death is the one who lives on earth, introduces itself into our bodies, and devours them; and Tolstoy describes it not with the eyes of an outsider but with those of one who is slowly dying. It suddenly enters the body of Ivan Ilyich: stays there, nestles in, accomplishes its consuming task, halts before him: looks at him and insists that he too look at it in the same way, fixed, petrified, straight in the eyes; look at it without doing anything and yet suffer unspeakably, both alone, shuddering. Every screen, temporary respite, or psychological evasion are of no help: for a brief time they seem to offer an escape, and immediately after they again become transparent, as though death could pierce through any sort of refuge and barrier. Living with death, Ivan Ilyich leaves behind the forms, appearances, and conventionalities which had so pleased him: he sees the sacred aura; and finally he lives a tragic life, which only a few of us know. The story of Ivan Ilyich is the symbolic story of every human being; but at the same time it is the story of Tolstoy who, in those years, felt himself invaded and penetrated by death, let it rise within him, and lived with it in pure obsessive solitude—staring at each other, sharing each other's thoughts—as no other person had lived.

The story of Ivan Ilyich comes to a close with a grandiose, full-bodied allegory. One night he has the impression that someone is pushing him forcefully, painfully into a narrow, dark, and deep bag, and is trying to push him ever more deeply inside and cannot quite manage it: on the one hand he resists and, on the other, he tries to facilitate the passage. During the last three days of his life, as he continues to thrash about inside the bag, he screams desperately: for three days and three nights in a row, without catching his breath, he continues to howl. He struggles like a man sentenced to death struggles in the hands of the executioner, knowing that he cannot save himself: from minute to minute he increasingly feels that, despite his efforts at rebellion, what fills him with horror is coming closer and closer. A voice inside him tries to show him that his entire life was a mistake: he rebels with all his strength against this sentence: but he understands that his conviction of being right prevents him from slipping out of the black hole. In the end, an unknown force strikes him in the chest and side: his breath cut off, he finds himself pushed farther down into the hole; and suddenly there, toward the distant opening, a gleam of light flares up, then an ever more radiant light. At that moment, all the pain and the terror of death ends. Death itself "ends," "is gone"; Ivan Ilyich becomes the master of death, just as Pierre Bezukhov was prevented from becoming that by a final weakness.

How should we interpret this ending? Does the common man, in whom we all recognize ourselves, at last repent for his blindness and his sin? Has he renounced his own justice, accepted death, and thus conquered death? Is the light that blesses him in the last lines the splendor of God that reveals the ultimate truth to him? I believe the ending is much more complex and problematic. Until his end, Ivan Ilyich has no merit whatsoever: it is neither his will nor his intelligence but rather an unknown force, which Tolstoy dare not mention, that allows him to get out of the bag. No God intervenes to save him or illuminate him: He is cruelly absent throughout the story, from beginning to end. Everything that happens here happens by the grace and will of death: it is death that frees Ivan Ilyich from the feeling of being just; it is death that fills the eyes of the man coming out of the bag with its radiant, deeply dark light, like the gleam of the candle during Anna Karenina's last instants. What this light means, what the "revelations of death" are, neither Tolstoy nor his readers can say. We can affirm only one thing. Precisely during these years of horror and terror spent in the solitary company of death, obscured by its shadow, Tolstoy found in it the one force capable of destroying it, of cancelling the distinction between darkness and light, and of helping him to come out into the splendor where all opposites dissolve. Tolstoy had never asked for nor received such a gift from any other human or divine power.

In the third and most atrocious of these trials, Tolstoy discovers in the depths of his "I" a smirking, blathering "man of the underground," who hates life and love: a double, similar to the person Dostoevsky had depicted, confined like a mouse in his sordid, fetid hole. During the years of *War and Peace* and *Anna Karenina* he had run to meet the world with loving arms: all the hatred, jealousy, fury, homicidal violence, nihilistic depravity he must have hidden and repressed in himself; the love for life having vanished, these repressed feelings violently gushed out into the light, and Tolstoy unleashes, exasperates, emphasizes them, as though no decent expression were enough to soothe him. But "The Kreutzer Sonata" is not a diary. With his admirable power of objective transposition, Tolstoy attributes his most unconfessable emotions to Pozdnyshev: clasps him close as no other character in his novels; and, at the same time, distances him from himself, makes him become somebody else, capable of obeying the rules of the story. We know his glittering eyes, which at times become flames: his half-smile or the smirk that curls his lips: the strange inarticulate sound, like hawking phlegm or a burst of laughter cut short; the strident, excited, maniacal, almost obscene voice. Without ever stopping, the voice confesses, accuses, accuses itself, describes his wife's murder. Meanwhile evening comes: night falls, in the carriage the candle goes out, the conductor douses it, the other travelers sleep: the train—this obsessive erotic nightmare—continues its interminable course; and in the night, the dark, the mechanical noise which envelops him on all sides, Pozdnyshev continues his interminable confession.

While hatred compels him to attack other bodies, Pozdnyshev seems completely possessed by his unconscious: his nocturnal logorrhea is his unconscious finding voice and expression. But, at the same time, he playacts: he dominates; controls, astutely doses the degree of his obsession, like the coldest, most hysterical and exhibitionistic of orators. Jealousy makes him desire to possess all the bodies and thoughts of all the others. When his jealousy is fatally frustrated, it imparts acuity to his sight, intensity to his hearing and to all his sensations; and confronted by the violence of those dilated, hallucinatory eyes, reality becomes transparent, reveals its mechanisms, its secrets, deceptions, and lies. We can fantasize that the jealous Pozdnyshev is none other than Tolstoy the artist; and that his prodigious capacity for interpretation was always a sublimated form of the jealousy of reality.

In the course of his nocturnal monologue, Pozdnyshev, in Tolstoy's name, throws mud on all the things that the creator of *War and Peace* had loved most tenderly. The luminous loves of youth: those looks, those smiles, that musical correspondence of bodies and souls, that ecstatic intoxication, that vibrant radiance which Eros still unknown but close by emanates around itself, as though to announce and veil its power: those moonlit nights when hearts open up—Pozdnyshev sees in all this only the base excitation of the senses, generated by too much food, by "all these jerseys," by naked shoulders and arms. As for sexual intercourse, it is a dark crime, which the two accomplices perform against each other. If the barriers between two human beings fall away, only the most ferocious hatred can be born, and Tolstoy sees the signs of this turpitude everywhere, in customs, music, and literature. Marriage, which Tolstoy had once excogitated to contain the fury of Eros, has become a fearful condemnation; the nausea, shame, tedium, and hostility of the honeymoon, the painful, irritating illnesses of the children, the quarrels over the children, the physical aversions between the spouses alternating with outbursts of bestial passion. The abject Pozdnyshev has only one moment of greatness, when his clairvoyance, hatred, and delirium culminate in the dream of mankind's total extinction.

Later in the morning, Pozdnyshev's voice grows calm. Some might imagine that he repents of his crime and his hatred, and that the account of his wife's murder was a catharsis through words. But, in reality, Pozdnyshev's story was a repetition of the murder: another murder committed with words, no less bloody than the first. The crime remains unavenged; and the Furies still whirl about around the corpse. But Tolstoy has not purified himself either. By representing his obsessions and objectifying the hatred concentrated in his heart for a lifetime, he nevertheless did not leave them behind. Like Pozdnyshev, he will go through the rest of his life with a poisoned, darkened heart.

III

The treatises in which Tolstoy tried to systematize his thoughts after the crisis were composed by a mediocre reasoner, a boring sophist and polemicist, a bad writer of passwords for the masses. As we go through these flat, rabid argumentations, we ask ourselves where Tolstoy has hidden his brilliant molecular intelligence. As though he enjoyed splitting himself into separate persons, he reserved it for the *Diaries*, which from those years on became the central undertaking of his life. Here speaks the inspired amateur philosopher: instead of laying claim to the architecture of a system, or composing a finished argumentation, or rounding it out neatly, the aphoristic thought finds pleasure in unilateral ideas, shines fervidly, then darkens, and starts again from scratch. Sometimes it seems to us that Tolstoy is trying out his pen on his notebook block, to see whether the ink secretes thoughts. He thinks as if he were gambling, advancing ever new hypotheses, putting down an even higher stake: a kind of youthful delirium lures him into its vortices; and with what intensity, fury, aspiration to knowledge, and desire for the All does he cultivate his delirium.

As happens with all inspired dilettantes, God is the beginning and end of his thought. This God is an *X*, an *as if*, an unknown: "But even though the meaning of this *X* is unknown to us, without this *X* not only can we not try to solve, we cannot even pose an equation." The mathematical terminology inherited from the times of speculation in *War and Peace* must not deceive us. If we understand it in its nucleus, the religious thought of Tolstoy in his last phase is the most robust and vital affirmation of negative theology ever to appear in the old West's exhausted heart. Like an Islamic or Hebrew mystic he affirms that he does not know God's name; and he does not in any way understand His nature. Any attempt to describe intellectually or to represent with images and words the *Deus absconditus* is bound to fail. Even the mystics' last refuge—God is one—gives way to his ferocious monotheism. We cannot affirm that God is one, because He is outside space and time, whereas one initiates number, which establishes space and time. If God is not one, He is not a person either (and much less one and three persons): He is not conscience, He is not will or reason: He is not the creator ("the world was not created"); He is not love—since love is only our yearning for Him. Since God is outside space and time, we cannot even say that He is omnipresent and eternal.

With his cruel deductive skill, Tolstoy carries negative theology to its extreme consequences, to that abyss of nullity and darkness toward which it was always headed. If it is impossible to define God, one might as well, he declared in a passage of his *Diaries*, free oneself of the notion of Him: "The more sincerely I think, sincerely about myself, about life and its beginnings, the less I need and the more I am perturbed by the notion of God. The closer one gets to Him, the less one sees Him" (September 27, 1894). A few days later he rejected this temptation, which has assailed so many religious spirits. "The devil was on the point of snaring me. In my work on *Catechism* he suggested to me that one can do without the notion of God, of God who is at the basis of everything . . . , and suddenly I was overcome by disheartenment and fear. I was fearful, began reflecting, thought things over, and once again found the God I was about to lose, and it is almost as though I had conquered and loved Him again." Certainly, temptation was defeated forever. But this does not change the nature of *Deus absconditus*. This is an extremely cold and unseizable point, lost in the depths of nonspace: a single star of absence, a single icy love, swathed in emptiness, woven from the void.

Is it possible to love a God who does not love us? Is it possible to address that frigid, nameless star, incomprehensible and unknowable, with an élan and fervor that are never reciprocated? Tolstoy knows how difficult it is: yet, now and then, he notes in his *Diary*: "For the first time, I have felt the possibility of loving God"; "This summer I experienced this feeling for the first time, really the feeling of love for God." It is the sensation that a child experiences in his mother's arms: he does not know who holds him, warms him, suckles him, but he knows there is someone but it is not enough to say he knows it—he loves it. "This is the only love that knows no stopping, no diminution, no sensuality, no tergiversation, no servilism, no fear, no self-satisfaction." There are moments—moments of suffering, almost of anguish, as has always happened with mystics—in which he is acutely aware of His passage. While he dozes, it seems to him that something in his heart breaks: or it is a shock or blow; or He slowly pours into him, as in John's Gospel the water gushes into eternal life.

He loves to turn to God and pray to Him. "If God did not exist, it would still be good to turn like this to the impersonal void." Sometimes he insists that one can only pray to Him without words: "To pray with words is to express thoughts about God. Now, thinking about God is impossible." At other times he writes his prayers in the *Diary*, hidden among the passages and colors of time. "What am I doing, thrown into this world? To whom shall I turn? Whom will I ask for an answer? Men? They do not know. They laugh, do not want to know—they say: 'These are bagatelles. Don't think about it. Look at the world and its pleasures. Live.' But men will not deceive me. I know that they do not believe what they say. They torment themselves as I do and suffer from the fear of death, the fear of themselves, and of You, Lord, whom they do not want to name. I too have remained a long time without naming You, and for long I did as they do. I know this deceit, and how it oppresses the heart, and how terrible is the fire of despair hidden in the heart of one who does not name You. And with whatever water it may be doused, it will consume their inner being as it consumed me. But, Lord, I have named You, and my sufferings have come to an end. My despair is gone. I curse my weaknesses, I seek Your way . . . , I feel Your closeness when I walk Your paths, or Your forgiveness when I deviate from them. Your path is clear and simple. Your yoke is benevolent and Your burden light. . . ."

The fact that God is so dark and incomprehensible leads to a consequence, which some mystics would have excluded. That dark remote star generates in men and in life the impetus of a desire and an uninterrupted movement toward Him, a vain striving to understand Him. "If I were able to understand, this would mean that I have reached Him, and I would no longer have anything to strive toward, that is, there would no longer be life." Negative mysticism arouses an insatiable *Streben*,* as a less Faustian spirit than Tolstoy would have said. So he records with extraordinary joy a dream, which is the exact reversal of Pierre's dream during his imprisonment: "Human life is not what I thought: it is not a circle or a sphere with a center, but a part or section of an infinite curve in which what I see, what I understand has the appearance of a sphere" (January 31, 1890). Or he insists, merging the image of the circle with that of the ellipse: "Life is never motionless, but it advances always and incessantly, it advances in circles, which, one might say, causes everything that lives to return, through annihilation, toward previous nonexistence. In reality, these circles, by their appearances and disappearances, form other circles, new circles, larger circles, which, they too rising and being annihilated, form even larger circles, and so on ad infinitum, upward and downward." The spirit animating Tolstoy is that of an ever resurgent Utopia: "How beautiful," he wrote to a friend, "is Schiller's sentence: 'True is only that which has not yet happened.' "

Alongside this religious tendency, the opposite tendency lives in Tolstoy's soul; and only the extraordinary vastness of his spirit permits him to be inhabited by these two contradictory impulses. God is no longer the very remote unattainable point that the mind cannot understand: He is the close vastness of the universe itself, the extension of all present, past, and future bodies and souls. Once to defend somehow God's loftiness, he has recourse to a curious comparison. "This is how I represent to myself the life of the world: a liquid, gas, or light circulating through all sorts of innumerable small tubes. This light is wholly the life force—God. We are these tubes, all beings. . . . " More often, even this fragile screen collapses: God is

*Striving—TRANS.

nothing else but life, ourselves. "What a mistake and how habitual: to think and say: *I live*. It is not I who lives but God who lives in me. *I pass* through life. . . . " "Our life and the entire world are God's respiration. He and I are the same thing." If God is the All, an intoxicated élan of expansion compels Tolstoy, as at the time of *War and Peace*, to come out of himself, broaden and break his confines, establish an ever greater, intenser bond with the All and lose himself in the single body of living matter. At times, he senses an obstacle: there is in his ego a certain imperfection, something crude, coarse, unrefined, some sharp corners (his very acute spirit of limitation) that prevent him from coinciding with the Immense. He hopes to refine his spiritual–vital matter and lose himself completely. But would he really lose himself? Or instead would he encompass in himself the entire world? "If I were not limited by the confines of space, there would not be matter and I would be everything, and there would not be life." In the great Tolstoyan Pan-like impulse, there is always the danger that the extension of the universe may become a prolongation of the narcissistic "I," which flaunts its shapes and colors.

When he abandons himself to the amorous impulse—an undifferentiated impulse toward everybody and nobody—Tolstoy physically senses the falling away of all limits and all barriers that keep him in the jail of his self. Then, he becomes God: he is His "organ, rib cage, and all of His body." His sensation is even deeper: he does not become God, he has always been God, because no one ever cut "the umbilical cord" that tied him to Him. Thus Tolstoy, who earlier had indefinitely distanced God from man, affirms man's integral deification. From his imaginary reading of the prologue to John's Gospel he deduces that the Logos is intellect: and he proclaims that reason is the truly divine part of man. With contempt, he rejects faith.

Although these conclusions belong to the mediocre aspect of Tolstoy's religious thought, he is animated by the grandiose boldness, or perhaps the grandiose and involuntary madness, of making two extreme religious conceptions coexist: the remoteness and nearness, the darkness and light of God, the failure of reason and its triumph; negative theology and pantheistic rationalism. He negates the Trinity, Christ's divinity and incarnation, redemption, resurrection, all dogmas, all sacraments, all symbols—the heritage that the delicate and patient hands of centuries had wrought to make possible something so absurd as the thought of God. With the mad childish arrogance of being the Fifth Evangelist (the only true one), he "improves," simplifies, rationalizes the Gospel, making it mediocre, verbose, without style, reality, symbols, and aura. Never as in these writings does Tolstoy seem to us so blind, vulgar, stubborn, limited, quibbling, crude, and fanatical. But we must not forget that his intentions are twofold. Now he is a mediocre man of the Enlightenment, who wants to destroy, as he had dreamed in the Crimea, any and all transcendence and metaphysics. Now the Voltaire in him writes, unknowingly, at the service of St. John of the Cross or the Attar. If he denies Christ's divinity with such Islamic violence, it is because he wants to abolish all mediations, all the bridges that, over the centuries, tried to bring God close to man. The God without name must remain up there, high up, in His darkness, His silence, His ineffableness, His absolute transcendence vis-à-vis man.

As when he was fifteen years old, Tolstoy thought that time and space were not substantial realities but simply forms of our minds. He never loved them. He thought them the sign of the fatal inferiority of human intelligence, which can think only through them, and is unable to imagine the infinite. And yet he believed that, despite the incarceration of these barriers, the supreme spark of our spirit was extratemporal and extraspatial; and he endeavored to think without them. He already found presentiments in his daily life: the dream, which with ever greater frequency visited him in old age, was a model of extratemporal and extraspatial life; in the dream he was simultaneously in Moscow and Kazan and conversed with people who were dead for a generation. During his last years he lost his memory: he did not remember his past, his writings; and he was happy about it, because it seemed to him he had finally freed himself of the old chains. Like his characters, he had known the only instants of full existence by living in the moments of the present: then, the memory of and repentance for the past were forgotten, the expectation or fear of the future did not hound him; with the vital plentitude of youth and the mystic's ecstasy, he embraced the moment, *was* the moment. Often he must have dreamed of a life thus composed of only ecstatic moments without relapses into time. He had no illusions: if he had been able to attain it, he would have possessed God's sight himself. He continued to think about death, which after many years still seemed to him something paradoxical and inexplicable. It was absurd to die. Now he morbidly caressed the thought of it, indulged in it, and wrapped himself up in it: now he was afraid of dying: now he wished for it: now he dreamed about a slow and tender death: now he feared that in dying God would be extinguished in him; now, looking at nature—the fresh grass under his feet, stars in the sky, the perfume of blossoming laburnum, the trills of nightingales, the buzz of beetles, the cries of the cuckoo—he thought that *on the other side* he would find the same vital exuberance. Before going to bed, he wrote in his *Diary*: "If I'll be alive tomorrow," "If I'll be alive." And on the morrow: "I am alive." For him every day was a tatter of time wrested from death; he lived it as if it were the last, forgetting past and future; lived it like a miracle that against all probability, continuously repeated itself again and again. Sometimes, the old dream of immortality tempted him again. "I tried to fall asleep and I cannot because I ask myself: 'Am I falling asleep?'—That is, I have full consciousness of myself, and consciousness is life. When I will be close to death, if I have consciousness of myself I will not die."

If he reflected on the totality of life, he saw it as a series of progressive incarnations. "In a previous existence, not being a man, I loved what constitutes man's spiritual being, and I passed from an inferior degree of reality to the one I loved. Now I love something higher and I will go on to the form of existence that corresponds to my spirit. And so there can be innumerable quantities of the forms of existence." Or perhaps it was better to think of existence as dreams, dovetail one into the other: dreaming that he had lived a previous life of which he remembered nothing: *this* life was the awakening from that dream: in this life, death represented the awakening from the new dream which was our life; and so on ad infinitum, slowly coming closer to unknowable reality. What had happened before this existence? He fixed his eyes on the dense fog of his past, in which could be discovered a few small islands, on which appeared men and objects, surrounded on all sides by that impenetrable fog. He searched there mainly to discover some memory or recollection of his previous life—gleams, flashes, intuitions outside time. He was certain that what he saw he had already seen at another time: what he loved he had already loved: all his thoughts he had already thought; and he had inherited his inner form itself from a previous life. His curiosity was equally aroused by what happened close to him, in a sphere or ellipse close to his. Once he traveled on the top deck of a streetcar, looking at the houses, signs, stores, coachmen, passersby on foot or in a carriage, and suddenly he understood with the greatest clarity that this world with his existence in it was but one of the innumerable worlds rotating in the universe.

In a few hours he would awaken from the dream of this life. His awakening would not last long, because immediately after he would live another dream. But, in that instant, his eyes lucid and wide open, he would understand that the sequence of human existences is a series of theatrical, phantomatic, and illusory representations, like the performances repeated every night in the theaters of our world. In that instant, freeing himself from the confines of his shape, he would leap out of space and time: the divine particle, which inhabited his body, would approach—no matter if only for an instant—God, striving for complete fusion with him. It was a desperate attempt to grasp the inconceivable: in which we still sense the echo of the great narrative intuitions of *Anna Karenina* and "The Death of Ivan Ilyich"—those gleams, those dazzles of light, which pierce one, passing from life into death. Then, one must go back to life. The *Diaries* swarm with contradictory hypotheses, as though the old gambler did not know what card to play. Sometimes he was certain he would be reborn in the same form: "In the world an *infinite* quantity of combinations and phenomena of all kinds is produced. I am one of them. I will disappear, but time is infinite and later on the same combination, the same 'I' must appear again at the end of an infinite time. Now the infinite time during which I will not be is for me the blink of an eye. Consequently I will always be, I will fall asleep and immediately after I will reawaken." Perhaps he would be reborn in a new form, distinguished from the others as he was now. Or—this was a hope in which he did not dare believe—in dying, leaping to the *other side*, he would find that time no longer existed ("time exists only in this form of life"); and he would lose himself in the flow of existence, in the fusion in God without intermediaries, the beloved Nirvana.

He read the *Tao Te Ching*; in it he found thoughts that he had imagined without knowing this book—the involuntary Taoist at the time of *War and Peace*. How could he help but share in the praise of flexibility and weakness, of mobile, formless water? "When man is born he is flexible and weak, when he is rigid and strong he dies. When trees are born, they are flexible and tender. When they become dry and hard, they die. Rigidity and strength are the companions of death. Softness and weakness are the companions of life." "This is how one must be—like water. No obstacles—water flows: a barrier, water halts. The barrier breaks—water flows: a square receptacle—it is square; round, it is round. And therefore it is more important than anything and stronger than anything."

So, in the *Diaries*, bringing the ideas of his youth to ripeness under the light of this pellucid Oriental mirror, he criticized all ethics of intelligence, will, effort, and good works. We must not set—he said—determined and precise ends for our life: nor plan this or that good work: "The works that must be planned ahead, the works to which one must turn one's mind before performing them, and which one must calculate, are not important works, are not vital works, they are works in which there is nothing good or bad, and therefore they cannot ransom anything." When we do good, we do it unconsciously and almost by chance. God's kingdom is not a ploughman who turns to look back: the man who does God's will always ignores what the visible consequences of his actions will be. His eyes are always blindfolded; and the blinder he is, the better he fulfills the celestial will: "The typographers who do not know the language compose better without trying to guess at the meaning in their own fashion. It is like this that one must live—without trying to guess at the meaning of that which one does—not make conjectures about works claimed to be necessary to God, but do one thing at a time, what God commands—compose letter by letter, and the meaning of the whole will not be given by me but by Him." The sole good work consists in opening the skylight through which one sees God. There is nothing worse than putting oneself out, tormenting oneself, struggling in the name of the Good—relying on our strength alone. We must not convert anyone. If we try to do so, we bring about very serious evils. As the Gospel said: "No one can come, if the Father who sent me does not call him."

What matters is to accept God's will. Desire nothing, obey, accept with love all that is asked of us: do what is necessary, what we need, what our vocation irresistibly leads us to. "You fret, you struggle, always because you want to swim in a direction that is not yours. Now close by, incessantly, and close to everyone, the divine descends, an infinite torrent of love, always in one and the same external direction. When you have exhausted yourself in attempts to do something for yourself, to flee, to be safe, abandon all the directions that are yours, plunge into this torrent and it will carry you, and you will feel that there are no limits, that you are forever tranquil and free and happy." When we become so mobilely and fluidly passive, we will achieve the heart's supreme quality: joy, calm, tranquillity, the capacity to act with ease and effortlessly, as though action were spontaneously pouring from the fount of Being. Then we will no longer propose great actions for ourselves: to love all of mankind, be industrious and abstinent. "One can perform a great wickedness, but all good works can only be small." What counts in every good work is its formal perfection: the love, attention, fullness, and precision with which it is performed.

Tolstoy did not apply this admirable breviary to his own life. He was not as weak as a young shoot, and mobile as water. He was not gay, calm, tranquil. He planned, set himself goals, acted goaded by purpose, with open eyes: he strove, tormented himself, tortured himself, tried to convert, attempted great actions. But coherence is the characteristic of gods, not of men. For us it is enough that the force of contradiction carried Tolstoy where no one would ever have imagined that he could go.

IV

In spring and summer Tolstoy rose early, trying to escape the prying eyes of other early risers who were visiting Yasnaya Polyana. In the pocket of his blouse he always kept a small pad: while he roamed the nearby forest, if some thought crossed his mind, he suddenly stopped to make a note of it: a thought about time perhaps, or death, or the future life. An hour later he came back, his clothes impregnated with the smell of the fields and woods: he carried some flower with him and every so often raised it to his nostrils to sniff it.

The visitor having come from nearby or afar—Chekhov, Rilke, Bunin, or Gorky, an English politician, an Italian psychiatrist, an apostle of some faith, an inventor of some invention, an Australian or Argentine journalist, a young Nihilist—came to meet him on the lane. He saw at first amid the linden trees a small white spot, like that cast by the sun on a wall through a thicket of trees. The spot became larger, passed alternately into the shadow of the linden trees and then into the light. It approached slowly, leaning on the cane, like a slightly weary wayfarer. Finally an old man with a huge white beard arrived, his step still youthful, his legs slightly bowed, dressed in a long blouse and pants so wide that one could mistake them for Turkish pantaloons. Tolstoy stared at the known or unknown visitor: from the forest of his eyebrows came a hard glance, not good, impenetrable, very acute, a "wolf's look," which gave the impression of a gimlet drilling into the mind; Turgenev said that it seemed one could see its tip coming out through the nape of the neck. Then the scene changed. Tolstoy assumed a strange paternal air: he bent a bit forward, proffered or rather threw at the visitor a large, wrinkled, gnarled hand in which he limply enclosed his. He smiled with an enchanting and good smile, a bit sad and full of compassion, while the visitor realized that that dreadful look was simply precise.

With the graciousness of an old gentleman, Tolstoy invited the visitor to come inside, pointed to a chair, and began to listen to him. As soon as the subject of the conversation became serious he lit up: his face quivered, his eyes shone brightly with all their nuanced colors; meanwhile he moved his carpenter's or stonecutter's hands, waved his fingers, slowly clenched into a fist, then suddenly opened them again and pronounced a beautiful folk word, rich in meaning and elegantly precise. If Tolstoy wanted to please, he could do so more easily than a beautiful woman: he played his verbal orchestra with its thousand instruments, spoke about Lao-Tze and Buddha, Pushkin and Maupassant, depicted murderous characters, recounted adventures from his youth, anecdotes of high society, alternating flute, violin, bass, drum, like an extraordinary man–orchestra. Chekhov, perhaps, was the most fascinated of all. He loved Tolstoy with a deep and ingenuous love: he tried to be liked by him; and, when he went to see him at Gaspra, he made very minute preparations and had a thousand hesitations about his attire. He tried on one suit, then another: came out of the bedroom to look at himself in the mirror. "No, really, these pants are too narrow. He'll think I'm a fop." He put on another suit and said to himself, laughing: "And these are wider than the Black Sea. He'll think I'm an impertinent oaf."

How many images of Tolstoy's old age have come down to us: thousands of images captured by Sonya's or Vladimir Chertkov's jealousy or a railroad-station photographer, paintings, sculptures, souvenirs left behind by the thousands of people who visited Yasnaya Polyana for a day or a week and wrote down their impressions. Often in the morning he was very gay: "How happy Papa is this morning!" Alexandra observed. Sonya, ironic, wrote in her *Diary*: "If Alexandra knew that her father is always happy for the same reason—because of that love which in words he denies!" Immediately afterward he played tennis for three uninterrupted hours. He got great joy out of riding the bicycle: it had been presented to him by the Muscovite Society of Velocipede Fans. When his faithful disciple Chertkov criticized him ("Does he not in this way put himself in contradiction with his Christian ideal?"), Tolstoy defended himself: "I feel that there is in this a natural fantasy on my part, and that there is no sin in amusing oneself simply, like a small boy." He read with interest the *Letters on the Velocipede Game Considered as Physical Exercise* by K. L. Popov; he went to the bicycle track at Tula, where he talked about the races with everyone. But horseback riding was his great passion. When he raced on his favorite Delirio, he leaped over ditches and ran through the densest forests among oaks and huge maple trees, choosing very narrow paths. When he came across a brook, he urged Delirio without hesitation and jumped over the obstacle. He rode up the steepest inclines at great speed: raced among thickets and trees, risking at every moment to kill or blind himself: "Everything all right?" he shouted, turning around. "Everything's perfect," his daughter answered.

To some people he seemed a chthonic demon, a mysterious god of the elements. Dressed in a sheepskin coat and felt boots, he had the air of a Scythian chieftain: when he suddenly appeared from behind the door with the light, swift step of one who is used to walking on the bare fields, he looked like a gnome. Gorky once saw him on the Crimean beach, sitting on the rocks with his chin resting on his hand—his silver beard flowed between his fingers—he looked into the distance, toward the sea, while small, greenish waves rolled quietly at his feet, almost speaking to the old magician. In a moment of exaltation Gorky imagined that Tolstoy, like a primeval god, would lift his hand and at that gesture the sea would coagulate, turning into glass, while the rocks in tumult would begin to howl and everything around him would become animated.

We also know sadder images. At the time of his religious crisis he sat at his desk amid copies of the New Testament and books of theological and dogmatic exegesis. He remained there until dinner time: his health waned, he suffered from headaches, lost weight, and one could see his hair turning white from day to day: he no longer had those fits of vivacity and gaiety which were everyone's delight, and his eyes stared sadly into the void, looking at something that continued to elude him. He worked like a peasant in the fields of

Yasnaya Polyana. He chopped trees in the forest, sawed the huge oaks at their base, transported them, and built *isbas*. He carried manure on the land of widowed peasant women, worked with a primitive plough, sowed wheat, rye, and oats, cut grass with his scythe with a group of peasants, and sent the hay to the poorest families in the village. In a small room adjacent to his study he set up a cobbler's bench. Every day at a fixed hour a cobbler came: and master and apprentice sat next to each other on their stools. Work began: the leather must be tarred, cobbled, and beaten, the soles nailed, the heels assembled.

He did not like to live in Moscow. His house was close to three factories. Every morning at five o'clock you heard the whistle of a siren: then two, three, ten, countless times; at that sound men, women, old people, children, who slept confusedly in damp cellars, got up in the darkness and rushed to the factory to do work which never seemed to end, remaining for twelve hours in the heat, suffocation, and mud. At eight o'clock another whistle: a half-hour's rest. At noon a third whistle: one hour for the meal. At eight in the evening the fourth whistle: the end. As if to expiate his guilt over that inhuman labor, Tolstoy rose in the dark, went down into the courtyard to draw water, pulled an enormous bucket on a small sled, filled the house's pitchers, chopped wood for the stoves, tidied his room, and shined his boots. In the afternoon, he left the house in worker's clothes. Crossing the frozen river, he went up on Sparrow Hill white with snow—from that hill Napoleon had contemplated Moscow—and there he sawed wood together with some old muzhiks who had become woodcutters in the big city. In those years he descended into the world's lower depths, where wounds, evil, and sorrow gather to fester: attracted by curiosity, pity, a profound feeling of guilt, and a no less profound complicity with the sordid and shady. He visited the small working-class streets, the wretched neighborhoods, the markets frequented by beggars and thieves, the houses of ill repute, the five-kopek dormitories. The spectacle was dreadful, because of its misery, filth, and vice: everywhere a suffocating stench, lack of space, alcoholism, and promiscuity; and on all those faces the same docility, the same fear, the same guilt. Like Dostoevsky in London, he met child prostitutes. He saw one of them, as big as his thirteen-year-old daughter Masha. Her dress was filthy and tattered, her voice hoarse like a drunkard's, her face gray, old, savage, her nose flattened, and she was smoking a cigarette.

Every day he wrote in his *Diary*: in fact two diaries, a smaller one that he reserved for the immediate stenography of his thoughts; and another where he elaborated the first notations. Sonya kept a diary, Tanya had another; also Masha and Alexandra; while the doctor and secretaries did not fail to write down in other notebooks everything that happened before their eyes. Some of them dreamed of spending the time of day reading to each other these diaries, where they deposited the minutest events at Yasnaya Polyana and the confused needs for improvement. Tolstoy tried to conceal the secret notebook from his wife's jealousy and hid it in a boot. But that was perfectly useless, for afterward he himself asked his daughter Masha to copy part of the *Diaries* and sent them to Chertkov, who would extract from them some moral pamphlets. So his life lost every trace of privacy: there was nothing that wasn't read or printed; everyday existence was like a theatrical spectacle for the enjoyment of the audience. And in any event, Tolstoy's *Diary* was not one of those examinations of the inner life, in which the soul is followed at every startled moment: he could only confess in the third person, transposed into a novelistic figure. In these pages which always speak about him, what is most striking is the meticulous rendering of accounts. He needed to be accompanied by a mirror more faithful than the keeper of an archive, which would record his every gesture. He, of all people, who had declared that he lived only in the present, did not allow the present to slip away and remain alive only in the memory, and wrote it down, annotated it, transcribed it, to be sure he had lived.

Tolstoy had an unusual, almost miraculous sense of form: form of the meticulous, spacious mind, form of brilliant, paradoxical thought, form of irony, the manifold or twofold form of the great novels: until the end of his life he insisted that what matters in the virtuous deed is its formal quality; however, in his activity as preacher and polemicist he gave proof of a deplorable lack of formal sense—confused, verbose, complaining, sentimental, querulous, litigious, prolix. Perhaps the reason for his wretchedness is a desire for which men have always paid bitterly. He wanted to be the nineteenth-century Christ; and he acted out the part of Christ for us. When he remembered family quarrels, he applied John's words to himself: "They have taken to hate me without motive." If he thought of his fate as an apostle in Russia, he described himself in his fashion—"insulted, martyred, crucified, despised by all and nevertheless just." He reflected on his doctrine, he was certain that he would arm son against father, brother against brother, like the doctrine of Christ. Despite the intensity of his religious intuition, his faith was hasty and impatient: he shouted with an ostentatious quarrelsome voice: he preached before the mirror, journalists, photographers, cinematographers, and the phonograph which the world's inventors laid at his feet.

He had admirably proven that no techniques for living exist: military strategy, politics, morality, and pedagogy are all immense illusions; and it was precisely he who, in order to overcome his anguish, deluded himself that he could give a direction to the lives of others and taught, educated, demanded, "tyrannical as a general." His conversion reawakened in his heart the almost monstrous aggressiveness that had tortured him during his youth, and which, with the feeling of being motivated by a good cause, now augmented gigantically. He again became the gruff, spiteful, and ill-mannered boy who "speaks the truth" and exposes the lies and illusions of the great—the lies that all subtle minds regard with ironic tolerance and amusement. With old friends and his cousin Alexandra, he was ignobly sincere, arrogant, rancorous, without consideration, charity, or respect. And besides why, in the name of what dream, all this rudeness, this rage, this attitudinizing as Christ? Tolstoyan religion culminates in the abject ideal of an ascetic Rousseauan commune. "To live all together: the men in one room, the women and girls in another. There must be a room to be used as a library, for intellectual work, and another to serve as a workshop. . . . Life, nourishment, clothes, everything will always be simple to the highest degree. The superfluous, the piano, furniture, and carriages will be sold or given away." On Sundays, meals for the poor, readings, conversation; and public confession, during which each member would relate his sins with meticulous ferocity.

We gladly forget these miseries for love of a story—"Father Sergius"—in which Tolstoy described his sins with the only courage he knew: that of narrative objectification. Behind the light veil of fiction, he denounced his inhuman pride and inhuman desire for self-perfection, which had forced him to burn all his experiences, so as to pursue an indeterminate escape route. By writing *War and Peace* and *Anna Karenina* he had achieved an incomparable glory, but he did not yet feel that he stood above all human beings: by converting and condemning his own past, he reached a plane from which he could despise everything and everyone, even his old self, of which he had become jealous. He denounced his histrionic imitation of the Gospel: pity and compassion for himself: his spiritual aridity, the radical absence of love which had overcome him on going so far ahead of all men; the drying up of every fount of love, the exhaustion of all of his soul's spiritual fire. Like Father Sergius, he needed others. All those visitors who arrived at Yasnaya Polyana asking him for the one word, the definitive word, salvation in this and the other world—satisfied a profound desire of his: never to remain alone with himself.

The family life he led from 1882 until 1910 was dreadful: there were years, seasons, months of remission; and yet we wonder how he, his wife, and children were able to endure such an intolerable burden for so long. The love that bound him to his wife had not ended: jealousy made him suffer like a boy; the never mitigated sexual passion, the desire for ownership and possession, the savage hatred, hysteria, the furious need to wound and offend whetted each other's daggers, leaving flesh and soul prostrate. He said to his wife: "Where you are, the air is poisoned." "Until death Sonya will be a stone around my neck and also the children's. Most likely that is what is needed. To learn how not to drown with a stone around one's neck." After having possessed her, the next morning he wrote in his *Diary*: "Slept criminally," "slept terribly," and going through these pages his wife received the full impact of these rejections. About his sons, he went so far as to write: "But who are they? My sons, my work from every point of view, carnal and spiritual. It is I who made them as they are. They are my sins—always before me. And I cannot escape from them in any way." They were his sins in two senses: they were the sons born from his concupiscence; while the vices he imputed to his own youth were embodied again in their lives.

To his three daughters he devoted the tenderness and violence of an Oedipal love so intense as to be without comparison even in an epoch as imbued with Oedipal passion as the nineteeth century. He no longer gave his manuscripts to his wife to copy: but rather to Tatyana, Masha, or Alexandra, who avidly vied for this favor, plunging Sonya into the horrors of jealousy. He could not tolerate men resting their impure glances on his virginal daughters. He had ferocious fits of jealousy when one of then, full of coquettishness, knowing that she looked pretty, came to show herself off dressed for a ball, and when he saw her again at the ball surrounded by a crowd of suitors. It seemed to him that the turpitude of every erotic thought and glance cast filth on his fatherly pride. When Masha got married, he wrote: "I pity her, as one pities a thoroughbred horse used to carry water. She does not carry water, but they have chopped her to pieces and besmeared her with dirt. What will happen I cannot imagine. Something monstrously unnatural, like making pâtés out of children." When Tatyana fell in love with a Tolstoyan, he said that all his blood flooded his heart "because of a strange, confused feeling of compassion for you and shame for you and myself": then he had the two lovers hand over their diaries and ruthlessly prevented all relations between them. Despite her father, Tatyana married Mikhail Sukhotin, whom she had secretly loved for years. The letter her father wrote her on that occasion makes one think of Pozdnyshev's fury in "The Kreutzer Sonata." "I can understand that a corrupt man will save himself by getting married. But why a pure girl ought *aller dans cette galère* is difficult to understand. If I were a girl, I would not have married under any circumstances." Falling in love was an ugly, unhealthy emotion, much more dangerous than such illnesses as diptheria, typhus, and scarlet fever, or vices like drunkenness, smoking, and morphine. If at least Tanya had married coldly, out of calculation! But the frightful thing was that she had falled in love with Sukhotin: "It means that there is suggestion, as if to say an illness of the soul. And in the case of an illness of the soul, one must not tie one's fate to someone else's, but lock oneself in a room and throw the key out the window." He had never hated women with such ferocity: he had never raged with such mad passion against the sweet female womb of life.

Gradually, as the years passed, he felt increasingly alone in his family and the world. "Pascal says: '*Il faudra mourir tout seul*,' but one must also live *seul*, with God." It seemed to him that he was despised by all those who surrounded him: nobody had any use for him, he was of no interest to anyone: his family did not read what he wrote, did not listen to what he said or answered irritably, did not see what he was doing or tried not to see it. "If you speak to one of them, even if he does not get angry, he will look at his watch and at the door thinking how long the muttering of this irritating unilateral old man who does not understand youth will go on." As for Russian society, he was confined to its margins. "I no longer have any of life's comforts, riches, honors, and fame. On the one hand, liberals and esthetes consider me mad or gone soft in the brain, like Gogol: on the other, revolutionaries and radicals consider me a mystic and charlatan: the men in government consider me a pernicious revolutionary: the Orthodox consider me a devil." Alone, confined to his hermitage, enclosed in his reflections, he still felt the great breath of love swell his breast like a sail—the juvenile narcissistic love that intoxicated with devotion was transformed into the love of others; and he magnificently wrote that to love a man one must love him not for something but "without reason." To enter into the soul of another and live his desires seemed even more difficult to him, perhaps impossible: he was afraid to give himself, to let himself go—the awful contact, the jolting encounter with the abyss of an alien soul. And, for the rest, how could he have succeeded? When he less and less tried to understand what the sensations, feelings, desires of others were? When he had more and more thoroughly wrapped himself in himself?

During the last years, he wrote a novel and a long short story—*Resurrection* and "Hadji Murad"—on the basis of contrasting principles. In the novel he renounced the complicated architectures, the play of refractions and reflections which were dear to him; he built it around a single narrative center, the story of the events involved in Prince Nekhlyudov's sin and expiation. Instead, the short story has many narrative centers: the technique of character presentation is slow and meticulous; and in it Tolstoy admirably expressed the nostalgia that seized him, during his activity as a reformer, for the open and fragrant wind of his great novels. He was filled with nostalgia for his youth: sometimes he thought he was still the same as then, when everything was possible in the multiplicity of possible worlds that offered themselves to his gaze . Prince Nekhlyudov was a part of his youth: the austere, ascetic Utopian who pursued a dream of redemption. To the young officers in "Hadji Murad," Poltoratsky and Butler, in whom he mirrored himself twice, he entrusted the other part of his youth: the warrior's ardor, the extrovert happiness of his years in the Crimea. Despite his new professions of morality, he had no reproach to bring against those old images: he loved them tenderly and made them pass with joy before the eyes of the imagination.

So completely antithetic, the two books expressed two different images of Eros. The road traveled by Nekhlyudov after he recognized his sin is gray, austere, arid, without joy and vital light: the road of abstract duty, which we perform alone, with nothing to lighten our spirits or calm us, no hand to comfort and accompany us. He lives by his will: whereas at one time Tolstoy was bitterly ironic about pure intentions, he now accepts and respects such melancholy decisions. Thus, all traces of the warm and amorous feminine world has vanished from *Resurrection*: we venture into the cold, austere, and mortally tedious virile time to which, according to Tolstoy the reformer, the future belongs. Our hearts quail confronted by this extremely gray future; and how sad it would have made the young Tolstoy, so ardent, so capricious, so incapable of bearing the slow pace of time! Woman's disappearance has left an unfillable void: precisely because there are no women, precisely because the womb's forces have vanished, Nekhlyudov can "expiate" but he cannot be "resurrected" as the title announces, deserted as he is by the springlike joy of the universe.

With an admirably cold touch and a miniaturist's preciosity, Tolstoy evoked in "Hadji Murad" a world saturated with Eros. The narrator of *Resurrection*, so cruel with Mariette, would have viciously condemned Princess Vorontsov, futile, smiling, flighty, dominating, a gambler and adulteress: but the narrator of "Hadji Murad" is irresistibly attracted by her vital light. Marya Dmitrievna, "with her thick braid, her high breasts, and the radiant smile on her freckled face," is the popular folk pendant to the princess: she is beautiful too, flighty, maternal, the bringer of order into the chaos of life. The world of men is the grim world of power, overseen by the horrible Czar Nikolai; the feminine world is still Natasha's world—tender, humid, mitigating, immensely powerful, like the conjoined forces of earth and sea. So, at life's extremity, with a tired hand that was unable to embroider an entire canvas of the Caucasian legend, Tolstoy returned to the years of industrious and demonic maturity when he invented a world, as in a new Genesis; and revealed to us that *War and Peace* was the heart of his existence.

V

The big house was full of women. Despite all of his virile rebellions, Tolstoy lived surrounded by skirts and jams, in that redolence of old woods, creams, unguents, fantasy, feminine gossip, and tears, as in his natural element. Among the women his genius found strength and nourishment. His wife had become fatter: extreme myopia imparted something caressing to her glance; her voice was high, clear, and modulated like that of a singer—whereas Tolstoy's voice was dull and without intonation. The passion she felt for him was even more ardent and exclusive than in the past. Patterning herself without realizing it on her husband's characters, she now resembled Anna Karenina: experienced the same passion–love, the same possession–love; and the impulse of Eros vibrated in her thoughts and dreams. She continually desired him. When she saw him unexpectedly—he came into her room while she was washing, or returned home from a horseback ride, or she saw him again after a week's absence in Moscow—she was swept with overwhelming joy: she loved his entire being, his eyes, his smile, the old hands she had so often caressed and kissed, his conversation. She contemplated his photograph with sadness; and she realized that she was irremidiably dependent on him.

She did not feel loved by her children, nor by the dark and inaccessible heart of her husband, who gave her nothing in return for the exclusive emotion she had devoted to him. Because of him, she had remained alone all of her life: he did not take walks with her, because he liked to meditate in solitude: he did not accompany her anywhere, he did not share any impression or sensation with her—he had experienced them all before when he had gone through the world in his youth—and being involved with his children always bored him. When he fell ill, Sonya sat day and night by his bedside and he accepted these humble attentions: but as soon as he regained his health, he pushed her away harshly. When she looked at his portrait, those eyes never ceased attracting her, she remembered reproaches and kisses, but could not recollect a single tender word or affectionate feeling. She had in her husband now a passionate lover, now a severe judge—never a friend. He lived so concentrated in his life that the entire world ceased to live; and only at night he slipped into her room and possessed her with untiring ardor. But, instead of passion, she would have wanted a serene friendship, a tender spiritual relationship, in which their hearts would have met in unison. She exerted all her strength. She read the *Diary* on the sly, to try to understand how to get inside him, and the *Diary* repelled her. She would have liked to copy his writings as in the past: but now Tolstoy hid them from her and entrusted them to his daughters, casting her out of his existence.

So her jealousy, like Anna Karenina's, reached its peak. At night she could not sleep: she strained her ears at the slightest sound coming from her husband's room—or went to scrutinize that aged face she had loved for so many years and which now was blindly lost in sleep. She hated her daughters ferociously: especially Masha and Alexandra who had robbed her of the privilege of copying his writings. Above all she hated Chertkov: she was physically jealous of him, as she might have been jealous of a woman, and on the basis of an old page in the *Diary* she accused her husband of having a homosexual passion for him. If the two of them were talking together in a room, she took off her shoes and spied on them from behind the door; when Tolstoy went riding, afraid he might have made an appointment with Chertkov, she rushed after him in her trap; if, finally, Chertkov arrived at Yasnaya Polyana in his carriage, she dashed to her room, pulled aside the curtains, got out her binoculars, to see if they were showing particular signs of affection. Then, the hatred, always pushed away and repressed, became concentrated on her husband. She could not stand the fact that he was happy after spending a night with her: could not stand his being amused by reading French novels; and if she copied his youthful *Diaries* it was above all to wound and offend him, to topple him from his apostle's pedestal, proving that he had lived in the mire. One time, in a fit of delirium, she imagined that anyone touching Tolstoy's hand was condemned to a slow death, contaminated by his perverse force.

While her husband grew older, Sonya still felt young. Everything about her—she wrote in her *Diary*—had remained young: her sensibility, her eagerness for work, her ability to love and suffer, her passion for music, the enjoyment she got from ice skating: her step was light and her body healthy, although photographs did not reflect the restless movement of her face, the splendor of her eyes, her elusive features. Despite her thirteen children, the role of mother and mistress of the house which she had played with so much enthusiasm, at the bottom of her heart she had remained a romantic *jeune fille*. She had an immense need for tenderness, caresses, pure, delicate, and tranquil emotions. Like a heroine in Tolstoy's novels, she loved nature which awakens and blooms every spring, the fabulous blossoming of the apple trees; and the vast moonlights when trees and meadows are immersed in the purity of silent snow. "This whiteness, this purity is beautiful anywhere, in everyone; in nature, in the soul, in customs, in the conscience, everywhere it is magnificent! What efforts I made to preserve it! What was the use of it? Would not the memories of a love, even a guilty one, have been better than this void and this whiteness?" She was tired of living for others: husband, children, grandchildren, the family; without a personal life, without time for herself, without reading, making music, thinking, and fantasizing. She would never want to repeat her youth. How much sadness was hidden by her impersonal existence, how tragic it was, full of abnegation, tension, effort, love, totally deprived of any solicitude on the part of others. Now—she was not old yet, there was still a little time—she wanted a life all to herself. She did not ask for much: to love her favorite things and persons, visit the places she liked and where her thoughts were at ease, use for something the superabundance of affection and energy she sensed in herself. She was fed up with being alone, while her husband played cards to relax his nerves: she was fed up with those odious exclamations: "Little *shlem**, of spades . . . Less three! Why did you play a spade, you should have passed! . . . You made a grand *shlem!*"

Her husband could no longer satisfy these desires, and did not want to grant her a life of her own; and Sonya, reading a Bourget novel, began to dream she was a woman with a "double love." At last her schoolgirl dreams were realized. She met Sergei Taneyev, an excellent pianist and composer twelve years younger than she. He was the incarnation of the music which Tolstoy had also loved in his ecstatic youth, and to which Sonya had remained desperately faithful: that music filled her existence, made her suffer, soothed her yearnings, stretched her soul in a passionate effort of understanding. Soon after she began to rave. It seemed to her that her dead son, little Ivan, had sent her Taneyev and protected her love: she saw the baby sitting on his knees while together they held out their arms in uncertain prayer. She had long talks with Taneyev, she told him things she did not dare tell her husband, photographed him, listened to music, Beethoven, Schumann, and Chopin, and her soul melted and was liberated by those sounds. She loved Taneyev's calm, measured, apparent indifference—so far from Tolstoy's violence. This gave her peace and seemed to bring her back to life.

When Tolstoy fell seriously ill in 1902, she watched over his pains, delirium, and terror of death. While the doctors, nurses, and daughters took turns at the sick man's bed, she, fearless, precise, and untiring, attended him at every instant. "Every evening I put my husband to bed like a child: I bandage his abdomen with a compress of water and camphor, prepare a glass of milk for him, put his watch and a bell next to him, undress him, tuck him in. Then I sit in the drawing room and read the newspapers until he falls asleep." When she looked at his emaciated face, his hair and beard all white, his skinny body, a dull pain gripped her heart and she was afraid that he would die. On the other hand, she looked on his death as a liberation: without him she would at last shed her shackles; live a free existence, without impossible devotion, without superhuman tasks, without geniuses to look after, without diaries to ransack, without labors, without jealousies, without sacrifices at every instant. She

*A slam in a card game—TRANS.

would live at last for herself. But then behind these desires for liberation she caught sight of a desolate existence. She would no longer rush in in the morning to see if he had slept well, if he had gone out, if he was in a good mood. What would she do with that terrible void, what did her freedom matter to her? What interest did her life have for her?

The last years of their married life were atrocious. Chertkov's return to the neighborhood of Yasnaya Polyana, the struggle for possession of Tolstoy's *Diaries*, the battle over the will and author's rights, the desire to play a great role in history—exhausted her, increasing her hysteria beyond all bounds. She wanted to kill herself: not silently in a corner—but theatrically, like her whole existence had been theatrical, after writing hundreds of letters in which she would explain to acquaintances and strangers the reasons for her action. Now she thought of letting herself die of exposure like the protagonist of "Master and Man," now of drinking the flagon of opium she always carried with her, now of throwing herself on the train tracks like Anna Karenina. Never, never, not even at the point of death was she able to free herself from the shadow of the man who had filled her existence.

While Sonya despaired and raved, her three daughters timidly stepped into life. The oldest, Tatyana, had been a withdrawn child, taciturn and a dreamer. To fill her solitude she had invented an imaginary and invisible "friend" who lived on an old lilac tree in front of the house. She climbed up the tree, sat on a branch, and confided secrets, dreams, and sorrows to her "friend." In time she became so accustomed and attached to her invisible double that she began stories in which she told her adventures. When she became fourteen and wrote the first pages of her diary, she was a different creature. Spontaneous, full of grace and vitality, of amorous joy, with something childish—she had a moving faith in the perfection of God's world. Whatever is—is right, she said in English, repeating old Handel's last words. She loved to walk in the flawed paradise of Vasnaya Polyana. She took a towel and went swimming in the Voronka: along the way she picked strawberries and flowers: she flung herself into the water with great shouts; and returned on Aunt Tanya's little cart. She went picnicking in the woods together with her brothers and cousins, lighting a fire, roasting potatoes on the embers, drinking tea with cake, and fishing. She awoke early to pick the first mushrooms, and halfway through the picking she drank milk in a watermelon shell. She cooked strawberry jam under the oak trees, although her mother was worried: "Sugar has gone up and costs twenty-two kopeks a kilo as against sixteen last year." And as they did every year, the children conscientiously licked off the foam. She went hunting for hare with the borzoi: raced on horseback all the way to Tula. And when the moon rose over the snow-covered world, like Natasha on the balcony or in the sleigh, like Sonya, like the adolescent Tolstoy—she walked with friends, holding them by the arm, in the mild celestial splendor.

Living in that virtuous and apostolic house, Tatyana's mind was full of frivolous desires. She contemplated herself in the mirror, fretting because she thought she was ugly: she sadly looked at her hands, "ruined, scorched, hardened," and at her nails broken by household chores. She liked new dresses, ribbons, frills. The first time she was taken to a ball, she exclaimed: "How funny you all look! You are all naked and covered with flowers!" Then dancing won her over: although her father warned her that anyone who dances the mazurka well "is worth nothing." She passionately loved the waltz, the mazurka, and the quadrille. She regarded as marvelous the open-air theater, which her father condemned as the peak of the "false." She was always in love with somebody: otherwise her heart was sad and empty: and she wished that the anonymous love that runs through the world would leave its flowers at her feet. One time, during a ball, she decided to flirt with a boy to attract him and in turn let herself be caught. She talked with him in the embrasure of a window, clasped his hand; and it seemed to her that the ballroom was divided down the middle: the two of them on one side and on the other the indifferent crowd. She heard the music as if in a dream: until he accompanied her to her carriage, solicitously begging her to cover herself well, "as if it really mattered that I should not catch cold." When he left, she thought she would forget him immediately but after three months she still regretted him. She went down Gazetny Street to pass in front of his door on foot or by carriage. "My life is nothing but waiting. For what? I myself don't know, but I never stop believing that *in one moment* something will happen and that life will at last begin for real." For a while she fell in love with Taneyev and she wanted to "mean more to him than any other." Then she read Chekhov's "The House with the Mezzanine" and wrote in her diary: "Chekhov, there is a man with whom I could fall madly in love!" It seemed to her that he had penetrated to the bottom of her soul as no one had ever done; and one evening she went to the house of friends, the Petrovskys, to look at his portrait.

But the great amorous phantom that occupied Tatyana's mind was her father. In his presence she was like a timid vigin ready to be sacrificed. She herself recognized this: "Yes, Papa is the greatest rival of all my beaus, and not one of them has been able to defeat him." She worshiped his beauty when he got on his horse and raced through the forest: she accepted all of his ideas with passionate conviction; it seemed to her that what he said was "so rational, so clear, so logical" that it was impossible not to think as he did. She was jealous of Masha, her younger sister. If her father wrote to Masha that he missed her, for some hours Tatyana had a heavy heart: if her father went to Masha's room before coming to hers, she was upset by it; she would have liked to become beautiful and intelligent to please him, or become ill so as to experience again his tenderness. She went so far as to write: "Masha is a liar, astute and at the same time sensual and falsely elated." Her father reproached Tatyana for her coquettishness, her love of balls and dresses: he was cold and hostile to her if she was the guest of relatives and friends for a few days; and he advised her to remain a virgin—this sovereign remedy in the entanglements of existence. She would have liked to lose her virginity as soon as possible: and yet she wanted her father to punish her and prevent her from having any experience of love and like a dark, punitive phantom keep her from any sort of love.

So, following her father's example, young Tatyana made every effort to realize his moral ideals. She was ashamed at having so many people work for her at Yasnaya Polyana and in the house in Moscow: shoemakers, carpenters, milliners, dressmakers, watchmakers, furriers, glove makers, jewelers, opticians, waiters, maids, coachmen. . . . She resolved not to go to another ball although she liked them so much: to give alms regularly; and to follow a vegetarian diet.

But, when her father admonished her that wealth is an impediment to living properly, she answered candidly: "I understand these things with my intelligence, I would like to live in goodness, but my soul remains indifferent to this goodness and rejoices when I am promised a new dress or a new hat." The impulse of frustrated love then became maternal love and was turned to her smaller brothers and her cousins. As soon as her mother was away, she looked after them: listened to their chatter, the uncertain racing of their tiny pudgy feet; and she looked after her sister Alexandra who was twenty years younger, as though she were her daughter. Her father had convinced her that marriage was not suitable for her: when she read "The Kreutzer Sonata" she decided not to get married; and yet she dreamed of having children and scrubbed her breasts with a brush and washed them with cold water to prepare for nursing an infant.

When she fell in love with a Tolstoyan, a certain Popov, it seemed to her that there was in her feeling something "murky and excited," and she despaired, thinking that this passion would only bring her sorrow. Tolstoy asked for both their letters and diaries: he read them: anguish and shame kept him awake for an entire night, and in the morning he went to Tatyana to tell her that there could be no doubt—it was love. Then he wrote to Popov to stop him from speaking and writing to her. Some years later, when she met Mikhail Sukhotin, a widower much older than she, Tatyana felt she needed his tenderness. Seeing him made her feel "joyous, light, and extraordinarily calm," although the thought of her father filled her with an obscure sense of guilt. She married Sukhotin and her life became happy: "a calm, sober, undeserved, unexpected happiness." It seemed to her that she no longer had a life of her own and that she was completely dependent on him. When she thought of her father, it seemed to her that she had betrayed him.

The youngest daughter, Alexandra, was unwanted, unloved. When she was pregnant with her, her mother wanted to have an abortion. Alexandra heard this from her nurse. When little Ivan died—a thin child, with a pale, transparent face, attentive eyes, a small blue vein on his forehead, and a sensitivity acute to the point of suffering—Sofya seemed to go mad with grief. Then she calmed, gathering together Vanechka's toys, examining them from time to time, photographing his portraits again; but then she started sobbing again and screamed that she would kill herself. She roamed about the house, unable to stay in one place. "Why? Why is the Lord so unjust to me? Why did He take Vanechka from me?" she cried. And one day, beside herself, she screamed: "Why, why did it have to be Vanechka and not Alexandra?" The girl, who heard those terrible words, grew up alone, without caresses, tenderness, affection, with strong impulses of love toward her sisters which, however, she did not dare express. Withdrawn into herself, she became shy and stiff: she was considered obstinate, while a kind word was enough to make her melt. Once she went into her father's study: he looked at her attentively, at length, and remarked with sadness: "My God! How homely you are! How homely!"

She spent her time fantasizing in the garden and courtyard of the Moscow house. The garden was large and shadowy: the neglected, grass-covered paths gave her the impression of being in a virgin forest, the walks seemed interminable, and the pergola seemed to her full of secrets. In the courtyard, there were a pair of carriage horses with the old coachman the Tolstoys had brought from Yasnaya Polyana, her father's mount, a cow, a cart full of hay and oats, enormous receptacles full of salted cucumbers and cabbages, countless jars of jam—while a shed contained Tolstoy's unsold books. In the countryside Alexandra devoted her full attention to the horses. She mounted them, drove in the carriage, rode without saddle, was thrown by them, bought and sold them, trained them. She did not have girlfriends of her age; and stayed with the boys, adopting their habits, enjoying their games, climbing trees, shooting, coming home with bleeding hands, bruised feet, and torn dresses. When she was melancholy, she locked herself in her room and sang, accompanying herself on the guitar. Or she listened to Aunt Tanya's songs. When her aunt sang, she silently approached the drawing-room door in her nightgown. Her aunt sang:

> The beautiful moment comes to mind
> When you appeared before me.

Alexandra knew every note: she was so agitated she could not breathe, everything around her seemed to take on a new meaning; she felt an unknown force grow inside her and her soul seemed to be lifted up.

She loved her mother when she was industrious, silent, and calm. Sofya Andreyevna kept all manner of garden tools in her room: in summer she cut the wheat around the house; in the autumn and spring she pruned the lilac and acacia trees. She liked to paint the garden tables, benches, and washstands. Her energy was inexhaustible: she typed, copied the portraits in the house with her brush; or, seated at the piano, with her not very nimble fingers, she repeated pieces of music from beginning to end, over and over, alway making the same mistakes. Alexandra could not stand her mother when she was nervous, hysterical, domineering "Countess Tolstoy." At those moments, her mother was unable to listen quietly to a conversation, could not concentrate or read a book. She was always in a hurry: life seemed to her full of insurmountable difficulties and frightful worries. When she entered the dining room, Alexandra immediately sensed with irritation the noisy rustle of her silk skirt: then she heard her tap the high heel of her small shoe nervously on the floor. That tapping pierced her heart and her brain: she was unable to remain calm: she was overcome by hatred and left the dining room. She couldn't bear her mother to be animated, cheerful, elegant, with white shining eyes and nervous gestures when Taneyev arrived—that little pudgy man with his shrill laugh and his red-tipped nose, who sat down at the piano to play one of Mendelssohn's *Songs without Words,* making Sofya sob.

Alexandra's ideal place was her father's study. Everything in it attracted her: the arched ceiling, the writing desk, the antique armchair which was so long that one could stretch out on it as on a small bed, the smell of leather and old paper which emanated from everything that belonged to her father. Tolstoy wrote sitting on a low chair, which had been Tatyana's during her childhood: he was myopic, he did not want to wear glasses and only in this way could he see what his hand was writing. He needed absolute silence: the slightest sound disturbed him; he could not stand barking dogs, the rooster's crow, the hens clucking. When he needed something, he pressed his finger on a bell shaped like a turtle or beat against the wall with his cane; and Alexandra immediately rushed to him. She too sacrificed her loves to her father's jealousy: she devoted herself to him unreservedly, with all her young Amazon's strength, as secretary, companion, and copyist. At two in the afternoon, Tolstoy left his work on his desk. They were small pieces of paper, pages torn from letters, small numbered strips: the words were unfinished, without punctuation marks, or put in the wrong place. "Be careful, Sasha," he said. "Don't lose any of them. Today I made a lot of little noodles." Sometimes Alexandra had to work all evening, part of the night, and the next morning. People said to her: "You're still writing? Quit, come on!" She would have liked to join the others, to play chess or *vint*, listen to the conversation: but, after a moment of sadness, she resumed her work. When he saw her up in the evening, her father sent her away. But at night, when everyone was asleep, Alexandra returned to the study and typed until morning. At nine o'clock all the sheets were neatly copied, as her mother had done in the past. Tolstoy shook his head and smiled; and that candid and astute smile was enough to make her forget all her labors.

VI

By now Tolstoy sensed he had reached the end, and he was grateful for all the gifts that his unknown and distant God, that cold point of light in space, had given him. "Nature moves me to the point of tenderness and the plains, the forest—the wheat, the work in the fields, the haymaking. I think—am I not living my last summer? Well, this too is good. I am thankful for everything—I was the object of infinite benevolence." He was no longer afraid to die: he watched with curiosity, in himself and others, the steps of death which in the past had seemed to him so terrible. When he fell ill—he had become very, very frail, and often lost consciousness—he thought that his illnesses were like death's birth pangs. His reawakening was not far off; from day to day his dreams became clearer and more reasonable, and from one moment to the next he would enter the true state of wakefulness, or a higher sleep. While he waited to pass beyond, he had the impression that a reversal had taken place inside him: the "Tolstoy" inside him was dying and a suprapersonal "I" had taken his place. Sometimes that "I" looked toward life: his strange eyes—cold, joyous, clarifying—brought about a synthesis of appearances: as in dreams, the faces, places, times, and spaces fused into one; his brothers became confused with his brothers, his sons with his sons. More often he looked ahead. Soon, as he had often thought and fantasized, he would leap outside time; and in that extratemporal instant, similar to the heart's leap in the state of sleep, he would receive a retrospective vision of his existence.

To die in his bed was not enough for him. He wanted to flee. To flee the jail that real life is: that web of falsehoods, constrictions, limits, fixations, and institutions that he had built for himself in eighty years as father of a family, writer, and apostle. He wanted to flee the worldly glory which suffocated him—showing, with a last mocking and humble act of pride, that he was superior to all earthly glory. He wanted to flee his own self: all the crystallizations, personifications, and shapes he had assumed, demonstrating that his true "I" did not have a shape, or had the same shape as a comet—an ellipse that vanishes in the depths of the sky, an uninterrupted force of flight. What the goal was did not matter: death, the abyss, the future, the desolate absence in which his God lived; or no goal. When many years before, he had studied the Gospels, he had translated Matthew's sentence "Blessed are the poor in spirit" with a strange restriction: "Blessed are the beggars without homes." Now he dreamed of nothing else. He wanted to become a "madman in Christ," a wretched mendicant, staff in hand, knapsack slung on his back, walking hundreds of kilometers from one monastery to the next, alien to everything and begging a piece of bread at the doors of the *isbas**. He had painted a self-portrait of his old age in the figure of the old vagabond whom Nekhlyudov meets on the barge at the end of *Resurrection*: in a shirt the color of ashes, a pair of cloth pants, a worn fur cap, and ragged Siberian boots; without a home, country, or church, without a name and without a God. "I do not accept any name. I have renounced everything: I have neither name, nor place, nor country—I have nothing. I am I and that is all. What am I called? Man. 'And how old are you?'—'I, I say, do not count the years, and there is no need to count them, because I always was and always will be.' 'And who are,' they say, 'your father, your mother?' 'I have,' I say, 'neither father nor mother besides God and the earth. God is the father, the earth is the mother.' "

On the night of October 28, 1910, the flight began. There was one last harassment on Sonya's part—her hands ransacking drawers, searching for secret papers: the last letter: the carriage racing through the dark: the wait at the Shchekino station: the discussion with a peasant on the train; the arrival at the Optina monastery, the

*Small log cabin—TRANS.

meeting with his sister at Shamardino convent. The man who fled with his *Diary* and without books toward an unknown goal was not the desperate, self-assured vagabond he had hoped to be; but rather an uncertain, perplexed, doubtful old man subject to the influence of his travel companions. So there was the new flight: the train to Rostov; and fever. When they got off at Astapovo station—a small wooden house painted red— Tolstoy was carried into the larger room. As he got into bed, he thought he was at Yasnaya Polyana and with his love of habit wanted all the familiar objects to be in their proper place: the candle, matches, note pad, the small lamp on the night table. He was afraid that his wife was pursuing him; and he gave orders to cover the window with a veil, because he thought he had seen a woman's shape looking at him through the windowpanes.

Alexandra got some warm water, added a bit of cologne, and began to wash his face with cotton. Tolstoy smiled, half closed his eyes; his face was tender and peaceful. When his daughter finished washing one side of his face, he turned the other and said softly: "Now the other. And don't forget to wash my ears." He became delirious: he thought he saw a person in the room who had not greeted him, mistook a friend of Alexandra's for Masha, his dead daughter, and with his thin, muscular arm took Tatyana by the hand and did not let go of her. He asked her to write his thoughts in the *Diary*, but dictated only incomprehensible words. Then he wanted her to read what he had dictated. There was nothing to read: but he insisted desperately: "Read to me what I have dictated. Why don't you say anything? What did I dictate?" Then he stopped; and restlessly stroked the blanket with his hands, smoothed it with his fingers, back and forth, back and forth, endlessly, as though he wished to engrave on it what nobody understood. Suddenly he said: "I cannot fall asleep, I am forever composing. I write and everything is linked together harmoniously." On the evening of November 6—only one candle burned in the shadowy room, and from the room nearby came a stifled murmur—his breathing was regular, hoarse, and frequent. At five in the morning his respiration grew weaker. It stopped, then resumed, more and more sibilant and irregular: until it suddenly stopped. Silence fell in the room—the interminable silence we hear only in the rooms of the dead.